Advance Praise

"This is a marvelous tale, whether the reader enjoys grand story-telling, expanding cultural horizons, or nuanced insights that emerge from the unique 'he said-she said' evolution of the book. At another level, *El Tio* is a brilliant case study in the real complexities of economic and sociological development that so often are absent in modern economic analysis. The book's journey is made all the more riveting by prose that is quick, clear and always engaging."

John W. Mayo, PhD, Professor of Economics,
Business and Public Policy, McDonough School of Business,
Georgetown University

"Prospecting in 1995, geologist Larry Buchanan found evidence of a gigantic silver ore deposit whose development would necessitate the complete removal of the small Quechua-speaking village atop it. . . . This book raises the question: when a people's traditional lifestyle is on the very margins of survival, how should the gains and losses of modernity be weighed? . . . *El Tio's* prophecy and his ambiguous gift completes the circle of meaning, providing context for a page-turning mystery that is both tightly structured and evocatively written."

Anne Chambers, PhD, Professor of Anthropology at Southern
Oregon University, author with Keith Chambers of Unity of
Heart: Culture and Change in a Polynesian Atoll Society

"Larry Buchanan and Karen Gans have written a fascinating personal account of discovery and transformation that interconnects a silver discovery, a small village, and their own personal views of science, culture, mysticism and religion."

Paul Klotman, MD, President & CEO, Baylor College of Medicine

"A deeply moving and timeless testimonial. . . . The authors' grace shines through as do the charm and dignity of . . . the townspeople themselves."

T. S. Kaplan, PhD, Founder and Executive Secretary of Panthera, the world's largest organization dedicated to wild cat preservation

". . . before I went to Bolivia and Peru, I tried to read about life in the Altiplano. The only information was as arid as the Altiplano itself. . . . With *The Gift* I have gotten to know an entire village, a whole new way of life. . . . It has adventure, humor, conflict, grace, death, prophesies, greed, mysterious spirits and baby llamas. . . . A real page-turner."

F. H. Curtis, Ed.D., former University instructor and avid armchair traveler

"*The Gift* takes you deep into an unknown world in such a delightful way, through the eyes of the people themselves. An eye-opener . . . unafraid to tackle politically incorrect subjects, but does so with a balanced, honest approach. This is a must-read for our polarized society."

J.C. Gelvin, geologist, President of Minera Plata Real

"Any writer who starts a book as Karen Gans does in her introduction with the words, 'My husband is so full of it,' has my attention. *The Gift of El Tio* is a rare treat of a story that pulls you in from the very beginning. The writing is compelling, and the people who touch Larry and Karen will stay with you long after you finish reading the last page."

Nicolle Wallace, author of the novel, Eighteen Acres

The Gift of El Tío

The Gift of El Tío

Larry Buchanan
Karen Gans

Fuze Publishing, LLC

This is a memoir. Circumstances and events described are based on the Authors' recollections, tapes and field notes, supplemented with information learned through discussions with the villagers and engineers. Of necessity, the dialogue is often reconstructed. For simplification, some characters have been added, others omitted, and most characters are composites. Names of corporations and characters, except those of the authors, J. Gelvin and C. Murillo, have been changed to ensure privacy. All of the situations described herein are intended to show the honor and decency displayed by all players in this momentous undertaking.

Fuze Publishing, LLC
1350 Beverly Road, Suite 115-162
McLean, Virginia 22102

www.fuzepublishing.com

ISBN 978-1-4507-3914-6

Cover Design by C. Schmetler and J. M. Dunnington

Design and Typesetting by Scribe Inc.

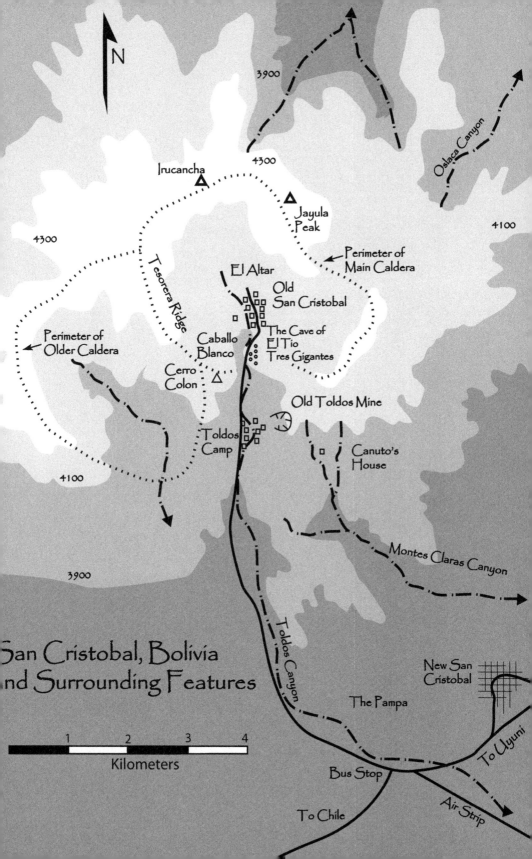

N

3900

4300

Oslaca Canyon

Irucancha △

△ Jayula Peak

4300

4100

Tesorera Ridge

Perimeter of Main Caldera

El Altar

Old San Cristobal

Perimeter of Older Caldera

Caballo Blanco

The Cave of El Tio Tres Gigantes

Cerro Colon

△

Old Toldos Mine

Toldos Camp

Canuto's House

4100

3900

Montes Claras Canyon

San Cristobal, Bolivia and Surrounding Features

Toldos Canyon

New San Cristobal

The Pampa

To Uyuni

| 1 | 2 | 3 | 4 |

Kilometers

Bus Stop

To Chile

Air Strip

Table of Contents

Part II: The New Town 1999–2007

Larry's Introduction

When my partners and I discovered an enormous silver deposit under an impoverished indigenous village in the Bolivian Andes, we unknowingly fulfilled a four-hundred-year-old prophecy that would wrench the villagers from their seventeenth-century homes of thatch and rock, thrust them headlong into the twenty-first century, and send my wife and me on a ten-year journey into the world of the Quechua.

Theirs is a culture of multiple gods and spirits, one with a profound respect for the earth in general, and curiously, for rocks in particular. The Quechua of southwestern Bolivia believe rocks are their direct ancestors, living souls that speak, think, feel emotions, and have distinct personalities. Most are benign, never failing to offer good advice when consulted; others come alive at night to cause grievous harm. Every mountain is a *mallku*, a wise god; every cliff, a demon or spirit; every rock, an ancestor. The god most familiar to the outside world is the Pachamama, their goddess of the earth, but there is another we came to know, a particularly cruel and peevish one named El Tío, who lives in the black interior of mountains guarding his precious veins of gold and silver.

It is natural that I would appreciate such a culture. I am an exploration geologist. My job is to search the remotest parts of the world for the certain rocks, the *right types* of rocks, those displaying the clues that El Tío's precious metals may be present. My team found plenty of those right types, directly beneath the little Quechua village of San Cristóbal, three miles high in the Bolivian Altiplano. We discovered nearly a half-billion tonnes of those ancestors of the Quechua, each tonne of them loaded with silver.

Our discovery was easy, perhaps too easy. The deposit lay on the surface, mineralized ledges cropping out everywhere around and below San Cristóbal. You couldn't take a step without tripping over silver-bearing rock. But somehow it had been overlooked by everyone: the Quechua, with their long history of silver mining to satisfy their Inca lords; the Spanish, desperate to return as wealthy gentlemen to the green hills of Andalucía; and the more recent Canadian and American geologists who combed the hillsides of the sierras, backed by all the money and science they needed. Even the generations of people who spent their lives in San Cristóbal, who lived in houses with foundations and walls constructed from silver-laden rocks, who played and walked on streets lined with cobblestones laced with metallic veins, didn't realize what lay around and under their feet. That treasure was unmistakable. It couldn't be missed, but somehow nobody had noticed.

On a crystalline cold day in January of 1995, I was prospecting with two other company geologists, Jon Gelvin and Carlos Murillo. We hiked over the desert ridges of the San Cristóbal Range, down near the triple-point where Argentina, Chile, and Bolivia meet, a hard four hours from the nearest bar, bed, or restaurant. Shadows stretched across the canyon walls while we chipped about 100 samples from cliff faces and rock exposures. But it was obvious; we didn't have to wait for the assays. The four hours or so we spent sampling were enough for us to realize we were standing atop what would turn out to be the largest silver discovery of the century.

A lousy four hours and we had recognized what centuries of explorers had failed to see. How was that possible? We weren't any smarter than those others who had searched these hills; we certainly didn't work any harder. Most people figure we were just lucky, but I think it was more than that. We had El Tío on our side.

Fourteen months and two million dollars later, the mining company I worked for had managed to purchase all of the mineral rights for twenty kilometers in every direction. By September of 1996, hundreds of test holes had been drilled on a grid with fifty-meter centers, each hole nearly three hundred meters deep. Every two meters a sample was taken for assay, about 150 per drill hole.

The data indicated the mineral deposit was disk-shaped, circular in outline about 1.5 kilometers in diameter, about 250 meters thick. It lay right on the surface making it amenable to a low-cost, open pit operation, where we planned to mine 180,000 tonnes of rock per day.

With the outline of the mineral deposit nailed down, the engineers calculated it contained nearly a billion ounces of silver, enough ore to last seventeen years of intensive mining. The computer models proved it feasible: the profits would be more than enormous and the mine would become a money-machine. It was a company maker, a world-class discovery, a perfect set-up. Except for that poverty-stricken little village right on top of it. If we wanted to make a mine, San Cristóbal had to go.

I spent many a cold night on the couch as my wife, Karen, and I argued about the injustice soon to be perpetrated by the company (her words), or the opportunities we were offering the people (my words). Neither of us would budge from our positions; we just knew the other was wrong. It was Karen who decided how to resolve the impasse: she and I had to move to San Cristóbal, live amid the people, get to know them, and document what the company was doing *to* them (her words), or what the company was doing *for* them (mine). Thus developed the structure of *The Gift of El Tío*: we took turns writing the individual chapters, allowing each of us the freedom to describe events as we saw them, offering our opinions from our personal viewpoints.

This book tells the story of the village, of the changes it suffered as the mine developed, of its customs; its gods, spirits and demons; and the rugged, enterprising people we came to love. It also tells the story of the unanticipated life-changes Karen and I experienced, how so many of our deep-seated opinions about justice and fairness, right and wrong, good and bad were proven to be naïve products of our cultural myopia.

For the sake of simplicity, some participants in events have been omitted, others added. Names of some locations have been changed. Except for our own, all names of characters were changed to assure privacy. Most characters are composites of several individuals.

However, one character's name remains unchanged, that of El Tío. He was born as an adult sometime after the year 1605, and has lived his life over the centuries beneath the surface of the earth, though he does come out from time to time, especially at night when he is hungry. Even in the absolute black of his subterranean home, El Tío's beard and mustache glow orange or yellow. His eyes are blue; his face, Caucasian, resembling those of his creators, the Spanish overlords who ruled by the whip in the mines of the Andes. In a blasphemous rewriting of *Genesis,* they molded a clay god after their own image and enthroned him to rule in this sunless underworld. They called him *El Diablo,* the *Dios,* the god of the underground. This god guaranteed torture and death for any exhausted native who dreamed he could somehow escape his *mita,* the impossible quota of toil in the Bolivian mines. And the miners certainly did come to fear him, for they soon learned the hard way that he had an insatiable appetite for human flesh.

"Here you will work beneath the earth, beyond the touch of the Santa María and the Saints, here in the realm of the Devil," the overlords said to the frightened workers. "Obey us you must, and fear him you should, for if you do not, this devil, your *Dios,* will devour you." The rumor is that the Quechua could not pronounce the Spanish *"Dios."* Over the years it became "Tíos," then "El Tío."

Time removed the Spaniards from the mines, their bones and blood an inadequate payment for their sins. But gods remain forever, and this god, El Tío, had promised that he had hidden a gift for those who continued to believe in him, a gift to be unveiled in the year 2000. The gift promised to change their lives forever. But true to the perverse nature of that harsh god, in accepting the gift the people must also accept the strings attached: the destruction of their village and loss of their entire way of life.

Karen's Introduction

My husband is so full of it. He can take a true event and romanticize it to the point I can't recognize it anymore. He tends to embellish reality too much, just so he can tell a good story. For example, he never had to sleep on the couch. Not once.

I want to assure you that I have made him go back and remove all the *colorful enhancements* (his words), or *lies* (my words), and the real story, the *true* one recounted here, is—well—you get to read the book for yourself.

Part I

The Old Village

1995~1999

Chapter 1

What Right Do We Have?

Karen

1995

"You want to move an entire town of indigenous people?" I withdrew my hand from Larry's. The sweetness of last night's reunion vanished.

"It could be the largest silver deposit in the whole world. Damned town's sitting right on top of it. You've got to understand, Karen, what this would mean for the people, for the country of Bolivia."

"*I've* got to understand?"

"Well, yeah." He shifted his body and rested his forehead in his hands, averting his eyes. "We have no choice. If it turns out there's an orebody there, we can't mine with San Cristóbal smack in the middle of it. That town's got to go."

"The town's been there for centuries. You don't *have to.*"

I searched the coffeehouse for comfort in the familiarity of the forest green walls, the philodendra hanging from the oak beams, and the shelves of espresso machines for the home. The aroma of fresh-ground coffee permeated the place.

Larry was studying me through his thick glasses as he sipped his latte. His face, burned by the sun and wind, looked misplaced in our Northwest winter. Outside, the rain fell.

He licked his chapped lips. "This discovery is just too important to walk away."

The night before when I'd picked him up at the airport, he couldn't stop grinning. "I think I've finally found it!" he'd said, slapping his once-white hat on his thigh and releasing a cloud of dirt. "Geologists spend their whole lives looking for a deposit like this one. Thirty years and maybe I've really hit it."

He strode through the airport amid a sea of business suits, his plaid flannel shirt torn at the left elbow and both knees of his faded jeans worn thin. The remaining bit of brown hair on his balding head, several weeks' growth of whiskers, and his mustache all looked a shade lighter from the dust. The other business-class passengers must have loved sitting next to him on this long trip from Bolivia to Ashland, Oregon, our home.

I wanted only to wrap my arms around him and keep him close to me for a while before he headed out again.

Now, this morning, I sipped my latte, buying time. I hated conflict, but too much was at stake. "How can you move a village? They've got to be rooted to their land," I persisted.

"They're poor, Karen." Larry took a deep breath. "San Cristóbal has fewer than two hundred residents, all women and children. The men have left for the cities to try and earn some money."

"But they've lived that way for hundreds of years. *Leave them alone.*"

"Maybe the men return at Christmas long enough to impregnate their women. Then they're off again. Meanwhile the women and kids survive on shriveled potatoes. There's no future there. They just watch their llamas eat grass all day."

"Maybe there's some way to help that doesn't destroy their culture. Maybe they have some skill, some resource that could be developed."

"Believe me, Karen. I sure didn't see any skills there. There are no resources other than this mine."

We avoided each other's eyes. Two university students sat down next to us with their laptops and Mexican mochas.

Larry spoke again, his voice soft at first, then rising, "Their chances of surviving are slim. Children die all the time. They have nothing. They want the jobs the mine would bring. The kids are wearing sandals made from old discarded tires. Sandals! No jackets! It's freezing there." His eyes widened as his words hammered me. "No electricity, no running water, no sanitation, no sewage."

"Yeah, well maybe they don't want their village destroyed. Maybe they find a form of happiness that you could never understand. You don't know. You haven't lived there. Maybe they have cultural traditions or a spirituality that supports them. Who are we to say their lives aren't okay? And who are we to make them leave everything they've ever known?"

A pained expression came over Larry's face. "Honey, you know I love you, and I know you are compassionate. It's just that you're not being realistic here."

I turned away and stared out the window. The school where I worked as a counselor was located only a block away. Faced with the many children I could not help, those living with drug-addicted parents who abused or neglected them, I had to be realistic every day.

I felt Larry's hand on my arm, soft as a caress. I let his touch linger, then pulled away and lashed out at him. "What makes you such an authority on this village?"

He sounded tired. "Look, I've been to every God-forsaken hell-hole you can imagine from Tegucigalpa to Tashkent, and I always ask the people I meet what it is they want. And you know what they answer every time? Every time? No matter their religion or their color or their culture? They inevitably say, 'I want a job.' Poverty grinds them down. That's the culture these villagers have, a culture of poverty, and they want out of it."

I glared at the National Republican Party button flaunting his conservative views on the rim of his filthy hat. Damned button had survived the trip. If I hated conflict so much, why had I married this man?

When I met Larry, he was recently divorced and taking time out from geology. He spent his days capturing the beauty of the surrounding mountains on canvas and wooing me with bouquets of wild flowers. A romantic at home and a world-wide adventurer, Larry was a real-life Indiana Jones and couldn't stay away from the treasure hunt for long. The quest beckoned and he returned to prospecting within the year.

As a youngster in the southern California desert, he had witnessed domestic violence and poverty. The world of rocks was safe. The desert became his refuge, and he, a loner, bicycled out to remote canyons for weekends to explore old mine shafts and tunnels.

I was born and raised in the first Jewish family to live in a blue-blood New England community. Having grown up as an outsider, I felt deeply for those who didn't belong. My passion was not rocks; it was championing the rights of the underdog. But Larry had experienced the path up and out of the underdog world and thought everyone should be able to do the same.

After a long silence, I rallied. "Didn't you tell me they were Quechua, descendants of the Incas? They must still have their language and customs."

"Well, maybe, but their Quechua customs or spirituality or whatever you call it sure hasn't helped them very much. If they don't change, they'll die." Larry looked away, then leaned in closer to me, his voice almost pleading. "Culture, spirituality— it doesn't feed the people."

"Maybe not their bellies," I said.

"Well, let them eat first and worry about their souls later." Larry paused for a moment and let out a sigh. "We have our warm homes, good food, and children with bright futures. They don't. We're comfortable. They aren't. So, what right do *we* have to sit here and say these people shouldn't take advantage of the only opportunity to come their way in centuries?"

We had both raised our voices a notch. Next to us a couple in their warm, purple Patagonia jackets looked up from their *New York Times*. The students were also eyeing us. I didn't care.

Outside, a dark-blue BMW displayed a bumper sticker *Live Simply So Others May Simply Live.* Holes broke through the clouds, revealing small, brief patches of blue.

I was on the verge of tears. I fixed my eyes on the table; my heart pounded. "I can't live with a man who destroys villages. By staying with you, I'm giving tacit approval. I *can't* do that." I shook my head as my sweaty hands ripped the napkin on my lap into shreds.

"Wait, wait, honey." A look of panic crossed Larry's face. "No need for this. If the silver is there it won't matter what you or I think. The company will go ahead. It's out of my hands."

The implications of my own words scared me. I didn't want to lose him, but I didn't know how to make peace with the situation. I needed to see what was going on firsthand.

"I'll come with you," I said with conviction that surprised even me.

Larry raised his eyebrows and studied me. "You'll come with me? To Bolivia?"

"I want to see what you're doing to these people."

"It's rough country. It won't be easy."

"I don't care. If you're going to move the village, we need to see what happens. We'll have to live there for a while."

"Live there? You mean that?"

"Yes."

"You're not going to like it." He sat without speaking for some time. Then he reached for my hand and took a deep breath. "Yeah, I'm . . . I'm OK with that. I guess we could try it, but just for a trial period."

My body relaxed just a bit. "Promise me this," I said, "You can't just move on to the next project like you always do and forget these people."

"Okay, that's a deal—*if* we make a mine."

"And I think we owe it to the people to document all the changes."

"Document the changes?"

I said nothing; just stared Larry in the eyes.

"Okay, okay, but I guarantee you these people don't have much to document."

"I think you might be surprised."

Chapter 2

Welcome to the Altiplano

Larry

October 1998

If a hell of a long way from anywhere is how you define *nowhere,* then we were certainly somewhere smack in the middle of it. Several hours behind us was a dirt-poor grassless village of scrawny llamas and kids with swollen bellies. Several hours ahead was a place where they dug salt out of the dry lake to load on llama caravans for the six-week haul to the lowlands. It had been this same nowhere for the past seven hours: flat, dry, a constant wind with its thick dust, a few clumps of sharp-needled grass and occasionally a scrubby *th'ola* bush growing half way to your knees. We had five more hours to go.

Three years had passed since that winter day when Karen and I decided to live here, and finally free of her school contracts, she was on her first trip to her new home. Karen was curled up in the back seat with a raging case of *soroche*, the altitude sickness. At 14,000 feet, no wonder. The headaches are the worst, but they dissipate with time. I munched on Guru Hoki-Wan green algae health bars and bags of dried fruits and nuts.

It was a five-hundred kilometer trek. Our driver, Marcos, said he had made the journey "fifty times too many." Marcos was strong and round and meticulous. He wore a wool vest and tie while driving, and was the only company driver who could change a flat out on the desert roads and when finished, stand up unwrinkled and free of dust.

He gripped the wheel and swerved; a tangle of beads and a Saint Christopher medallion danced below the rear-view mirror.

Karen appreciated Marcos. He spoke slowly and used school-perfect Spanish. He was one of the few people she could understand with little effort. Besides, he understood English pretty well, even though he pretended he didn't.

Karen leaned forward between the two front seats. "I just can't believe they would vote to leave their homes. How could they do that? What do you think of the vote, Marcos? Was it a wise choice?"

He thought for a moment. "I do not necessarily support such disruptions to small villages, but for this one, it is a good thing."

"Why good for this one?"

"Most villages have some agriculture to support them. They have water and suitable soil. Here there is nothing. Any change will be an improvement."

I was tempted to say, "I told you so." But instead I offered, "I think the company convinced them their new life could be so much better. I'm sure there was skepticism, but the promise of jobs and a couple of fancy new trucks sure put a stop to that."

Karen arched her back and frowned. "The company gave them some trucks? And they voted in favor?"

"Well, the trucks, and other stuff: training, titles to the land—"

"Titles?"

"There were no papers showing the people owned their homes. But if they agreed to move, the company promised to give clear titles to their new houses in the new town."

Marcos looked over and added, "Titles. That is a treasure."

Karen shook her head. "For a promise of a house and a few trucks, they would abandon their ancestral homes?"

Marcos chuckled. "And the trucks were not even new."

"They were used?" I was genuinely surprised.

"Old trucks, new paint."

"Well," I conceded, "at least the village can make some money with them, hauling things, doing jobs for the company."

"True enough," Marcos said, swerving around a hole filled deep with flour-like dust, "until they fall apart."

"Larry, I just can't believe your company would do things so shoddily. They are mistreating the people, tricking them like that," Karen said.

"Now wait, the company also set up a foundation for them. Put in three million dollars, right up front. The people themselves have complete control over how to spend it. It's supposed to create permanent jobs for when the mine eventually shuts down."

"Like what?"

"They're talking about greenhouses, a hotel, even a gas station."

"Yeah, I'll believe that when I see it," Karen said.

I looked over to Marcos. "I wonder if the people are happy, or maybe a bit excited to leave San Cristóbal. It's amazing the vote was unanimous in favor of the move."

"Well, *ingeniero,* not quite unanimous. There were actually two votes. In the first one only eighty-five percent voted in favor."

"So it passed, right?" Karen asked.

"No, not really, señora. In these remote villages *all* must agree. It must be unanimous or no action is taken."

"Then how did it pass?"

"They held a second vote. Maybe the village leaders put a lot of pressure on the *contras.* I do not know what they said or did, but it must have worked. The second vote was unanimous."

"Larry . . . ," Karen said in that voice I hated.

"Hold on Honey, this is the first I've heard of this."

"Do you suppose the company threatened them?"

"Of course not."

"Or bribed them?"

"We don't do things like that."

Marcos drove with his eyes straight ahead.

For the rest of the afternoon, every half-minute interrupted by a bone-shattering bounce, the Toyota crawled its way across the Bolivian high desert, heading south and then west through as lonely a piece of country as exists outside the moon. The meager annual portion of ten centimeters of rain mostly evaporated before it even wet the ground. The ruts and potholes restricted speed to about twenty kilometers an hour, at least on the good stretches. A few black mountains rose out of the western haze, dark islands floating in a calm sea of white salt.

I was half daydreaming with eyes shut, thinking of the last conversation I had a couple of years ago with Wilson Córdova, the CEO of the La Paz subsidiary of the company. During a fine dinner with expensive French wine I made the mistake of remarking that Karen wanted to write a book about our experiences here. Poor guy had enough problems; he sure didn't need a book written about the mine right now, especially one by someone he suspected of having an anti-mining bias. I tried to reassure him. "I doubt she will ever write it. She hasn't even been to Bolivia yet and probably won't for a long time."

"But if she does write it?"

"I know Karen. She's as honest as they come. She will see for herself all the good we are doing here. And I'll be around to point things out; make sure she sees the truth."

Wilson squeezed his napkin into a tight little ball. "I hope she listens to you," he said.

Six words. I heard only three: *Make it so.*

Marcos braked hard and pulled to the side of the road. Dust enveloped the Toyota. Karen raised her head to stare into the gritty yellow cloud swirling around us. As it settled, we saw an old man sitting by the side of the road unhurriedly fixing his broken bicycle frame. In such remote country I would never pass a stranded person without stopping to see if help is needed. The next time it might be me out there, and I don't like to walk that much.

"No, no problem. All's well," he answered, leaning into the driver's window, with dark eyes both alert and amused. Years of wind and sun had burnt his face into etched mahogany, radiating bronze from deep inside. The depth of the wrinkles gave testimony to a lifetime of harsh conditions. One side of his face was puffed up by the wad of coca tucked in his cheek. His gums were black and a trickle of green saliva dripped down one side of his mouth.

He was at home, delighted at the sight of a couple of middle-aged gringos who definitely were not from these parts. His cheap Chinese bicycle had broken a support, he said, now fixed with splints of brittle *th'ola* sticks held tightly in place by some wire found along the road. "I left Río Grande at six this morning. I have business in Huari. There is much money to be made." His name was Efraím something. He shoved more coca leaves into his mouth.

After eight hours of peddling, he had at least six more to go, through deep sand and across rocky ledges, every bit of it against that damned wind, carrying a load that would choke a Volkswagen. Old Efraím would arrive well into the night. He had a poncho and a hat. He may have been old, but he was one tough guy.

Karen asked, "Would you like us to take you anywhere?"

"No, señora, *pero gracias.* No, I'll just go on. My business awaits me. It makes a month and I have *la carga.* This time it will sell," he said, pointing to his bundle. "But maybe if you could spare some *aguita*?"

I handed him a bottle of water as Karen asked, "Is it always so windy here?"

His answer became a greenish smile. "*Sí,* it is perpetual, señora, the perpetual wind." As he packed the unopened water into his bundle, he turned to look me straight in the eyes and added, "Thank you for the gift."

"It is nothing, only water."

"Oh . . . yes, the water. Thank you for that as well." He smiled, and peddled off north as we headed south.

We were close now, maybe a half hour. We turned north into the bone-dry canyon of the Río Toldos, dodging the occasional boulder poking out of the sand, passing the abandoned Toldos

Mine where the company had built dormitories and dining facilities for the contractors and engineers. A field of parabolic satellite dishes sprouted in the desert like gray mushrooms. Eight or nine identical white Toyota pickups with red flags tied to their radio antennae sat in straight lines, parked with their backs to the buildings. A huge generator ground away, twenty-four hours a day.

We snaked our way up a rocky, yellow-orange rise, bumped down into a gully and started to climb again.

After another bend we passed into the shadow of a narrow canyon and parked at the base of three massive rock slabs towering four hundred feet into the air with vertical and at times overhanging walls. They were red, hard as silica, and knifed thirty stories high into a clear cerulean sky. A condor circled slowly, looking for breakfast.

"The Tres Gigantes," Marcos said as we stared up.

"My God, so magnificent," Karen said. "Listen to the wind, as if they're talking to us."

"They are the guardians of the village. The people say as long as they stand, no harm will come," Marcos said.

There was so much I hadn't mentioned to Karen. Routine sampling of all rock exposures in the district indicated the Tres Gigantes were also mineralized with silver. The engineers were debating if they could mine them as well. It was possible the guardians might be ground into dust and sent on a boat ride to Korea for smelting.

The road climbed a switch-back around twisted and gaping rock formations, tortured at birth by violent surges of explosive volcanism. Jagged, toothy mouths opened to the opaque throats of caves and crevices. Marcos crossed himself, said a prayer, stared ahead and kept driving up the canyon. We splashed across the sickly green trickle of water of the Río Toldos, passed a football field, and drove into a little square plaza paved with cobblestones. We parked for a moment beside the white-washed church wall.

A group of women wearing what looked like a dozen skirts and long leggings were in the plaza filling buckets with water from the single spigot. Small kids ran to their mother's sides and all eyes turned toward us. In an instant the mothers grabbed their buckets, turned their backs, and pulled the kids into their dark adobe houses, shutting the doors behind them.

Karen stared into the now-empty square. An emaciated yellow dog lapped water from the dripping spigot. "Are they shy?"

"No, they are afraid," Marcos said.

"Afraid of what?"

"Us."

"Us? But why?"

"We are outsiders."

We drove up Sucre Street, one of three in the town, bordered on each side by single-story adobe or rock houses. Each was no larger than three by three meters, small when you considered most families had anywhere from three to seven surviving kids. Each family unit commonly occupied two or three such houses, all facing a walled-in patio. Most houses had no windows looking outward, and those that did were closed.

Grass covered every roof as a soft, yellow-brown thatch. Each house had a single, loosely fitted, weather-beaten wooden door, for some reason most of them painted green. Flattened tin cans patched the numerous cracks and holes. House walls were a mixture of brown adobe and rust-colored rocks. Few families could afford to paint their walls, and thus the town was mostly various shades of earth and stone, a camouflage perfectly blended into the surrounding hills.

As I suspected, Karen found it charming: narrow cobblestone streets, little munchkin houses clustered in irregular rows, grass thatching with wisps of smoke coming from numerous black stovepipes stuck in the roofs. "Isn't it interesting how they can make their homes out of native materials? They are so resourceful," she said.

"Enterprising all right," I said. "Mud huts with grass roofs sure are cheap to build, but they aren't the cleanest places to live."

"But look, it really *is* clean here, not even a piece of paper or tin can lying about."

"In a village this poor, even a tin can has value," Marcos pointed out.

As we drove to our new home, I was sure every crack in the doors held eyes busy checking us out. One little girl peered from behind a rock wall. We stopped in front of the house the company had rented for us, the best in town, Marcos said, costing ten dollars a month. Six attached adobe rooms encircled a flagstone patio. Three of the rooms were for our use. We began to unload the many bottles of drinking water, the boxes of health food, school supplies, and medicines.

A dark man, stocky, middle-aged, dressed in a frayed gray suit, staggered his way down the uneven cobblestone street, pausing occasionally to rest his head on his forearm as he leaned against a wall. His pants were unzipped. As the unshaven, squinty-eyed man stopped uncertainly before me, I gagged in a mist of stale beer. He thrust out a damp, limp hand, and greeted me with something like, "Buenffm muffl."

"So very pleased to meet you," I said in my best Spanish. I lied of course. I wiped my hand on my pants.

"Miruffle snoruf," he replied, going into a long, incoherent monologue, breaking three or four times to spit. Although he was friendly enough, the booze got to him before he got to us, so we had no idea who the hell he was or what language, if any, he was speaking. He staggered down the street and disappeared into the plaza, leaving us looking after him in confusion.

"The director of the school," Marcos said. "He said you should visit him some time and take his photograph."

Chapter 3

Los Angelitos

Karen

November 1998

The afternoon wind carried strains of mournful music up the slope from the cemetery. Singing mingled with sobs accompanied the steady beat of drums and instruments I couldn't identify. The villagers were filing into the stone-wall enclosure, skirting the graves, their arms overflowing with wreaths of plastic flowers, purple ribbons, cardboard boxes, colorful woven *aguayos*, and plates of food. Some carried lit candles set in tin cans.

Having climbed in slow motion up this hill for a closer look, I sat breathless on a large rock looking down into the enclosure of graves. The first of November, *El Día de los Muertos.* These would be the last days the villagers paid respect to their loved ones in this cemetery where their ancestors had rested for centuries. The moving of the bodies to the new cemetery near the yet-to-be-built town would begin in several days. At least the damned company had enough smarts not to begin the digging before the celebration.

I removed my down jacket and sweater. I roasted in the afternoon sun, but as soon as I stepped into the shade of a boulder, I shivered, and put them on again. The pounding of my head and somersaulting of my stomach from the *soroche* mingled with tingling excitement of discovery. I really wanted to leave my perch and join the villagers, but would my entrance be intrusive? Would they shrink from me as they had when we arrived in the village? How would I communicate with my beginner's Spanish?

The villagers were setting up the cardboard boxes. In front of some graves they stacked the boxes into pyramid-shaped altars while by others they placed them side by side to create simple tables. The *aguayos*, spread over the boxes, served as tablecloths and on them, the villagers arranged plates with pastries. They lit incense, the smoke carrying a sweet aroma all the way up the hill, and draped purple ribbons and plastic flower wreaths around the crosses. For sure, no live flowers could survive in this desolate desert. Groups gathered at these altars, crossed themselves, and lowered their heads, their lips moving. Then they shared pastries as a plate was passed around.

I summoned my courage and approached the cemetery entrance. I wished Larry were with me, but he'd stayed down at the mining camp after lunch to finish up some work. I didn't want to draw attention to myself, but of course, that was impossible. A woman in dust-covered blue jeans, a puffy down jacket, hiking boots, sunglasses, and a floppy white hat struck a sharp contrast with these Bolivian women in traditional dress. Full skirts, blouses and sweaters layered their bodies with an apron to top off the colorful collage. Stick legs emerged from beneath the folds. Despite the afternoon wind, their black bowler hats perched on their heads like minor miracles. Their bronze faces and rosy cheeks were framed by thick, black hair braided down to their waist, where a colorful ribbon tied the two braids together. My fair skin was greasy with sun-block and my auburn hair retracted in tight curls from a recent permanent.

But as odd as I appeared, no one seemed to notice, or if they did, they paid no attention. As I wandered about the cemetery, men and women turned their backs to me. Only the children stared. If I acknowledged them with a nod of my head or a smile, they slipped behind their mother's skirts or disappeared amid the adult group. Though I felt like an intruder, I did not want to leave. I tried to eavesdrop on the conversations, but the Spanish, mixed with the clicking sounds of Quechua, was incomprehensible.

The villagers knelt before the smallest mounds of earth. The engineers had told me at breakfast that today the *angelitos* would be honored. They had to be fed two to three years after their deaths since such young souls were unable to care for themselves. Tomorrow the villagers would honor the *almas*, the souls of those over eighteen. But those words had meant nothing to me until this moment. Now standing here, the number of tiny graves overwhelmed me. Some families appeared to be honoring more than one. How did they endure so much loss?

Death was not familiar to me. My father had died when I was a child, but I was not allowed to attend his funeral. My mother feared it would be too upsetting for my ten years. We never visited his grave. Here, there was no choice. You couldn't hide from death, couldn't pretend it didn't happen.

The villagers shook bottles of orange soda, keeping their thumb over the opening, and then released a spray of sticky liquid all about the graves.

A little red truck with a wheel missing rested on one grave; on another, a deflated ball. A doll on yet another caught my eye. The plastic had yellowed and cracked. Stringy hair covered its missing eye and the hole where an arm had once been. Who knew how long it had lain there comforting the child resting below the surface?

I got down on my knees and said a grateful prayer for the health of our four children, now in their teens and early twenties. I prayed for the soul of the owner of the doll; I prayed for her mother; I prayed for all the mothers.

A hand rested upon my shoulder. I looked up into a woman's eyes, her face, worn and wrinkled. She reached into her pocket and pulled out a frayed photograph, a precious item in a town where photographs had to be scarce. In it a man and woman stood side by side while in front of them stood four children, stiff and serious, no one touching. She pointed to a tiny girl, at most three years old, standing to the left of her siblings, her big brown eyes staring into the camera. The woman pointed to the grave, shaking her head so that I might understand.

I was grateful for the few Spanish words I had. *"Lo siento,"* I said.

"Gracias," she responded in a soft voice.

I wished I had more words, but even if I did, what would I say? How sad it was that so many children die in her village?

How fortunate I was to live where we had medicine to prevent such deaths?

I gave the woman a weak smile as she offered me a plate of small breads of different shapes and sizes, some covered with coconut and others glazed with sugar. I helped myself to two braided breads. She handed me two more.

"*T'anta gua gua*," she said.

"*T'anta gua gua*," I repeated, wondering what she was talking about. I thanked her and walked out of the cemetery and down the hill to the village, wiping the tears from my cheeks.

Larry didn't say, "I told you so," as I spoke about the number of tiny graves. He listened intently to my experience at the cemetery. Reaching into the pockets of my down jacket, I held out the four little breads, crumbled a bit despite my attempts to keep their shape.

"*T'anta gua gua*," he said.

"What?" I asked.

He walked into the kitchen and returned with a plate stacked high with similar pastries. "A gift from the mining camp chef. *T'anta gua gua*, Quechua for 'little girls' braids.'" He picked one from the plate and bit into it.

"Aren't we supposed to put some of these out for our dead relatives' souls? Their *almas*?" I asked.

Larry bit into another. I frowned.

After some hesitation, Larry agreed not to eat all the pastries, and together we figured out our dead, placed five breads on a plate and laid it on a bench in the courtyard. I gave thanks that in our combined years, we'd lost so few loved ones.

"You know, the mining engineers told me the villagers had to ask their dead for approval to move the cemetery and town," Larry said.

"We could learn from these people. I think while we're here we should practice the rituals that the villagers follow."

"Such as?" Larry studied me with a cautious look.

"We have to buy a llama fetus."

He rolled his eyes.

"Well, remember Marcos said that when a family moves into a new house, they always bury a llama fetus under the front door. Something about the body being an offering to the evil spirits. They stop at the door and eat so they don't go inside and bother the people."

"Honey, I have no idea where we'd get one of those."

I pulled some Bolivianos out of my pocket and handed them to Larry. "Then how about some beer?" I asked.

"You don't drink beer."

"Marcos told us that they also spray beer around the house as a gift to the gods, to ensure good health and wealth."

"Hmmm, well, a beer doesn't sound bad."

Larry left and after five minutes returned with a story about Lourdes Alí, the lady next door.

"She doesn't have much to sell though she certainly has more now than before the company started exploring: one can of tuna, a roll of toilet paper, two candles, but she does have lots of beer." He held up two bottles. "Kinda chubby," he went on, "with a huge gold tooth right in the front of her mouth."

"At least she has teeth," I said, thinking of the number of gaping holes I'd seen in the adults' mouths.

"When she talks she looks like a flashing traffic signal."

I couldn't help but laugh.

"Well, she sold me the beers, but then said I couldn't take them with me. I'd have to drink them all there in her store. Must be some kind of cultural ritual, I guess."

"You can buy them, but can't take them?" I asked.

"Yeah, she said she didn't know me and that the bottles were worth more than the beer itself."

"But you have two bottles."

"Yeah, I had to pay her triple the price to carry them away." He handed me a bottle, opened the other and took a drink.

I shook my head. "No, we're not supposed to drink them. These are for the gods." I took my bottle, popped the cap, put my thumb over the top, shook it vigorously, and let the spray cover the courtyard walls and floor.

Larry looked on as if I were nuts. "Tell me again why we're doing this?"

"We're appeasing the gods by feeding them. Seems hungry people have hungry gods. If this beer is what it takes to keep our home safe or help keep a child alive, then I think we should do it. For the gods."

"Multiple gods. Cool. I'll drink to that," Larry said as he took another long drink, then splashed what was left on the adobe walls.

Chapter 4

Maybe the Dead Ate Them

Karen

November 1998

As the sun set on our first full day in the town, Larry and I hovered around our propane stove warming our hands. We sipped *mate*, a tea made from the coca leaf, supposedly a cure for altitude sickness. I inhaled the steam, my parched mouth and throat craving the moisture. My lips were already chapped and the skin on my fingers, cracking.

Despite the harsh elements, there was something cozy about our new home. The rich, dark wooden floors, imported from the Bolivian tropics, shone throughout the rooms. The sink and two-burner propane stove defined our kitchen at one end of the main room. Photos of our four children and cat hung on one of the green adobe walls.

I didn't feel at all deprived, at least not yet. We were the only house in town with running water. Whoever constructed the house had tapped into the main pipe that fed the spigot in the plaza.

At the other end of the room, chairs crowded around an oval table. This room would lend itself to evening classes in English I hoped to hold for the engineers and the teachers. Rows of shelves allowed us to store all the supplies we'd dragged down from the States: pads of paper, markers, pens, crayons, pencils, games, books, and boxes of survival foods. Hearing what Lourdes Alí's store had to offer, I was glad we'd brought it all.

The cold intensified with the night. Huddled around our stove, we sipped more tea. As the discomfort from my throbbing head and queasy stomach diminished, we played gin rummy until the hanging bare light bulb died with the town generator at ten p.m. Turning off our little propane heater and grabbing a flashlight, we made our way across the courtyard to the bedroom next door.

The construction of these huts impressed me. The adobe walls had to be at least a foot thick, keeping out the intense sun and evening frost.

In the bedroom, frayed, white, floor-length curtains embraced two windows, windows with cracked glass, but nevertheless, glass. A large wooden bureau stood in the corner of the room, and having a strong need to nest, I had already placed our clothes in the drawers. A photo of an austere gentleman looked down from the adobe wall. Someone had gone to the trouble of placing a vase of artificial flowers up high on a corner shelf. A calendar on the wall dated several years back added to my sense of timelessness.

"Not bad accommodations," I said to Larry as I stripped off several layers of clothes and scurried to put on thermal underwear. I hopped under the four blankets that smelled of llama wool.

"We're lucky," Larry said. "Our neighbors don't have any of this."

Larry threw off his clothes and jumped under the blankets in his little bed. I caught a glimpse of his white body in sharp contrast with his sunburned hands and face. We'd moved the two twin beds next to each other with the hopes of claiming some intimacy, but I couldn't imagine how anyone managed, including the villagers, when it was a challenge just to breathe.

The wind howled outside the thick mud walls. Suddenly awake, I felt the heaviness of the woolen blankets like weights upon my body. The sheets felt rough and the dried grass mattress made my skin itch. I resisted scratching. A moment ago sleep embraced me, but there were restless dreams in Spanish. Even in my sleep, I struggled to understand the language. The effort was intensified by a feeling that with even more concentration, I should be able to understand. Images of tiny graves haunted me. My heart raced, my breath was shallow and rapid; my body, distressed.

"You awake?" I asked.

"Yeah."

"Can you sleep?"

"Sort of." A pause. "Not really," Larry said. "It's the altitude. Happens to me every time."

I felt him searching for me under the blankets. He touched my hand.

"You're cold," he said.

"Uh-huh." I shivered.

"Come lie near me. I'll warm you up."

"Is there room?"

"For you, always."

I threw the covers off me and a blast of icy cold air chilled my body.

He lifted his blankets creating a tent. Wrapping the blankets around me, he pulled me close. He was naked and warm. I sank into him molding myself to the contours of his body. He gently kissed my forehead. His mouth was on mine. His breath was warm. But I couldn't breathe. I gasped and pulled away. The coldness hurt in my lungs.

"It's like trying to kiss underwater." I laughed.

"The local folks sure have it down."

"We'll have to ask them how they do it." I smiled at the thought of how well that question would go over with our new neighbors.

I was torn between my need for oxygen and my desire for him. His hands were under my thermal top now, stroking me gently. He slipped off my thermal bottoms.

I gasped for air again, breathing more deeply.

By now my lover's wise hands were busy. The cold was gone. The thin air no longer mattered. He was upon me, kissing me all over, both of us covered by the tent of blankets, immersed in the smell of llama wool and love.

The next morning I awoke to the sound of Larry moving about in the courtyard. I sat up in bed long enough to feel the frigid air and see my breath form clouds in front of my face.

"Get up, sleepyhead," Larry said entering the bedroom. He carried a heater as if reading my mind.

I sat on the edge of the bed and gingerly placed my bare feet on the icy floor.

He bent over and kissed my forehead, then walked over to the cracked window and carefully raised it. "Our windows even open."

A gentle breeze stirred the curtains, carrying with it the stench of urine.

"Where's that smell coming from?" I asked.

"We have a room with a view. The gully is right below us," Larry said, staring out the window.

"And?"

"Welcome to the third world." He smiled at me. "Have you noticed how people just walk up that hill along the gully, the lucky ones with toilet paper in their hands?"

"Oh, so that's the public restroom?"

"Sort of. I don't know why they choose to go above the town. Every rainy season there's a Big Flush and the waters wash everything back downward into the streets."

"I'm glad we have a toilet."

Joining Larry at the window, I studied the two-foot wide ditch with only a trickle of toxic, green water in it.

"And do you know where our toilet leads?"

"Don't tell me. The gully?"

"Yeah, there's the pipe sticking out of our wall."

The day we'd driven into town, a small girl and boy were kneeling by the gully. The terrain was flatter there and the gully, more like a tiny creek. Like preschoolers all over the world they were enjoying this large sandbox full of damp, moldable earth. The knees of their baggy pants were covered with wet sand, the sleeves on their sweaters equally damp and sand-covered. Every so often, the boy reached up and wiped his runny nose leaving a mixture of grime and yellow snot on his red wind-blown cheeks. There were squeals of excitement as the little girl scooped up the wet earth and plopped it onto the growing pile by the gully's edge; then the second child followed. The two giggled and jumped up and down as the pile grew.

Out in the courtyard, the sun was already beginning to remove the morning chill. I glanced at the dish where I had placed the braided breads the day before. Only a few crumbs remained. Larry watched me. A grin spread across his face.

"You ate those," I said.

"I didn't touch them. Scout's honor." He placed his index and middle fingers against his forehead.

I studied him.

"Maybe we have rats, or it was that bird." He pointed to a tiny golden bird that sat on the thatched roof chirping away. "Or," he teased, "maybe the dead ate them."

"Maybe so." I smiled.

I crossed the courtyard, walked past the large cement sink, and entered the little bathroom warmed by another propane heater. Thankful for plumbing wherever it might lead, I sat on the toilet only to jump up with a howl. Too close to the heater, the plastic toilet seat had partly melted. A three-inch pink welt formed on my thigh. Near tears, I moved the heater as far away from the toilet as possible.

Larry appeared at the door. "I'd better show you how that shower works."

He squeezed into the tiny space. In the corner of the bathroom was a contraption of brass and aluminum tubes in a big metal box hooked up to another propane tank. Larry held a match to the pilot light while turning various handles. The whole contraption shuddered, some jets burst into flames and a trickle of hot water was forced out of a showerhead. I disrobed and jumped in. Standing under the water, I closed my mouth tight to prevent any hostile microbes from entering and washed off the layer of dust I'd accumulated from head to toe.

How did the townspeople clean themselves? We'd seen the women break the icicles off the spigot near the town plaza, fill their plastic pails with water, and haul them up the cobblestone streets, dripping and splashing their way back to their adobe houses. I shivered at the thought.

"Don't come out without dressing," Larry shouted to me through the door. "We have company."

I peeked out. Larry was surrounded by five or six children, all under twelve years. Some were toddlers. They looked like kids in photos of the depression era. Their frayed sweaters had rolled up cuffs, their pants were too large and patched, and each nose runny.

When I made my appearance, Larry was reading, and the children had lined up, their backs to a wall. All were holding candles and mumbling to themselves with eyes shut. The youngest sneaked a look at me with his huge brown eyes.

"What are they doing?" I asked.

"Not sure, really. They don't talk much. Praying, I think. They came to the door and asked if they could pray, and I said 'Sure, why not?' Next thing I knew they walked in and—well—they've been praying ever since."

"How long will they do this?"

"I have no idea."

In Spanish, I asked the children their names. Nobody answered but most stopped praying. They just stared at me. I asked them why they were praying. All looked down at their feet. I asked them if they liked their school, played soccer, if they lived in town. Did they have llamas? There were no answers, all eyes cast down, hands to their sides.

I walked back to Larry. "What should we do?"

"Pretty somber group. Let 'em pray, I suppose."

I looked again at the children. They had resumed praying. I went into the kitchen when another knock came from the door.

Larry led Iván Quíspe, foreman of the mine crew, into our kitchen. Of medium stature, his broad face, dark skin, and high cheekbones indicated his indigenous origins. His competence with Quechua, Spanish, and English spoke of the three worlds he straddled. His appearance was western: jeans and a plaid shirt and a blue cap with the insignia, *Cia. Minera Altiplano*, the Bolivian branch of the company, stitched across the front. His fingers were thick, rough, calloused, those of a man used to hard, physical work.

He glanced at the line of children as he walked in. His large sad eyes studied his shoes as he refused our offer of granola bars and tea. He'd come to see how we were doing. Sensing my limited Spanish, he did his best to show off his English. "Señores," he said in a quiet voice, "you don't have to stay up here. In a very comfortable house in the mining camp you want to live?"

I recalled seeing a white wooden house up on a knoll as we drove through the mining camp. With its picture window and green shutters, it belonged in Akron, Ohio.

"Thanks, Iván," I said, glancing about our spacious kitchen and office, "but we have everything we could need here."

Now Iván urged Larry. "*Ingeniero*, don't you think in the mining camp your wife is to be more comfortable?"

"We appreciate your offer, but from here she can just walk over to the school to teach."

Iván scrunched up his forehead as if trying to understand. "La señora wants to teach? Here?"

"Yes, if they will let me," I answered.

"Why?" Iván asked.

"We want to get to know the people," Larry said.

"What is there to know? These people are not so educated."

"There's so much culture here," I said.

"Culture?" He sounded surprised.

"Well, just the way they celebrated *El Día de los Muertos.*"

"You liked that, señora?"

"I don't know that I liked it. It's just interesting."

"Interesting?" Iván repeated my word, mulling it over. "You know, many people say these old customs are, um, how do you say? Primitive? They say they are just old superstitions."

I glanced at Larry and asked, "Like believing their dead are still with them? Or burying a fetus when they move into a house, spraying soda or beer?" *Had the beer left a scent on the walls?*

"Well, yes." Iván was watching our faces closely as if expecting some shocked expression.

"Damned waste of good beer," Larry said, catching my eye.

Iván turned to the door and as if making one last effort to convince us, said, "Well, of course, it's your choice, but these people will molest you."

His translation of the word *molestar* threw me for a moment. "Bother us?"

"Actually, they seem shy of us, at least the women," Larry added.

"But they will. The villagers I know. Good people, but they never leave you alone."

Larry walked with him to the door but stopped at the children. Each child held up a plastic bag. Larry asked, "What are these kids doing?"

"Praying for the *almas,* the souls of your family."

"Why?"

"At this time every year they do it. From house to house they go. They pray. The families give them food, sometimes *t'anta gua gua,* sometimes candy, sometimes actual meals. Whatever they can. Two or three days they do this. They never quit."

Hearing this, I dropped two granola bars in each of the waiting bags.

Iván stared at the line of children and warned, "You will tire of it. You will see."

Chapter 5

Alone on a Dangerous Sea

Larry

November 1998

We were determined to meet the neighbors. Sticking to the sunny side of the narrow street, we walked the half block to the plaza. A black cat jumped from roof to roof trying to catch a lone bird. A couple of skinny dogs lay in the sun. A mother called her kids in the distance; the haunting sound of Andean flutes was broken by the braying of a burro from the other side of town. A thin layer of acrid smoke bathed the village in blue-gray.

The few women we greeted with "*Buenos días*" silently turned their backs as we approached, resuming their activities only after we had passed. Maybe our cameras frightened them. Marcos had mentioned the women in small villages reacted with a gut-level reluctance to being photographed.

Small houses lined three sides of the plaza. On the fourth was the largest building in town, the two-story, whitewashed church. Like most of the rest of town it had a thatch roof, but unlike the small homes, its walls were massive, at least five feet thick at their base, slowly tapering to two or three feet at the top, giving the church a permanent, solid foundation. A similarly tapered wall encircled the huge building, forming a narrow courtyard between the church and the plaza.

A pair of triple-decked bell towers rose from the south side of the courtyard wall, each with numerous greenish-black bells. The easternmost tower leaned perceptibly. Cracks at its base suggested it was not long for this world. One tower lacked a bell, purposely left empty from the days of the Spanish colonialists when unfinished churches were spared taxation. The entrance was a green wooden door kept from falling to pieces by cast-iron braces and bolts. Shrunken and warped by the sun, the door looked as old as Jesus himself.

We pressed on it, but pulled our hands away as it was opened from the inside by a frail man standing a full hand shorter than Karen. His faded suit, worn thin, was patched at the elbows. Although he looked sixty, he was probably in his forties. His build was that of a skinny thirteen year-old.

"So pleased to meet you, welcome to the church of San Cristóbal. My name is Santitos Colque Colque. Welcome, come in, come in, I am the guardian of the church. You know we have many thefts in the Altiplano. Oh, yes, it is a big business as collectors want the paintings and bells and—come, let us walk to the church. Come, come, I will guide you," he said, and before our reply, added, "The church was built sometime around 1620 by slave labor brought by the Spaniards from Argentina. They built it atop a Quechua ceremonial site so the one true God could reign forever over and above the gods of the Quechua. Look, those bells in the towers, they are engraved, forged in 1776. This church, the entire building, is a registered historic site. Yes, from some group in Europe, Europe—the Patrimonial Mundial or something. I think."

In both body and speech he fidgeted, jumping at the slightest sound or movement, be it rustling of the wind or the turn of my head. He was a mouse with too many cats in his neighborhood.

"This church, our village, was a refuge for the Spanish travelers between central Bolivia and the Pacific. The village was founded here because of the spring. It is such a good spring. Very dependable. The mule trains loaded with silver from Potosí would stop here to rest, to get food, and then hike down to the port at Antofagasta. So much silver they hauled."

He went on, "Once or twice a year Father Aurelio comes from Uyuni to perform mass and marry all the young couples and collect some funds. This is a Catholic church, but quite frankly the Quechua gods are welcome, for on an occasional Tuesday we have Quechua ceremonies, and the spirits and demons are all here, of course, how could it be otherwise? But not El Tío, not that god, we would never let him into such a holy place." Santitos seemed to shudder.

"El Tío?" I asked, "Who is that?"

"Oh, he is *El Diablo*, señor, he kills, he tortures, he is pure evil. Pray to the saints that you never meet him."

We hadn't walked more than fifteen feet from the gate in the wall. I understood about half of what he said.

"He's cute," Karen said as we approached a small door on the side of the church.

From inside his jacket Santitos pulled a cast-iron rusty key the size of a wild-west six-shooter and likely twice as heavy. With both hands he inserted it into an equally rusty lock. It wouldn't turn. Santitos leaned his body into it and with a few snaps and crunches, the door slowly opened to a choir of creaks and screeches.

Karen peeked into the dark interior. Like me, she hesitated a moment, then gently stepped inside.

It was as cold as a meat locker, kept insulated by a floor of rough flagstone and the thick mud walls, plastered and white-washed. Holes in the roof allowed water to enter, staining large swaths of the interior walls a light brown, but in many places the walls glowed a faint blue or pink, as if a rainbow were trying to pierce its burnt lime coating.

Perhaps this glow came from the north end of the building where pale light reflected off an entire wall covered by a mass of polished gold and silver. It stood at least seven meters high and five wide, with niches holding silver statues, saints, ornaments, and plates engraved in Latin and Spanish. Statues of five or six of the saints were draped in the pontificalia of embroidered white and purple robes. The holy mother was there, and of course, the mandatory statue of Jesus on the cross.

The little mouse was right; it was worth a fortune.

"It was a gift of the Viceroy of Arica in 1792," Santitos said, and then whispered, "It is pure gold, carried by mules all the way from the Pacific. You can see why they need me to guard here. This is my life. I am the only one who the Bishop trusts enough. I am here every day, even when nobody wants to come in.

"I am also the sacristan. I do not get paid for it. Visitors like you often give a little something to help me. But there are almost no visitors so I am very poor. Just a little something they give, whatever they can spare means so much, usually a few coins, sometimes only an onion or two."

Santitos spoke non-stop as we toured the sacristy and other rooms in the church, all similarly dark and cold. He placed both hands on the baptismal font, caressing it like a mother her first born. "Made of local alabaster," he said, reluctant to take his hands away. A corner darker than most was filled with an antique foot-powered pipe organ, "a gift of the King of Spain himself, from 1779. Brought here on mules all the way from Antofagasta."

Our eyes became accustomed to the dark. Rough-hewn benches sat in parallel rows on the flagstone floor. Beams of white light cut the darkness from numerous holes in the roof.

"Come, you must meet our *Patrón*, our San Cristóbal himself." Santitos motioned for us to enter a small room to the left of the altar.

It was big enough for only four or five people but with a high ceiling rising up to the grass thatch. An ornate glass case in a carved wood frame filled half the room. Several dozen candles, some still burning, covered a table before the case. Santitos walked up and pulled a purple velvet curtain aside, saying, "Here is our *Patrón*. He is beautiful, no?" He knelt and prayed before his saint.

Inside the case a life-sized statue of a tall, muscular man stood in a field of flowers. A well-trimmed black beard and long, curling hair framed a face beaming with holy serenity. Flowing white, gold, and purple robes draped loosely over his body. He leaned with both hands on a wooden staff, apparently to aid his footing in a rough passage. On his right shoulder balanced a cherubic little boy. Both the *Patrón* and the boy were graced by halos.

"San Cristóbal, our *Patrón,* was a tall man, so much bigger than me," Santitos said. "He became a Christian late in life when an old hermit told him of a river where many people had drowned while trying to cross. Perhaps with his great strength he could serve God by helping people to the other side.

"One day he carried a small child through the swift waters, but for some reason the child was so heavy, heavier than any other person, even heavier than all the adults combined. It was a struggle, but he brought the child safely to the other shore.

"Then, señores, can you imagine, the child turned into the Christ who told him it was the weight of the world he was carrying."

"Do you believe this story?" I asked him.

"There can be no doubt, no doubt at all. Is not the world heavy, señor? The weight of everybody's sins must be very heavy just by itself, but to add the weight of all the rocks and buildings and animals, you can just imagine."

"Yes, but. . . ." I let it die.

"So that is why San Cristóbal became the patron saint of all travelers," Santitos added.

"He must be our patron saint, too," Karen said, "We are always traveling somewhere."

"Honey, it's a *statue.* It's made of wood and paint. It's all a myth. Even the flowers are plastic, for God's sake."

"It's more than a statue, and it's not just a myth," Karen insisted, "It is a spiritual connection to a world we only vaguely understand."

"Why do people delude themselves so much? Why not just trust reality?" I countered.

"Look at his face," Karen said, pulling me toward her and pointing at the saint, "It seems almost alive. The eyes—look—I swear he is moving, observing us, listening to us—look."

His eyes didn't move for me. All I saw were two marbles of blue glass. "Hell, even their saints are foreigners. It would be nice to believe like our little friend here. It would make life so much simpler, even peaceful I suppose, but you'd have to give up your free will and a big chunk of your intelligence. It ain't worth it."

Karen stared at the people's *patrón.* "It's wonderful to believe in such things. Life isn't all rational."

"Yeah, well, it seems to me it's the irrational that causes most of the problems in the world." I didn't wait for Karen to reply when I asked Santitos, "What happened to your *patrón?*"

"He was martyred, tortured to death by the *Romanos*. Every saint must be tortured, no?"

Just as we had intended, we had met one of our neighbors, but I wanted to get outside into the sun. We thanked him profusely and promised to return soon, after slipping him fifty Bolivianos, about seven dollars.

His smile was bigger than his face. "Do come again, señores, come any time. I am here at your service. My name is Santos, Santitos Colque Colque. I know the history of the church of San Cristóbal. Come again and I can tell you of the bodies buried under the floor, of the treasures buried with them, of that which is hidden behind the walls. I know it all. That is why they call me 'Santitos'," he said, all the while pumping our hands.

He accompanied us to the green wooden door in the wall around the courtyard, talking constantly, "Look at that sky, so blue it is. Isn't it beautiful? We who live here on this rocky island, I often think, are like castaways: leagues and leagues from anywhere, vistas without end, alone on a dangerous sea. But the *patrón* is our safe harbor, and he will be here in your time of need. When you need him, he will welcome you."

Chapter 6

Goblins and Gods

Karen

November 1998

Nothing worked: the little cook stove on which I heated my water for tea kept blowing out, the jets to the gas heaters that warmed our freezing fingers and toes constantly plugged up, and the shower spat out scalding water—better scalding than freezing. I tried to be grateful, knowing that my neighbors had none of this, but the discomfort overwhelmed me. I was still waking up at night gasping for oxygen and disturbed by nightmares of death. An itchy, red rash appeared on my legs from the dryness or from the detergent not rinsed from the sheets. Who knew which? And to think it was my idea to stay here! Larry would have chosen the mining camp had I not insisted that we live in the village to better document the changes.

Larry shuffled the cards for our nightly rummy session. I glanced at my Timex: eight thirty-five. It would be our last game before bed. I winced as I tried to pick up my cards with cracked fingertips.

The propane heater hissed under the table, warming our feet, and a yellow bulb strung on a wire overhead cast a shadowy light upon the cards. Each card, a copy of a Van Gogh painting, added a spot of color to our drab surroundings. I had bought Larry the deck when he was an aspiring painter, before he returned to geology full time. Clutching a replica of "Starry Night," even a poor one, comforted me now.

A knock on the courtyard door interrupted our game.

"At this hour?" I looked again at my Timex. Eight forty-five.

Larry, ducking so as not to hit his head on the frame of the kitchen door, headed out to the street where I heard him speaking with a man. Then he returned to the kitchen.

"I think this guy is asking for a ride to a bus stop. Says his name is Senóbio Condori. Something about his baby, his wife and a stove, but I'm not really sure." Larry pointed to the man who was now standing stiffly in our courtyard.

"What are you talking about, stove?" I asked.

"There's no bus service to town because of the sharp curves in the road so the bus lets everyone off somewhere down in the plains below town."

"Can we say no?"

"Guess we could, but we want to get to know the villagers, don't we?" He smiled as he zipped up his jacket and put on a woolen hat. "He said it won't take long, just *un ratito*."

We headed down the canyon, the stranger in the back seat. Although his features were indistinguishable in the unlit vehicle, it was clear that Senóbio was a small, thin man, not much bigger than I. Dark hair framed his angular face, and his smile revealed a full set of straight teeth, not a single one missing. His hands danced as he sculpted pictures to accompany his story. Thankful that he enunciated his words, I grasped some of what he said. His wife left by bus two days ago for the distant town of Soniquiera to buy some supplies and a stove. It was a twelve-hour ride.

"I hear, *profesora*, that you will teach English," he said.

"Yes, I am hoping to, but the school is always closed."

"Unfortunately there are many holidays and strikes, but it will open in *un ratito*. I know because I am a teacher. I teach English."

"So you speak English?" For a brief moment I hoped to have an English interpreter to help me at the school.

"No, I don't *speak* English. There is no way to learn to speak here, but I do teach it."

After a long pause, Senóbio continued, "Many of us teachers would like to learn to speak, *profesora*. Perhaps you can help us."

I'd never taught English before and I'd assumed this identity of *profesora*. No one even questioned it. I took a deep breath and replied, "*Con mucho gusto.*"

"I also teach Quechua to my students," Senóbio added. "I do not want our culture to be lost."

This comment sparked interest in Larry who had not said a word since we started down the winding road. "Quechua culture?" he asked.

"Yes, I am planning on writing a book one day." His hands framed a rectangular shape.

Larry and I glanced at each other. "*Qué buena suerte!*" Larry said. "Karen and I would like to document the culture of San Cristóbal and the changes with the move. Perhaps you can help us."

"Yes, yes, we can help you!"

"We?" I asked.

"Yes, my grandfather, Juan de la Cruz, the keeper of the customs. A very wise man." Senóbio tapped his head with his fingers. "I will introduce him to you. He knows all the stories of the people."

The headlights bounced off the rock walls casting eerie forms as we bumped along the rocky road. Looking out the side window, I saw nothing, just black. In front, the headlights flashed for an instant on cracks and crevices of a cliff face, now all shades of gray in the artificial light. A shiver went through me. Shadowy forms appeared and disappeared as if the rocks themselves were moving. We rode in silence.

Larry was driving fast, but he had driven this route many times and seemed confident. I looked behind me and could see Senóbio's hands clutching the back of Larry's seat like a steering wheel. His eyes, now visible to me, widened like a frightened animal.

"*Ingeniero*," he said, "there are several bad bumps ahead, just beyond this curve."

Larry slowed down a bit. There were no bumps.

Senóbio continued to stare wide-eyed at the cliffs flashing before him. "This is a very bad part, *ingeniero*, very dangerous," he said. He fingered a metal chain around his neck, what appeared to be a cross.

The bumps were no worse than on the rest of the road.

As we passed the cliffs, Senóbio peered out the side window and I followed his gaze. I saw nothing. He then turned to the back window as we drove on. I felt unnerved, as if someone had told me a ghost story.

"Why did you say dangerous?" I asked.

"*Pues*, we just passed El Caballo Blanco," Senóbio said, resuming his position of staring ahead, his hands now more relaxed at his side. "By day it looks like a big white rock, there by the side of the road. But by night it becomes a white horse, huge, very angry and it will kill you if it can. Many of us have seen it. Many from the village, women, children, it matters not, have been killed by it. Tonight it did not awaken."

"So we are safe then?" I asked, not sure what to make of all this.

"No, not yet," Senóbio warned, pointing to the cliffs flashing before us. "Look at these caves. There are so many places for the *achachilas* to live. No, we're not safe yet. Three kilometers more, it's better, but we are never safe, even on the *pampa*."

"*Achachilas* are . . . ?" I asked.

"They are devious spirits that live in the rocks. They look like many things, like dwarfs with horns or animals with cleft hooves. Often they are very ugly, but they can fool you, too. They can appear as a horse or a llama or as a pretty little girl, and then suddenly change and attack you. They delight in tormenting us. They are watching right now, looking for ways to harm us."

I looked out my window, fully alert. "Harm us, how?" I asked.

"They chase our llamas and sheep, make them stray long distances where it takes sometimes days to find them. They pull potato plants out of the ground. They make young girls get pregnant. If an old person sees one, he can be made blind, or dumb, or his hair may turn white. And," he paused, "they cause road accidents."

I reached over and placed my gloved hand on Larry's thigh. "Better slow down," I said.

He glanced at me, rolled his eyes, and then lowered his speed.

"What can you do to avoid these *achachilas*?" I asked.

"Nothing. There is nothing you can do. The saints will protect you if your faith is strong."

Larry gave a nervous little laugh. I realized that I'd wrapped my arms around myself. Senóbio was silent and serious. As silly as it seemed to me, I was glad we were driving away from the rocks; not that I believed these *achachila* guys were real or anything, but the whole idea creeped me out.

We drove along the sandy road, now flat and even. The night sky twinkled with low-hanging stars casting enough glow that we could see the dusty earth going on forever and ever before it rose in the distance to form shadowy hills.

"If this desert floor were any higher," I said, "our hair would be singed by the stars."

Senóbio pointed out the Southern Cross, seen only in the Southern hemisphere. He explained that it was not very much like a cross, but you could see at least the three bright stars and the weaker one on the right. He said he could find himself anywhere, and knew which way was east and west just by the time of night and the position of the stars. I was glad someone knew where we were.

I fingered my Timex trying to see the little hands in the dim lights of the Toyota's dashboard. Nine-thirty. I found comfort from this marker of time. As absurd as I knew it was, it grounded me in this Dali-esque landscape.

After we'd driven in silence a while, Senóbio said, "Please stop here. This is where the bus will come."

There was no indication that this patch of land was any different from the patches before it or the patches to come. No sign. No bench. Nothing.

Larry killed the engine.

"The bus will be here in *un ratito*," Senóbio said. Cold air rushed into the vehicle as he opened the door. He got out and climbed up one of the dunes to get a better view.

The wind blew hard and the sand pelted the windshield. I checked my Timex. Nine thirty-five. It felt later. Larry yawned. We reclined in the seats, trying to stay warm and rest while Senóbio stood watch outside, his thin jacket wrapped about him.

"What do you think?" I asked Larry.

"About what?"

"About *achachilas* living in the rocks and things that go bump in the night." I widened my eyes to stress the *spooky*.

"I might have to go fight those *achachilas* to get the silver."

I wasn't sure if he was kidding or not.

The door opened sometime later and Senóbio climbed into the back seat. He rubbed his bare hands together, and then blew warmth into them. I glanced at my watch. Exactly ten.

"Maybe the bus broke down," Larry said.

"No, it will be here soon, *un ratito más*," Senóbio said with certainty. He waited just a few minutes before returning to his look-out point.

Larry muttered to himself, "I could be asleep in bed. Warm." He turned the engine on for a few minutes letting the heat blast.

We were quiet, each of us studying the starry night through the front window of the vehicle. I reached over and grasped his furry gloved hand.

A shout from Senóbio. Ten-fifteen. Lights appeared in the distance. There was nothing to obscure the view and we watched the lights disappear and reappear for a good twenty minutes. Yes, it was a bus, about half the size of the buses in the United States. A tortoise-like hulk, it crept over the desert hills. It looked old and tired, as if it had traveled many miles. As it approached we could see numerous bundles tied to the frame on top. Senóbio trudged over to the car to let us know this was the bus, and then stationed himself by the roadside so the driver would stop.

The bus pulled up in a cloud of dust, lurched to a halt, and leaned to the right. We watched as the driver opened the door and Senóbio spoke with him. Then the door closed and the bus crept away leaving him standing alone in a second cloud of dust. He returned to the vehicle and climbed in, explaining that the driver had said the bus from Soniquiera was on its way. It did have a bit of trouble, but was okay now. It was coming.

He paused before asking, "Maybe we should drive on the road toward Soniquiera?"

Larry's eyes widened. "No," he said with more assertion than I usually heard. "We'll stay here."

As Senóbio walked back to his post, Larry said, "I'm half-tempted to just go home and leave him to meet his wife."

I looked at Larry in disbelief.

"Well," he said, "he's managed before without us."

"Where would they sleep?" I asked. "They have a baby and a stove."

"There's a small adobe hut not too far from here."

He was right. These people had survived without our help, but leaving seemed pretty heartless.

'No, I couldn't do that," he conceded. "Let's see what happens." We snuggled as best we could with the gear shift between us.

A single light approached in the distance.

"Probably a motorcycle," Larry said.

We could see Senóbio standing at his post jumping from one foot to the next.

Ten-fifty. I took off the silly watch and jammed it in my pocket. As the vehicle got closer we could see it was a small bus like the one before it, but with only one headlight. It crept along under the weight of many bundles and squeaked to a stop.

The door swung open and a woman stepped out, a bulging cloth strapped to her back. The bus driver untied the ropes which held the bundles on top. Larry and I both sighed with relief.

The woman pointed to various packages, including a metal stove, and the driver took them off and then tied down the remaining bundles once again. Weary faces peered out the windows as the bus crawled away.

Larry and Senóbio somehow squeezed all the items into and atop the Toyota. Senóbio introduced his wife, Vañia, and the two climbed into the back seat. His wife pulled the bundle around from her back and I could hear the sucking sounds of an infant at her breast. I'd have loved to have seen her face, but it was just too dark. The woman whispered in Quechua.

We began once again to ascend the winding canyons. Larry asked, "Senóbio, these *achachilas*, do you think they'd get in the way of our mining silver here?"

Senóbio shifted to the left and forwards a bit so that he could place himself between the two front seats. Fingering his cross and his wide eyes scanning the rocks, he said, "No, *ingeniero*, no, I don't think that would be possible."

"Why not?" Larry asked.

"Because El Tío would be angry if anything got in the way of the gift."

"El Tío? Isn't he the one who Santitos was so afraid of?" I asked.

"He is the god of the underground. He rewards us with springs of fresh water and silver veins, but *only* if we respect him. He can be angry, but also pleased if we show him the respect he is due."

"But I thought your god was Pachamama," said Larry.

"We have many gods, *ingeniero*. We have the Catholic god, of course, and also the Pachamama. *S*he is the god of everything above the earth like the weather, the sunshine, the winds and the lightning. El Tío is the god of things below the earth, of earthquakes and volcanoes as well as gold and silver, like the vein your company found in San Cristóbal, *ingeniero*. This is the gift from El Tío."

Larry was glancing at the rear view mirror trying to make out Senóbio's face.

"Hundreds of years ago," Senóbio went on, "at the time of the first Spanish, El Tío told our people that he was hiding a gift only for those who believed in him, and prophesied in the year 2000, that gift would be revealed. He said it would be buried somewhere here, around San Cristóbal. He said it would be a gift of silver, the largest and richest silver deposit in all of Bolivia, unlike any ever seen before. He said it would bring a new life to the people who continued to believe in him, a new life of wealth."

Larry and I tried to absorb what Senóbio was telling us.

Finally I asked, "Do the people still believe in El Tío?"

"Of course, *profesora*, we believe in him. That is how we have survived for so many years. We have held to the old ways."

"But how do you know that this silver deposit is the gift?" I asked.

"Well, it's almost 2000, is it not?" Senóbio asked. "Is not the silver here in San Cristóbal just like he promised? He said we would be so rich we would live in new white houses shining in the sun from all the silver we have. The engineers are talking about a new town with houses such as these, are they not? It must be the gift, *profesora*, it can be no other."

"So, many people believe that the silver was prophesied by El Tío?" I asked. "Does that explain why they voted to move the town?"

"Yes, *profesora*, we would be punished if we refused such a gift. The town must be moved." He paused before adding, "And we are very poor. I am one of the few men with work and my salary is one hundred dollars a month. We need the jobs the mine will bring."

I wanted to ask Senóbio questions. I wanted to know how long his family had lived in San Cristóbal; how they all felt about leaving the house they'd built themselves, the earth where they had cleared the rocks in order to plant their crops, the places they had performed Quechua ceremonies. Would he leave his teaching position to work in the mine? I felt frustrated by my limited Spanish and too exhausted to even try to ask these questions.

Larry rubbed his hand over his balding head as if trying to smooth out lots of wrinkled thoughts. "This Tío was sure right about one thing. This deposit is the largest ever found in Bolivia. It's enormous." He grew silent again in thought.

We drove the rest of the way home. The only sound was the suckling baby.

As I undressed that night, my watch fell out of my pocket. It read midnight as we climbed into bed.

"What if the prophecy's real?" I asked. "You've discovered the silver very close to the year 2000."

"Coincidence."

"What if it's not mere coincidence?"

Larry was silent.

When I awoke the next morning, my stomach was growling, a good sign because altitude sickness had robbed me of hunger. I imagined a hot breakfast, an omelet or maybe even pancakes. It would be a short ride to the mining camp *comedor*.

Out in the street, we found our Toyota covered in bubbles. A man was lugging a small plastic bucket of water. He must have already made half a dozen trips to get enough water to make the vehicle that soapy. As he approached, we guessed it must be Senóbio.

He smiled when he saw us, showing off his perfect teeth. His high cheekbones, an Amerindian nose, and almond shaped eyes came together in a pleasing way.

"*Gracias,*" he said shaking our hands. "Thank you for everything last night."

We stared at the mounds of bubbles on the Toyota and at the small bucket Senóbio carried up from the faucet in the plaza about fifty yards away.

"I'll be done in *un ratito.*"

I glanced at my Timex. Eight-forty and the *comedor* closed at nine.

Chapter 7

The Doctor and
the Gua Gua Banana

Larry

November 1998

It sounded like a cat coughing up a couple of hairballs. I groaned, rolled over, and tried to go back to sleep. A few minutes later I heard it again, coming from the front of the house. Karen and I crawled out of bed and peered out the door. No cat. Instead, a short, square-jawed man with hair sticking out in all directions bumped down the cobblestone street on a motorcycle, gathering speed and then popping the clutch when he passed our front door. The bike coughed and sputtered, then died with a little hiss of blue-white smoke. The man was dressed in a frayed suit jacket, wool vest, and thin, cotton pants. He pushed the bike back up the slight incline to the top of the street and tried the whole process again. It didn't catch.

Three women with little kids clinging to their skirts stood watching on the sunny side of the street.

He had a square face, not rounded like the women's, nor thin and elongated like many of the men's. Like most descendants of the Quechua, he had no facial hair. He must have been an athlete—his body was all muscle. I surprised him by walking over to help push the cycle up the hill.

"Thank you," he said, trying to catch his breath. "Matilda is getting old. She is like my wife: stubborn, but when she is happy she is very reliable." He smiled, showing a mouth full of thick, strong teeth, except for two missing on the left side.

I answered between gasps for air, "Wives can be like that. Not sure which is better, a happy motorcycle or a happy wife."

His eyes sparkled. "Well, if they are both happy, a man can have two good rides."

It's hard to laugh at 14,000 feet.

At the top of the hill he again turned the key, stuck it in gear, and prepared for the bumpy ride ahead.

"I am Octavio Lopez Colque," he said, shaking my hand and patting my shoulders in Altiplano tradition. "Thank you for the help. I am the *Enfermero Auxiliar*. There is young man injured out on the *pampa*."

Karen crossed the street from the shade of our doorway to join the three *chola* women leaning against the sunny wall, adding her floppy, white sun-hat to the line of three slightly tilted bowlers. The three women nodded to Karen, said nothing, then returned to watching us. At least they nodded; a small improvement on the turned backs of the past few days.

I pushed the cycle and Octavio was off again, popping the clutch halfway down the road. Again the engine failed to catch.

He slumped near the base of a wall, soaking up the sun. I walked down the hill to join him, letting the heat evaporate the sweat from my shirt.

"No ride today," I said.

"No, not today. It is probably too late anyway." His head drooped down nearly to his knees. He spit between his legs.

"I'll radio the mine camp. There may be a mechanic or a vehicle you can use," I said. Sure enough, one of the geologists had a vehicle and was willing to take him to the remote ranch out in the *pampa*. After telling him a vehicle was on its way, I asked, "You said it may be 'too late' for the young man?"

"He was struck by lightning. It is common, sometimes three a year. It is so flat out there; the herders have no place to hide. They almost always die. The storms are so powerful with strong hail and lightning. Did you know that llama attract the lightning? It is their wool, it builds up electricity. Below a cloud you can hear it hissing. Many llama are killed every year, and, of course, the young people as well. They are only children, often only ten, maybe fifteen."

Octavio continued his story in a didactic voice devoid of emotion. He seemed tired, or resigned. "Here in our village, about 40% of our children die before they are five. They are dirty and they don't eat well. When people have a sickness, they come to my little office here in San Cristóbal and I diagnose their problems and dispense a few medicines. It isn't free, but it isn't expensive either, and with the small amount of money I bring in, I buy more medicines for the next time."

"There is a company doctor down at the mining camp now. I think his name is Islas," Karen said.

"Yes, Javier Islas. He is a good man."

"Does he help?"

"Yes, this company is different. It is a Gringo company. They care more than do the local ones, or the government." He leaned over and let a ball of spit slowly drop to the ground, creating a bit of a puddle between his legs. "It has always been the case for as long as I can remember. The government is corrupted. All of it. We can never trust them. The Americans just want things to operate smoothly, with no social problems, so they help us more."

"Really? You trust foreigners more than Bolivians?" Karen asked.

"No. No, not 'trust'—well, maybe—but the Americans are certainly more generous."

"Surely some in La Paz are honest with you," I said.

"Yes, of course, a few. But most of the rich only trick and abuse us. They are powerful people. At least the Americans are new to us and we have no history with them. But they are not perfect, either. For example, I have 150 llama. The Americans do not realize how delicate they are. If we are forced to move them they will try to return to their familiar pastures, but if fences prevent them, probably half will die. The company has offered us nothing in case of that happening. Nothing. I will have to hire even more old women to guard them, and they offered nothing for that either. I fear the changes that are coming."

"I doubt the head office in Reno has even been told of this," I said.

"Probably not. That is because they listen to the managers in La Paz. They do not come to speak with us. Everything your country hears comes from the mouths of those who care only for themselves."

Octavio spit on the ground again. I did the same. It seemed appropriate at the time. Karen looked away.

"But that is not the worst," Octavio added, "not only will many llama die, but so will many of the old people. People are like llama. They need something familiar."

A dog came up and curled into a ball next to our feet. I swear you could see the fleas jumping around him. Octavio nudged him with his foot. The dog moved a few feet away and lay down again.

The village was awakening to the morning. Women carried plastic buckets to the water spigot in the plaza, kids kicked a deflated rubber ball down the street, a cat jumped on a roof and stretched out on the warm thatch. Just to our left, Lourdes Ali opened her empty store in the front room of her home, sweeping her dust onto the street. She stood and stared at us a moment, her gold tooth shining bright in the sun, then wiped her hands on her aprons and disappeared back inside.

We leaned against the wall and waited. Octavio pointed out the haze settling like a gray stain over the village. "Smoke from the llama dung," he said. "Not enough *th'ola* to burn around here. Most of the chimneys in the village are cold now. It takes the old women around eight hours to hike far enough to find tall *th'ola*, and even they cannot find enough."

"So they burn dung?" Karen asked.

"Yes, it burns, but the smoke. . . ." He fanned the air in front of his face.

The sound of a truck downshifting reached us as it climbed the canyon. Octavio grabbed his medical bag and small backpack. "There is something you may be interested in señora, and you, *ingeniero*. We give lectures to the women's group. You should attend the Friday meetings with Doctor Islas and me. We talk to the women on many subjects, mostly health issues, cleanliness, diets, that type of thing. But they are of little benefit; of what use are nutrition classes if you cannot afford the food? And the women do not pay much attention, I am afraid. But if you come, you will be welcomed."

A beat-up Land Cruiser stopped in front of us. Octavio jumped in, gave his *saludos*, and sped off down the canyon. We were left with a couple pools of spit, a dead motorcycle, and an invitation to a meeting of the women's group.

"God, I feel like such an ugly American," Karen said as we watched the truck disappear.

"Why? It was an ugly American who got him the ride today."

"No, not that. The way the company acts."

"But he said he trusted the company, kinda."

"Yes, but it's not Reno that runs the day-to-day affairs. I know you trust your friends there, but they are probably in the dark about a list of things, the details that somehow get lost, like the llama and the old people."

"I can assure you that it is not the company's intention—"

"Is there any way you can help Octavio with his animals? The people of Reno respect you, they will listen."

The Friday lecture to the women's group was at the Wilson Córdova Social Club, a long, skinny single room down near the south end of town. The building, roofless for as long as anyone could remember, consisted of four walls with the sun beating down on a packed dirt floor, providing a useful garage for Octavio's recalcitrant motorcycle.

As CEO of the company, Wilson Córdova authorized funds for the clubhouse roof last April, and as *padrino* of the project, he received the honor of having the club named after him. Rumors spread immediately that the contractor substituted some wood beams of questionable quality and used rusty sheet metal he found nailed to an old shed, making a nice profit for himself in the process. Like most rumors in the village, we never found out if it had any basis in truth. Despite its numerous holes, most people considered a roof not only an excellent improvement, especially during the rainy season, but they also agreed that a metal roof was very modern, unlike the grass thatch so common in the village.

Karen and I poked our heads into the black room, its darkness cut only by thin lines of dusty rays terminating as yellow ovals on the walls and floor. I heard someone coughing. As our eyes adjusted, we noticed three walls were lined with a rough board bench, and on it sat at least ten *cholas* with as many toddlers and babies. Even the babies stared at us.

We squeezed onto the bench near the door, nodding and smiling to the ladies around us. A few more women with children entered, hesitated for a moment when they saw us, then sat, passing a few whispers to their friends. It took a few minutes for their talking to resume, mostly in Spanish interspersed with Quechua. Others were quietly knitting, some played with their children. The *cholas*, some stunningly beautiful, were wrapped in their multicolored hand-woven *aguayos*. Each woman who entered the low door bowed gracefully, holding onto her small bowler hat. Six or seven women sat on blankets spread on the dirt floor, breast-feeding their babies, allowing the toddlers to cry or crawl, explore, run, and fall. Several children rolled around in the dirt. The oldest woman was maybe 35, but I was surprised to see several who were younger, maybe 16 or 17. I felt my body melt, they were so lovely. None of the village men were present.

Spectators in an alien world, Karen and I shrunk our bodies and hugged the wall.

A raised platform about two feet off the floor lined the far wall, and in a corner Octavio and the mining company doctor, Javier Islas, tangled with wires and cords to attach a generator to a TV set.

The well-educated, handsome Doctor Javier Islas, the most eligible bachelor in town, began to perform his magic. This tall, slim, well-dressed young man stood in front of the village women, speaking of the complications of *gua gua*.

"*Gua gua?*" Karen asked a young woman beside her, who pantomimed patting a swollen belly, then pretended to hold a baby, finally twisting to turn her back to us.

When Doctor Islas spoke, at least half the women stopped murmuring and whispering long enough to listen even though many of them probably couldn't understand him. The doctor spoke in Spanish of hemorrhaging and infections during *gua guas*, and how each *gua gua* should be spaced two to three years apart. The younger women paid close attention, staring at the doctor like U.S. teenagers might at a rock star, but without the screams. They were glad to be here in the same room with this tall, young man with the well-trimmed beard.

After speaking a sentence or two to the ladies, Octavio translated the lecture into Quechua. The high point of the presentation arrived: the generator was turned on and the big color TV came to life, illustrating in full color the perils that accompany a 20th-century *gua gua*.

I must admit to not paying much attention. After a few minutes the lights came on. Doctor Islas repeated several times that he fully understood his next subject would be a bit sensitive. He had learned from his talks with their husbands that they felt it was good for the women to learn such concepts as nutrition, cleanliness, and medical care, and that they even agreed to the spacing of the pregnancies, but not all of them were comfortable with discussing such things as birth control.

"But how can I talk to you of spacing your *gua guas* without also speaking of birth control?"

The women giggled. Some squirmed a bit on the bench, but most seemed more interested than before.

He held a bruised banana in one hand as a grinning Octavio handed him a rolled condom. The condom rolling down the banana was met with giggles, whispers, and some derision, but also with downright opposition.

"You can't trick us like that," one of them said. "We would never let our husbands wear one of those."

"But this is not a trick," the young doctor said.

"You think we are fools?"

"No, of course not, but—"

"You people from La Paz, you think you know everything."

"This is science—"

"My husband has something much better than a banana," said another, to a round of laughter.

Javier looked for help from Octavio, who just shrugged his shoulders but couldn't hide the smile on his face.

A younger *chola* who obviously had not been paying attention added, "How can you eat the banana if it is wearing the raincoat?"

The sheet metal roof reflected the laughter, so infectious that Octavio's eyes were tearing. The toddlers stared at their mothers, unsure whether to laugh or cry.

Sensing the meeting was essentially over, Javier turned on the VCR again to show a film about breast-feeding, quieting the crowd. He and Octavio came over to sit near us.

"It will be a slow, very slow, process," Javier said, shaking his head, chuckling to himself.

"Maybe a generation or two," Octavio said.

"Yes. At least."

A collective sigh came from the four of us on the bench.

"I spoke with Reno about your animals," I said to Octavio. "They said they will look into it. I have heard nothing since."

Octavio nodded in slow motion.

"And the young man struck by lightning out in the pampa? The one last week?" Karen asked.

"Oh, yes. Yes, the boy . . . he died. We arrived to find the mother holding him. She would not let go. She was crying . . . so much. She had set up a little cross and was burning incense. It was difficult. After a while we tried to take the body to Uyuni, but she refused. The husband, too. They said the boy had to remain on the spot where he died. It was ordered by the gods."

"How strange. Why would the gods require that?"

"So that El Tío could eat. The Pachamama, El Tío, all the gods, they are always hungry, all the time. Like the people. The family believes El Tío asked the Pachamama to strike the boy, to kill him, so he could consume the body. If you remove it, El Tío will become angry."

"They buried the boy there, out in the *pampa*?" Karen asked.

"Yes. We watched them."

"So El Tío could eat the body?"

"The mother said the cross would protect his soul."

Chapter 8

The Profesora and the Hokey Pokey

Karen

November 1998

I clutched Larry's hand like a kindergartner as we climbed the hill to the school. My three years of university Spanish seemed worthless. To stave off the panic, I practiced conjugating the conditional. "If I were to teach English here, I would. . . ." If only I could take a deep breath.

A bell reverberated throughout the town adding to the cacophony of braying donkeys and crowing roosters. As if choreographed, groups of children spilled from their adobe huts and scampered toward the school. The children were immaculate, their faces shiny from the morning's scrubbing, the boys' black hair parted and slicked down and the girls' neatly braided. Their uniforms also sparkled: white smocks for the girls, and white shirts, blue sweaters and grey slacks for the boys. I looked down at my already dusty jeans and jacket thinking how I was the only one in town with hot running water.

The frigid morning air penetrated my layers of wool and down despite the sun. At most, these children wore a sweater. I had on my heavy leather hiking boots. They wore sandals; the lucky ones had socks. A few smiled at us. Some dared "*Hola,*" the bravest tried out a "*Goood* Morning," but most looked down at their feet. Once they passed, we heard whispers and giggles.

The school was a lawsuit waiting to happen, at least in the United States. Comprised of two single-story rectangular structures facing a courtyard, the adobe walls were crumbling and the windows were shattered. No one seemed concerned, either about jagged edges of broken glass or about the sharp, rusty tin gate which opened into an area where the students had planted a tree, the only tree in the town, which stood just three feet tall.

Children ran about stirring up the dust or stood in small groups chatting. Two boys rolled over and over on the earth like puppies in a play fight. A few teachers gathered in the corner of the courtyard, conversing. No one cast an eye in the direction of the tumbling children.

A neatly groomed young man in grey slacks and a pullover sweater bent over a short-handled broom sweeping dust and pebbles into a pile. He welcomed us with a warm handshake and directed us to a small room adjacent to the Director's office. Here Larry and I sat on two wooden chairs and waited. The cold flowed out of the mud walls and into our backs and feet. I shivered. I looked down at my Timex and noted that it was already nine. Teachers entered and left the room, signing a notebook to indicate their arrival.

Children's laughter filled the school yard. Every so often a wide-eyed face peered at us from around the corner, giggled, and ran. We waited. I had been in American education systems my whole life as either a student or school counselor. I lived punctuality and accountability.

At about nine-thirty, the Director arrived, shook our hands, and invited us into his office. He offered us two chairs and then sat across from us behind a large wooden desk, placing his folded hands on the empty surface with a sense of importance. A Bolivian flag was draped across the wall behind him. Beneath the flag hung a photograph of a somber Sanchez de Lozada, President of Bolivia at the time.

The Director, proud and tall, a stouter man than most of the men, attended to his appearance: a neatly pressed dark-grey suit, shiny black shoes and perfectly parted black hair.

I stared at him. Was this the same man who greeted us in a drunken stupor when we first arrived in town? He did not seem to recall having approached us that day and his meticulous appearance did not resemble the disheveled drunk Marcos had called the Director. *Could Marco have been wrong or was this another example of how things often were not what the appeared to be?*

I glanced at Larry, wondering if he, too, was questioning whether this was the same man, but Larry was already engaged in conversation.

The two spoke while I tried to decipher their words. Anxiety didn't improve my foreign language abilities. I guessed Larry and the director were doing the customary polite talk about weather, number of children in the school, the mine.

There was a pause in the conversation. I took a breath and in my best university Spanish stated, "I would love to start teaching English."

The Director looked at me expressionless.

"I sent a letter through the company. Did you receive it?"

"Ah, *sí,* the letter. We did receive your letter. Of course. Thank you."

"Well, what do you think?"

"About what?"

"The letter. My teaching. Do you have certain classes you would like me to teach?" I asked.

He bit his lip and squinted at me.

I looked at Larry, panic in my eyes at the thought that I couldn't make myself understood. Larry repeated my message, different words.

The Director still appeared a bit confused for a moment, and tapping his fingers on the bare desk, he studied Larry and me. Then, as if finding the missing part of a puzzle, he nodded his head up and down and beckoned us to follow him outside. There on the window, a single sheet of 8 x 11 paper revealed the week's schedule. He pointed to several little boxes marked "*Inglés*" and suggested I go to whichever ones I wanted.

"The teachers?" I asked.

He bit his lip again.

"Do the teachers know I will be teaching?" Had they discussed how my time could be used best by the staff? Larry tried to translate. The Director looked off into space, twisting his mouth and wrinkling his brow.

"Señor," I said, hoping to communicate one last request. "Permit me to observe some of the classes so that I may learn how your teachers teach."

This he seemed to understand. "*Con mucho gusto,*" he said and before we could continue this struggle to converse, he directed us to several wooden chairs placed in the courtyard. He excused himself as a young teacher appeared playing an accordion.

At least two hundred children filed into the courtyard. The teacher next to me explained that many students came from *estaciones,* or ranches, often more than a day's walk from the school. During the week, these students lived in the town, going home weekends if they could walk the distance in time to return on Monday. Some stayed with families here; some lived alone in empty houses, accepting handouts from sympathetic villagers.

"See how motivated these people are, Larry? Can you imagine our kids walking a mile to get to school?"

The children formed lines, twelve of them according to grade level. As the grade level increased, the numbers of students decreased so that by the last year there were only eight students, six of them boys.

The teacher with the accordion began to play the national anthem and the children stood at attention and sang with forceful, proud voices. One student came forward clutching the Bolivian flag, attached it to the pole, and with much concentration raised the red, yellow, and green colors into the air.

"We should encourage more patriotism like this in our schools," Larry said.

"Good luck." At the moment, raising the flag was not considered politically correct in our liberal town.

A toddler sat on the lap of the woman next to me, clapping to the music, a picture-perfect child, sparkling clean in a bright yellow sweater, neat brown pants, and a beige cloth hat with a large rim perched on his head. He studied me with wide, serious eyes and clung to his mother's chest.

He whimpered when I smiled at him. My strange appearance obviously disconcerted him so I looked away.

"Your child?" I asked the woman in my broken Spanish.

She nodded. "I bring him to work with me since my husband and I both teach. Our parents live in Huari so we have no one to watch him."

"His name?"

"Clemente. He especially likes civics hour when the children perform, and he also enjoys being in the classroom."

A girl no more than nine stepped forward and stood in front of the assembly of students and staff with marked composure, her hands neatly folded in front of her white smock, her black braids extending down to her mid-back, her dark eyes looking up to the sky. With a vibrant voice the child lifted her hands upward as if imploring the gods, and recited a poem with such sincere passion that I found myself searching for a tissue to wipe my tears. I had no idea what the words meant. She finished her poem, bowed her head as she received the other children's applause, and returned to her place in line.

"Wow, talk about culture," I said, looking at Larry. His eyes stared at the ground as if deep in thought. It was obvious that it was time for him to leave, so we kissed good-bye and he slipped away. I was on my own.

Civics hour was more like two hours. The sun had risen higher in the sky, and its rays were scorching my fair skin. Light-headed and a bit dizzy, I wondered whether my hat and sun-block could protect me at this elevation. I had to make myself focus.

Now standing in disarrayed lines, the children shifted from foot to foot and whispered to their neighbors. The teacher in charge walked among them, slapping a thin stick on the open palm of her hand, turning their wiggling bodies to face forward and placing a finger in front of her lips, uttering a hush. Finally the events were over and the lines of children filed into their classrooms. I stood wondering where to go. From behind me I heard, "*Profesora, bienvenido.*" I turned to find the familiar face of Senóbio, the man whom we'd given the ride to fetch his wife in the middle of the night.

He appeared more professional here in his grey slacks and shiny black shoes covered with a thin layer of dust. His beige sweater added no bulk to his slim body. He held himself so straight that he appeared much taller than I recalled though in reality we stood eye to eye.

"Right now I'm teaching Quechua to the younger children." He grinned as he held his palms down, indicating the height of his students. "Would you like to see?"

He beckoned me to follow him into the classroom, dark and cool as a cave. The children had already entered. Not more than eight years old, they dashed about the room chasing each other and jumping over the desks like monkeys. Their shouts echoed off the adobe walls.

I was wondering how I would ever be able to tame these wild creatures if it came my turn to teach when Senóbio took his place in front of the classroom. He said in a loud voice amplified by the adobe walls, "*Buenos Días, alumnos.*"

The children raced to their places and standing at attention, responded, "*Buenos Días, profesor.*"

I found the one adult-size chair in the corner near the blackboard. The children sat down, reached into their backpacks, and pulled out their frayed paper notebooks. Many clutched pencils that were mere stubs, each attached to their shirts or smocks by a short piece of string. I was to learn later that pencils were a precious item in a town without money and the consequences of losing them could be severe. All eyes were upon Senóbio now. The children were ready.

Could learning happen in this sterile room? It consisted of rows of aging wooden desks that could seat two to three children each and a well-used blackboard, the surface nearly effaced. Nothing more. No shelves of books or games; no reams of paper, markers, pens, or pencils; no classroom hamster or rat; no plants lining the window sills. No computers, televisions, or CD players. Just worn wooden desks and an equally worn blackboard. Senóbio had attempted to add color to the room by hanging some paper mobiles the children had made.

I could not understand all that Senóbio told his students, but I gathered he was explaining the importance of Quechua. He led the children in a song, their eyes following him as he bounced back and forth across the front of the school room. His energy was contagious, and they sang with all their being, no holding back.

I knew the song! It was *Frere Jacques*, but the words were not French. I guessed they were Quechua.

The young voices repeated each line until they could sing the entire song. Then Senóbio taught them in Spanish.

A smile spread across Senóbio's face when I offered to teach the English version. He handed me a precious stub of chalk, asking me to write the words so he could copy them. As I scratched the English words upon the blackboard, I heard the children's pencils writing in their notebooks. Then in my off-key voice, I sang the song in English. The children stared, wide eyed and serious. I invited them to sing after me.

"Are you sleeping, are you sleeping, Broter Yon, Broter Yon?" they repeated.

There was great applause when we finished. We all smiled and laughed. Senóbio moved on to teach reading. Holding the only book there was, he wrote the Spanish words on the board in script and the children copied them. They sounded the words out together for a few minutes, then the room grew quiet except for more scratching of pencils on paper. After some time, faces looked up and bodies started to squirm. Senóbio called upon different students to come to the board and write a word. As each one finished, the class applauded. Should one falter, Senóbio called upon a friend to help and the two received the applause.

I thanked Senóbio, letting him know how impressed I was that he was teaching the children songs in Quechua. He reminded me that he planned to write the book about Quechua culture and we agreed that he and his grandfather, don Juan de la Cruz, would meet with Larry and me to teach us the customs. In return, I would help him with his English classes.

I couldn't wait to tell Larry how remarkable these children were, so eager to learn, so attentive, so quick to grasp new material despite the lack of resources, and unlike the competitive mindset in the United States, so willing to cooperate and support each other.

We met daily for lunch at the mining camp *comedor*. I found Larry sitting in one corner frequented by the engineers and the mining camp doctor, Javier Islas. Iván Quíspe, the labor foreman, and Marcos, the driver, joined us. I related how impressed I was with the little village school. Larry listened intently, a look of empathy on his face, but many eyes studied me with bemusement. Two men muttered something under their breath and laughed.

"I'm glad you are impressed, señora," Iván said when I finished.

"You're not?" I asked.

"Well, it's just that the education in the rural villages is so much poorer than in the cities."

"But the children are so motivated," I said.

"Mm," said the doctor. "Malnutrition is prevalent here. I can't imagine how these kids can even focus."

I looked down at my untouched plate—a dry hunk of meat, a corncob with kernels bigger than I had ever seen, and chewier too, shriveled purple potatoes and a pile of sticky, white noodles. *Hungry children? Malnutrition?* I was tempted to shovel the meal into a bag and bring it to the school.

"But isn't that what's so incredible?" I insisted. "Despite lack of food, resources, *everything*, the teachers teach and the kids learn."

The men eyed each other, but I knew they would treat me with utmost politeness. I was the chief geologist's wife—and a *gringa*.

"Even if they are motivated, they can't get very far," said Iván. "Most boys go into the military after high school. Very few go further." He placed a shriveled potato in his mouth and chewed a moment before saying, "And I'm sure you noticed there aren't very many girls in the high school."

I felt defeated before I even began. Larry reached under the table and took my hand.

I tried one last time. "The teachers are teaching Quechua language. At least the villagers are keeping their culture alive."

"Yeah, when they're sober," said one of the engineers. The other engineer chuckled in agreement.

Marcos sat across from me. He was quiet. He would never contradict the engineers, but he looked directly into my eyes and smiled faintly as if reassuring me that he understood my concerns.

The doctor also looked at me with sympathy as if he didn't want to disappoint me further. "Señora," he said, "if the children finish high school, they can read and write and do simple math, but none of it is very advanced. They can sing songs and do traditional dances, but they are not equipped for modern life."

My second day at school found me standing in front of thirty-two large, dark eyes, all waiting. It was my turn to teach. Rosa, the teacher, was a round lady who spoke in a husky voice which made the Spanish even harder for me to understand. She wore a single braid rather than the traditional two worn by the *cholas*, and presented a professional appearance in her pink sweater, gray slacks and a clean, shiny pair of black flats.

I looked toward the chalk board. No chalk. Rosa dashed over with a tiny stub and handed it to me with a look of apology. I scratched a lopsided, unidentifiable United States upon the board and made an *x* to identify home, Ashland, Oregon. I took a deep breath and in my beginner's Spanish attempted to contrast home and their little village. Several children giggled when they heard my accent, but when I began to describe the green trees, the autumn rains I left behind, and the snow that fell in the mountains as winter approached, I sensed I had sparked their curiosity.

Living in the southern hemisphere, the children were fascinated that their spring was my fall. I contrasted not only the difference in seasons, but how hard it was for me to live at this altitude in a dry desert. I sounded like Darth Vader as I dramatized my breathing. They listened as if I were an academy-award performer. The room was silent except for my stuttering Spanish.

From my backpack, I pulled photos of my town and passed them around describing my favorite place, Lithia Park, with its ponds filled with ducks and swans. The children sat on the edge of their hard seats and strained their necks to see. There were Spanish equivalents of *ooh's* and *ahh's*, exclamations, *Qué bonitos!* How pretty! as the children marveled at the photos, then passed them back to me.

"Any questions?" I asked as I tucked the photos back into the backpack. The children sat in silence. The thirty-two expectant eyes stared at me, once again waiting.

"No questions?" I asked again.

Then, after many moments of awkward silence, the teacher said, "*Inglés, por favor,*" indicating she wanted me to teach English.

I had no idea what to do next. I may as well have been from another planet. I felt my face redden. I stared at the posters of hand-drawn body parts on the wall: eyes, ears, tongues, noses and hands. The children were studying the five senses.

That's when the idea flashed: we could learn the Hokey Pokey. I pointed and said, "Eyes, ears, nose, arms, legs, feet, hands, fingers." Some watched but never opened their mouths. Others mimicked me in perfect English. We learned "right," "left," "in," "out," "shake" and "turn." We moved aside the rows of chairs and, standing in a circle, I began to sing while demonstrating the motions, "You put your right hand in; you put your right hand out." The children imitated me and sang along. "You put your nose in, you put your nose out, you put your nose in and you shake it all about." I exaggerated sticking my nose into the circle and shaking it. Lots of laughter. "You do the Hokey Pokey and you turn yourself around. That's what it's all about."

They were mine, all sixteen children following my words and motions. When we stopped, they all applauded and shouted, "Hokey Pokey! Hokey Pokey!" We Hokey-pokeyed for what seemed like hours. When at last a bell rang for recess, we stopped and the children applauded once again. The door opened to the courtyard and the light poured in.

So began my teaching career in this remote Bolivian village. When the children saw me, they sang, "Hokey Pokey!" Soon the teachers sought me out. Would I come to their class at this hour? Could I do it today and tomorrow? Some of the teachers stayed with the class while I taught, others disappeared.

I tried to recognize faces and learn names, a skill I'd never been good at even back home, but the similarities made my task even more challenging. There were names like María Alí Quíspe and María Quíspe Alí, Jorge Muraña Cayo and Jorge Cayo Muraña and to top it off there seemed to be several María Quíspe Quíspes and Jorge Muraña Murañas.

As I stood at the cement basin in our little courtyard one afternoon attempting to wash the accumulated dust out of a once-white shirt, I asked Larry, "Why do these children have such long names? And why do they all have the same names?"

Larry leaned against the adobe hut watching me. He explained that the first last name was the father's and the final name was the mother's, then added, "Not a large gene pool up here. When the mining engineers come through, maybe once every twenty years or so, they add some foreign genes, a few anyway. The Chilean drillers the company brought in have already left behind a few babies. Otherwise, I'd guess lots of cousins marry cousins. Doesn't make for the brightest bunch of people. It happens in all poor, isolated communities."

"They're some very bright children here," I said, once again on the defensive.

"Sure. Most of them are as intelligent as anybody else, anywhere, but malnutrition and in-breeding takes its toll." Then he added, "I think they find you so novel, so different, dynamic. You're doing wonders with them."

"It has more to do with the kids than with me. They're not jaded like our kids back home."

Larry unwrapped a granola bar and took a bite. He eyed me with a smile. "Are we about to discuss *how rich in spirit* these kids are?"

I frowned and splashed some icy water at him. "Maybe not rich in spirit, just not spoiled by so much material crap, not competitive, more cooperative. They seem connected to family and community in a way that our kids are missing." I wrung out the still-dingy shirt and hung it on the clothesline strung across the courtyard.

Larry finished chewing the granola bar and, opening a bottle of water, took a swig. "No existential angst. Life's pretty simple. Survival. Pretty much do what your mom and dad, grandma and grandpa and so on did before you. No big decisions about what you want to be when you grow up."

"And what's wrong with that?" I asked.

"Nothing, if you don't mind poverty and lack of opportunity. I bet if you gave these kids a choice between life as it is here and life as it is in the United States, they'd choose the U.S."

"Because it looks good," I said. "What we don't have always looks better."

"And I say once again," Larry stated with an air of confidence, "the mine will bring changes. Who are we to keep impoverished people from having a choice?"

Chapter 9

Soledad

Karen

December 1998

We heard a knock.

Who was it this time? The villagers had begun requesting many favors: "Please, *ingeniero*, I need a ride. I had to leave crates of beer I bought in Uyuni down below the mining camp." "Please, *ingeniero*, are you going to Uyuni?" "Please, my *abuelo* lives out in the *pampa* and I need to bring him some supplies." "Please, I need a hot shower." (This one from a teen-age boy who did indeed need a shower.) It was difficult to say no.

The knocking persisted.

"Maybe we should pretend we're not here," Larry said. "It's the downside of having the only working vehicle in town. The upside is that we're getting to know the villagers."

We gave in. I opened the door.

A young woman, no older than sixteen, stared at me with big, wide eyes. She hugged a thick book in her arms like a beloved baby.

"*Con permiso*," she asked with the customary politeness of her people.

"Please." I led the way into our courtyard.

Dressed in dark green sweats with *Nike* scripted across her jacket, sandals made from worn tires, and a pirated *Nike* cap over her shoulder-length, straight, black hair, she resembled many of the youth in the village. But unlike other girls her age whose shirts and slacks showed off their emerging feminine bodies, her clothing hid her form. Her solid confidence made her seem a little masculine in this culture where young women were often shy and reserved.

"My name is Soledad." She reached out her hand to shake mine. "*Bienvenido a San Cristóbal*," she said, then patted my upper arm. She looked at her feet and we stood in awkward silence. Then she raised her head and spoke, "*Profesora*, please, I want to learn English."

"I'm happy to teach you English, Soledad. Aren't you in school?"

She nodded.

"I am teaching English there," I said, trying to recall whether I had already visited her class.

Her eagerness changed to disappointment. She shifted from foot to foot like an impatient child. "Please, *profesora*," she implored. "I want to read in English. I want to read *this* book." She clutched the massive book even closer. She spoke her Spanish with deliberate enunciation as if she had already assessed my limited language abilities and was willing to accommodate me.

"May I see it?" I asked.

The worn, brown cover and the bent corners of the pages looked as if it had been through many hands. Page after page revealed photos and drawings of minerals.

"Why, that's Barry and Mason's *A Textbook in Mineralogy*," Larry said. "Look, it's stamped Oxford University. Must have been some geologist who passed through here."

When Soledad saw Larry's excitement, her face broke into a huge grin revealing two front teeth partially rotted away. She covered her mouth with her hand, but kept smiling.

As Larry browsed the pages, Soledad moved next to him to glance over his arm at the pictures of sparkling crystals. Her eyes lit up as he explained in Spanish what several of these illustrations depicted. He spoke of mountains, volcanoes, veins, gold and silver, pointing out geological details. "*Andesitas . . . fallas . . . dique. . . .*" The Spanish words began to lose me. These two shared not only a fluency in Spanish but also an interest in rocks, something I'd never been able to get excited about.

I took down two children's paperback books from the shelf, *Is Your Mama a Llama?* and its Spanish counterpart, *Es Tú Mama una Llama?*

I stood waiting to introduce my books. They stopped chatting and looked up as they closed the hefty text. I handed Soledad the thin paperback children's book in Spanish.

"You can read me this book in Spanish and I'll read it to you in English," I said.

She looked at the skimpy book in her hands and back at the treasured text Larry was still holding. She threw me a disconcerted stare. Then, thumbing through the little book with a closed-mouth smile, she said, "*Qué bonito.*" How pretty!

"I'll help you in English. Will you help me with Spanish?" I proposed again. "And maybe," I said eyeing Larry for some non-verbal agreement, "maybe Larry can teach you some geology."

Her face broke into a smile and once again she raised her hand to cover her rotting teeth. Her face lit up when she said, "*Con mucho gusto.*"

We shook hands, sealing our contract. Larry handed her the mineralogy text and said, "Sometime we can walk the hills together and I'll tell you about the geology of this area. There's a lot of silver in those rocks."

"Of course." She nodded as she once again clutched the heavy volume to her breast. "I know."

Soledad became a frequent and welcomed visitor. Our reading of children's literature was short-lived, both of us finding it more exciting to just sit and talk. She had only to see me squint or wrinkle my brow to know her Spanish had lost me and would need to rephrase a statement. I, in turn, did my best to give her simple lessons in English by labeling the world around us.

One early morning, Soledad found me sitting in our courtyard bundled in layers of long underwear and down, attempting to play my *charango*, a string instrument of the Andes that seemed to be a cross between a ukulele and a guitar. This instrument looked like it just crept out of the desert. It was still covered with a fine layer of fur and crowned by an armadillo's head with its two tiny ears laid back upon the instrument's neck of richly grained wood.

I loved this instrument, which when played correctly, created the rhythms of the traditional Andean music. I'd bought it in La Paz with the wild fantasy that I would learn to strum while the students accompanied with drums and flutes. Unfortunately, my musical talents were as limited as my ability to learn language. And my cracked fingers didn't help. Though Soledad delighted in my attempts to make music from this ten-stringed instrument, I was very eager to hand it over to her.

"I love music," she told me as she strummed the strings and adjusted the pegs, bringing the ear-wrenching, out-of-tune instrument to near-perfect pitch. Forgetting her self-consciousness, she smiled her broad black grin and began to play. As I watched fascinated, she switched the rhythms with ease, explaining the different names and origins of each tune. She never used written music. There wasn't any in town.

"Where did you learn to play?" I asked.

"All the kids here learn to play instruments in school."

One day, without a second thought, we invited Soledad to join us at the *comedor* for lunch. She vibrated with excitement as we headed down the hill to the camp. When we entered the building, fourteen engineers stopped eating and looked up. The room fell silent.

Iván, hands in pockets, shuffled over to us. He glanced sideways at Soledad, making fleeting eye contact with Larry, and said in a low voice, "*Ingeniero, profesora*, um, maybe this señorita would be more comfortable in the kitchen."

"I don't think so," I said, puzzled by Iván's suggestion. "She's our friend. We've invited her to lunch."

Soledad touched my sleeve, whispering, "I'll go."

"Wait," I said to her.

The *comedor* was so quiet we could almost hear the engineers chewing.

Iván squirmed as he waited for us to respond. He repeated, "If your friend wants to eat, I will ask the cook to fix her a plate. She can go to the back door of the kitchen and enter there."

I could feel Larry tensing by my side.

Was I hearing right? My face reddened, my teeth clenched, it was no secret that I was pissed. Maybe we all should leave, but there were no alternative places to eat, no restaurants, no grocery stores. I was hungry and I guessed that Soledad was too.

Soledad tried to reassure me that she was okay, it didn't matter. But as she left for the kitchen, her shoulders slumped, and the usual bounce in her step faded. Of course it mattered. I understood that this was their culture and that I was a guest in their country, but to this day I regret not having stood up for Soledad.

Larry and I took a seat among the engineers. "We've gone back to the 1950's in the South," I said under my breath.

I shoved my plate aside and sat fuming. The engineers kept eating but every so often glanced over at me.

I needn't have worried about Soledad. Her self-confidence was indomitable. After lunch, she invited Larry and me to walk the hills surrounding the town. "I will tell you the stories of our rocks."

We started out through the village and headed toward the steep hill beyond the gulch. Her enthusiasm and equanimity put me at ease.

Larry and I walked in slow motion trying to catch our breath as Soledad scampered up the rocky hills like a mountain goat. She hopped and jumped from boulder to boulder and balanced precariously on steep cliffs.

From far above us she looked down, then climbed back to us with ease, slowed her pace, and reached for my backpack and the down jacket I'd already shed. "*Profesora*, I'll carry those." Putting the pack on her back, she offered her hand to help me over the rocks. With tiny steps one foot in front of the other, I made my way up the steep incline, heart racing, my breath shallow and fast. I sipped water from the plastic bottle I carried.

Larry bent down every so often and picked up a stone. "Rock break," he shouted, then sat on the nearest outcrop while he examined it. "It's an old geologist's trick. Any time you need to rest, you just stop and pretend to study a sample."

I was glad. I needed the rest more than anyone.

We neared the top of the ridge to the west of town. Larry called it Tesorera. I perched on a shale ledge, gasping, feeling sick from the climb. Soledad breathed easily, unaffected. We sat on top of the world, enveloped by a sky of deepest ultramarine passing on forever until it faded into pale blue topaz at the horizon. I looked around for a tree, even a small one, something that showed life in this barren desert, but there were only shin-high bunches of *th'ola* bush scattered amid the rocks.

Suddenly without a word, Soledad leapt up and dashed down the side of the hill. We watched as in an instant she disappeared, then popped up again as she darted up the next hillside. She ran at full speed, leaping with long, graceful arcs over the clumps of *th'ola*. Her bounds left her floating in mid-air, and when one foot touched the ground, the other was already stretched far in front. We waited a moment until she surfaced again. Then she walked slowly back, cupping both hands to her breast. Upon reaching us, she opened them ever so slightly to show us her prize. A baby bird with an unusually long neck stared at us through dark eyes which seemed to occupy most of his tiny head.

"What is it?" I asked.

"A baby ostrich." She stroked the little bird's feathers with tenderness. She smiled when she caught my look of amazement, then ran back down the hill to return the baby ostrich to the place she had found it.

"She can outrun an ostrich?" Larry marveled.

I had heard that it was common for the young men of the town to hunt for *vizcacha*, a rodent which could be eaten, and for ducks and their eggs by the river. They caught these creatures by hand and cleverness, not by use of weapons. Clearly, Soledad took her place among the best of these hunters despite her gender.

She returned running up the canyon slope to the ridge line where we stood. She wasn't even breathing hard. "I live in the most beautiful place in the world," she said.

"Yes, I think you do," I agreed.

Larry pointed at some rocks. "You can see from the colors they are mineralized. All those orange and yellow stains are from various base-metal oxides. The soils are naturally full of lead and arsenic and other metals."

The outcrops near the top fed their colorful rocky fragments to the talus flowing below them, weaving a toxic tapestry of red, yellow, orange, white, brown, and black. Amid these earthly colors, dirt roads zigzagged their way as far as we could see, leaving a pattern of white, dusty scars on the colored slopes.

"So many roads?" I asked.

"Drilling," Larry answered. He described how the company had built roads on a grid everywhere within a thousand-meter radius of the town. Every fifty meters they scooped out a flat platform and drilled a hole, leaving rectangular patches of barren earth.

Tall mountains and ridges of red and orange and yellow surrounded the canyon, sheltering the town.

"*Abrigado*," Soledad said referring to the Spanish word for jacket, *abrigo*. "These mountains have protected us for centuries." She swept her arm across the expanse of rocky hills. "They have kept enemies away and cradled us against the harsh winds of the Altiplano. All of the rocks have a name and a story."

"I'll say," said Larry. "Look at that black rounded mass over there. It looks like a dacite dome. You can see how the magma forced aside the surrounding sediments."

"Yes, that is El Altar where the spirits live in many small caves. That is where we do a special ceremony every year, a *ch'alla*, to keep the spirits content, to show respect."

Larry shook his head, muttering, "And it all has silver. . . ."

Soledad did not respond to Larry's talk of silver. She was looking down at another rock near the entrance of the town. Located on the edge of the *cancha de futbol* where the town played soccer, it made a perfect seat from which to watch the games. During the soccer matches, children covered this rock like ants swarming a piece of candy. It stood forty feet in the air topped by a mushroom-shaped cap which provided shade at the base of the stem, a cool escape from the intense desert sun.

"The Achupalla, there, is a very special rock," Soledad said. "It is where young lovers go for a provisional marriage. They are not really married."

"What do you mean not really married?" I asked.

"At the Achupalla, they're given permission to live together until the priest comes from Uyuni. We must be married in the church. The priest comes only once a year to perform all the ceremonies." She laughed. "It is a busy time for him. He must perform all the ceremonies at once: the baptisms, confirmations, marriages, deaths, all of it."

Larry asked, "Why this rock for these ceremonies?"

"Oh, because the Achupalla is a woman who gives birth to the *piñas*, smaller rocks which turn into pure gold and silver, but only if you believe strongly enough. We use *piñas* in our *ch'alla* ceremonies where we make offerings asking for good health or wealth." Soledad sounded completely satisfied that she'd answered Larry's question.

She then turned to the South. Looking past the scars in the hills created by the maze of roads, she pointed toward the three monumental rocks we had seen upon our entrance into the town. "The Tres Gigantes," she said, nodding her head in their direction. "They are three brothers who walked close together in the time before the sun. Then the sun came one day and they were turned into rocks. They kept watch against the bad people of Tupiza. Even today they stand guard, welcome weary travelers, and protect the townspeople. They are our favorites."

I could see why. This was a different view than the one we saw from the Toyota the day we arrived. Easily visible from any point in town, they rose out of the mountainside and reached for the heavens. They were my favorites, too.

"Has anyone ever been able to climb them?" I asked.

"Nobody has ever been to the top," Soledad said, "except a *cholita.*"

"*Cholita?*" I asked. "That's a little girl."

"Yes, she was carried up by a condor and left on top of the highest one."

"How did you get her down?"

"We didn't."

Perhaps hearing this in a coffee shop back home, I would have accepted it as a quaint myth; here among these majestic and mysterious peaks, I didn't doubt for a moment Soledad's words. I felt sad for the baby.

Soledad continued, "The rocks are our ancestors. They have souls. They will protect us as long as we respect them and listen to their opinions."

Larry's eyes were scanning the area, but I could tell he was listening. "Did you know all this?" I asked him.

"What I do know is that those three guys," he said pointing to the Tres Gigantes, "are probably the three most important rocks in the entire mountain range for unraveling the genesis of this orebody. Ancestors or not, they hold vital information.

"I sampled those rocks to the right," he said, indicating an area away from the town. "No silver. Nothing in them. Then I sampled those on the left. Silver, lots of it. The Tres Gigantes mark the boundary between ore and waste."

Soledad's eyes darted back and forth between us as Larry and I conversed in English. Larry turned to her now. In Spanish, he gave her more geological details about how the silver originated in the area. It was the kind of puzzle that thrilled him. "All the rocks around the town, in fact, the town itself, the streets, the walls of the houses, the floors, all are laced with silver."

Soledad's only response was, "I know."

On our way back down, Soledad picked up two rocks at the base of Achupalla, handing one to Larry and one to me. She said, "May these *piñas* give you much *riqueza*."

How heavy the rock was for something as small as a mango! Layers of sand-size grains, yellow-orange, with white square crystals sparkled in the sun.

Larry brought the rock close to his eye for further inspection. "Barite crystals," he said. "Barite always comes with silver. These rocks undoubtedly are mineralized."

Soledad listened intently as Larry spoke. "I know."

The next morning, Soledad knocked on our door with a few sheets of checkered graph paper upon which she'd scrawled something in blue ink.

"For you, *profesora*." She handed me what appeared to be a poem, then turned and left.

Desde Jayula de viso yo

El jardín dónde nací
San Cristóbal tíerra Linda
Su riqueza sin igual
Tres hermanos
Tres gigantes
El qué guardan mi pueblo.

Larry and I translated it.

From Jayula I have seen

The garden where I was born
San Cristóbal lovely land
Her riches without equal
Three brothers
Three giants
They guard my village.

Chapter 10

Digging Up the Dead

Larry

December 1998

Six men from Oruro in identical blue uniforms and white face masks stood to their hips in opened graves, pulling out bones and bits of hairy flesh to be transferred to zinc-coated coffins, each coffin shining new in the sun, each with a white ceramic cross attached, and each sporting a metal tag assigning a number to the body. There was a faint though distinct odor, like a long-abandoned root cellar where desiccated potatoes had molded into piles of gray-green powder. I retreated upwind. This was tough to take.

A condor spiraled overhead, skirting the edges of rising columns of warm air. *Lucky guy*, I thought. There weren't many of them anymore. Like the wild ostriches and rabbit-like *vizcacha*, they all were feeling the effects of change.

"That makes four," a blue man shouted. "A new record. The deepest must be at least a hundred years old." Four bodies in one grave, each on top of the other.

Karen pulled me closer to her. This was my first time in the cemetery. I suspected it would be the last. It was being moved to the new town site after sitting undisturbed for over four hundred years on a narrow bench half way up the slope of Tesorera Ridge.

Surrounded by a five-foot high rock wall, its only entrance was an archway capped by *paja brava* grass to protect the soluble adobe. The arch supported a pair of weathered wooden doors that you had to push slightly to the right and lift at the same time to open to an enclosure fifty meters square. In one corner was a dark, one-room adobe chapel with a single lead bell, said to have been forged in the 1700's.

Many graves were merely little mounds of hardened dirt with no markings. Some were identified by a single, large rock; others by little sticks or crosses woven out of grasses. Most graves, however, did have more formal crosses made out of two pieces of wood nailed together, now sun-bleached and sandblasted, the painted words lost to the winds. No matter the markings, every one carried the surveyor's bold inventory number written in magic marker, like "SC1-171," grave 171 in quadrant 1, San Cristóbal, Bolivia.

Senóbio, our friend from the school, had brought us here. His slender, almost feline body picked its way around the emptied holes and piles of bones. He muttered to himself as he approached, "*Triste, qué triste. . . .*" Sad, how sad. He looked into the graves with red eyes, shook his head slowly, then moved both hands to his chin to support his head.

"The graves . . . the graves, so many," he said, swaying slightly back and forth. With fists clenched, he said the digging was difficult. When describing the shallowness of the soil, a flat palm was held near his shoes to indicate depth. It was rocky, he said, one fist hitting the other.

"We needed to save space," Senóbio said. "But only family members sleep together. The latest was just last month, Luisa Alí Mamani. She was sixteen. She and the baby are resting in the same grave. She died giving birth to her second child." He held both hands to indicate a swollen belly.

"Couldn't you just have expanded the size of the cemetery to give more room?" I asked.

He pointed to the lone cross atop the small chapel. "Everyone must be buried within the shadow of the cross." His matter-of-fact manner left no room for more questions, and he walked back to the diggers.

A large rock of swirling orange and yellow color lay at my feet. I made mental note of the clays, pyrite and other alteration products which confirmed it was clearly mineralized.

Karen pointed to Senóbio. "Did you see his face?"

"Look at these rocks."

"Something is tormenting him. Did you see his face?"

"No, I was looking—"

"Please, talk to him." I watched her back as she walked over to Senóbio. I picked up another rock and followed.

Senóbio stared down into a hole as the men in blue removed a pelvis and some ribs, laying them out in parallel rows on the pile of yellow-brown dirt. He sat beside the bones. He shivered, zipped up his jacket, and wrapped his arms around his body. He hunched over, making himself small, as if unsure in this dark world of unfamiliar spirits.

"Triste, triste," he repeated once again. It didn't seem to matter to him that these men in blue were experts, that they had done this work before; it didn't seem to matter that they were careful to pay due respect as they handled the bones and other more fleshy remains; it didn't matter that the Quechua *yacho,* after divining the patterns of the falling coca leaves, said the spirits approved of this move, or even that the Uyuni priest had performed a special mass, desanctifying the cemetery. Sitting amid the broken and disturbed remains of his people's history, to Senóbio it didn't even matter that the Bishop of Potosí himself had blessed the move as well, saying it was the price the village must pay for a better life. To Senóbio, this was sensitive, delicate, serious, and indeed, very personal business.

He motioned for us to follow him into the coolness of the little adobe chapel. He lifted one of dozens of burlap sacks stored in heaping piles in the far corner.

"They have run out of new coffins right now. Look at this," he said, as he slowly pulled back the layers of burlap to disclose a jumble of dried, dusty, pale gray human bones. He crossed himself and kissed his fingers.

"These . . . your family?" I asked, afraid of the answer.

"Sí, mis parientes."

"Dios mío, que difícil," Karen said, putting her hand on his shoulder as he stood with head bowed.

The chapel was too small; the cold, too cold and the dark, too oppressive. I felt sick. This was my doing.

"I gotta get out," I said as I backed into the sunlight.

Karen and Senóbio followed. Our path was blocked by an older man standing by the chapel door, his back to us as he observed the men in blue. He wore a black leather jacket and other western clothes and carried a long wooden staff decorated with silver, wrapped with colorful ribbons. Nearly whispering, Senóbio spoke to him in Quechua, then introduced him as his grandfather, "*Mi abuelito,* Juan de la Cruz Copa Quíspe." This was the man Senóbio had promised to introduce to us on that long night waiting for his wife and a stove.

The old man slowly turned his head our way, catching the eastern sky in a glint off his eyes, his white whiskers short and stubby, glistening bright in the morning sun. Don Juan de la Cruz was short, and stocky compared to Senóbio's slim, sharp-edged body. Unlike his grandson's set of perfect teeth, don Juan had only a few loose, stubby ones, worn down and stained greenish-black by a lifetime of chewing coca.

"Don Juan is the oldest man in the village. He is *Cacique Principal*—the main chief—of the district. It's his duty to oversee all issues concerning respect for traditions and the performance of ceremonies," Senóbio said while don Juan grinned, nodding his head in agreement.

You couldn't shake hands with don Juan; his many years of arthritis made it too painful, so he offered us his wrist to grasp. It was bony and hard. He patted our shoulders in return.

Senóbio explained while don Juan watched our faces with his cataractic eyes: digging up and moving an entire cemetery filled to capacity with at least 620 souls—at least that is how many can be remembered by the living—fell into don Juan's list of obligations. Every morning he hiked up the ridge to the cemetery to spend ten to twelve hours a day watching the workers tear down the rock walls and dig up the bodies, his eyes alert for any sign of disrespect. He had a job to do; he had to be certain the digging proceeded correctly so the *almas,* the souls of the dead, did not punish the living for the disturbance.

"Today all is well, they are doing it properly, not like last week," don Juan said, his laughing cut short by a hacking cough. "Then, we had problems, oh, such problems they were. They had reburied about twenty bodies in the new cemetery in a long trench dug with a tractor. A tractor, can you imagine? But the trench was not in the right direction, so the *almas* could not rest properly."

"In the wrong direction?" Karen asked.

Senóbio answered for his grandfather, "Yes, children are the future thus they must be buried facing east, to see the rising sun. Adults are the past, so they must face west, to the setting sun. We made them dig the bodies up again and bury them in the proper direction."

Don Juan laughed. "The diggers, oh, how they cried. They protested and were upset, but we told them if they want our cooperation, they must obey our traditions. They quickly did as we demanded. It had to be this way. It had to be."

Don Juan put a little red rag to his mouth to catch gurgling, hollow-sounding coughs, folded the rag into a square and shoved it into the breast pocket of his jacket. He breathed with difficulty, not from the altitude but likely from asthma, a common disease in the smoke-filled homes of the Altiplano.

He leaned over to Karen. A smile added more wrinkles to his face. "You didn't ask about the living," he said, while cocking his head and giving Senóbio a wink.

"The living?"

"Yes, you know the children are the future and the adults the past, but what of the living?"

"I don't know."

"Oh, in the meantime the living simply work themselves to death," he answered, laughing so hard he doubled over, coughs again cutting his laughter short. He straightened up and turned his gaze to the cluster of little adobe houses among the crooked streets below us to the east, down at his birthplace. "We are moving the cemetery because of the silver beneath it," he said looking at me, this time without the smile, then added, "We are also going to move the entire village. All of this is required if you are to make the mine."

"Yes, the silver mine," I said, quite without the enthusiasm I normally shared with the engineers in the company. Somehow I sounded as hollow as don Juan's coughs.

"It is necessary for the mine to succeed for all of us to become wealthy," don Juan replied.

I squirmed a bit. I couldn't tell him that the townspeople won't get any of the silver. They probably won't even get to see it, let alone touch it. Only the company and the Bolivian government would control the final products from the mine. But in return, the people would get jobs, and high-paying ones at that, and the company must pay royalties on the production, a percentage of which would go to the local community. I hoped that was what he meant by "wealthy."

Don Juan waved his staff over the maze of pits now dug in the cemetery. "One night soon we will be asking forgiveness for disturbing the *almas* of the ancestors. Then is when we will pay respect to them by crawling on our knees around the cemetery three times, begging forgiveness for awakening them from their sleep. It is necessary for the good of the village and for our own souls."

What do these almas, these souls, have to do with it?

Don Juan continued, "The dead are active members of our community. Oh, they are so important, more than you can imagine. Of course, they must be consulted for their opinions on any major decision."

"In this way, if we appease the *almas* and the *espíritus*," Senóbio said, "they will not punish us."

The dead were dead, and the living were moving away; nothing was going to change that. Still, my belly felt tight and my heart pounded. A mild shiver rippled my body.

"Maybe you should come," don Juan said, looking straight at me with those same wrinkles creasing the edges of his eyes.

"Me?" I asked, as I looked at the perimeter defined by the partly destroyed walls. It looked awfully long.

"Yes," don Juan answered with a wide smile showing his green teeth and gums.

"At night?"

"Yes, exactly at midnight."

"Umm, three times?"

"Two is insufficient and four, too many."

"It sounds like something you should do," Karen said, holding my hand.

"I'm not so sure," I said. *How the hell do I get out of this?* Everybody was looking at me, waiting for an answer. I asked, "It helps the village?"

"And you. We will inform you of the day," don Juan added, without waiting for my answer. He walked away leaning on his staff on the uneven ground.

A cool wind began to blow. Gray clouds covered the western sky. Senóbio said the rains would be early this year. A storm was building up, electric and heavy; you could smell the rain, it wouldn't be long before it fell.

We went up to don Juan and presented him with a banana, a bag of nuts, and a plastic bottle of water, all that we had brought up with us. Don Juan rolled the banana over in his hands, inspecting every side of it, smelling it, saying, "It has been years. . . ." We offered our *saludos*, shook his wrist, patted his shoulders, and walked out through the arched adobe entrance. We did not shut the doors behind us.

Drops of mixed sleet and rain began to pelt our backs as Karen and I picked our way down the path. I didn't look at the rocks on the way. The silence was oppressive; I wanted Karen to say something. About halfway to the village I finally said, as if to dispel any doubt Karen may have had, "I know it's hard now, but everyone will benefit from the mine: the country gets the taxes, the company gets the profits, and the people get good jobs and a modern new town."

"Maybe, but it comes with a price," she answered, "and so far it looks like the only ones paying for it are the villagers."

We were silent the rest of the way.

I soon forgot my promise to crawl around the cemetery. I was busy with about a dozen trips to outlying mountains within a hundred kilometers of town to see if any additional orebodies might be present. We found none. The San Cristóbal deposit was unique.

On the second of December Senóbio approached me. "Tonight is the night we must ask forgiveness," he said.

"But the bodies have all been removed."

"Souls will not rest until freed."

I followed don Juan and Senóbio up the ridge just before midnight, each of us chewing handfuls of coca leaf. We sat in the now empty chapel, drank a few beers, smoked a few cigarettes, stuffed more coca into our mouths, and before I knew it, I was on my knees outside the cemetery wall.

After an hour of crawling in the dark on the rocky ground and begging forgiveness for disturbing the souls of the dead, my knees were bloody and the wind left me so cold that even my violent shaking eventually faded.

A sharp rock cut into my left knee at about the same place I had gashed it the last time around. I cussed, pushed the rock to one side, and crawled on asking forgiveness from some strange gods I didn't even believe in, trying to hug the cemetery wall to avoid the winds. I crawled and chanted, mindlessly, over and over. The shadowy forms of don Juan and Senóbio were now well in front of me, pulling slowly ahead leaving me farther behind in the dark. They would probably lap me within the next half hour.

Freezing to death in the dark gave me no fear, probably because I was stoned from all the chanting and from the tons of coca leaf I had chewed before starting to crawl. That coca leaf, *la hojita*, they call it, was about as tasty as grass clippings. I chewed and chewed but felt not a thing, then don Juan suggested I light a cigarette and put the ashes in my mouth—yeah, the stuff worked all right.

The whole scene seemed a bit odd and decidedly uncomfortable. By the time I finished two passes, my mind was as numb as my body and only the occasional stab of a *th'ola* bush or sharp rock kept reminding me to ask forgiveness again and again.

My two companions had out-crawled me from the start and already had finished their third and final pass. They were waiting, protected from the wind in the shelter of the chapel, no doubt chewing coca and drinking beer.

O.K., so it was right for them to ask me to come. Since I started this whole mess, I probably did have a moral obligation to be there, but it was only my sense of *machismo* that pushed me to finish it. I put myself on automatic and once again chanted, "Please forgive me for disturbing your home, please forgive me for disturbing your rest."

Crawling on my final pass, I reached out and touched now-familiar rocks as I went around, the same rocks I had felt twice before. I could remember specific ones—some rounded and grainy, others like glazed pottery, obviously silicified and probably loaded with silver.

Finally, I finished. I pulled myself up by the gate and stumbled my way toward the small chapel. It was over, the ceremonial cleansing, if you want to call it that. I had fulfilled my debt and showed my respect to the souls of the dead in this foreign land. I hoped they appreciated it.

For me there were no life-changing revelations. Angels did not open up the heavens; there was no celestial music; God did not speak. The ceremony did not make me into a believer in the Quechua gods. My soul did not soar with the eagles or condors or whatever. My spirits remained untouched by any profound metaphysical nonsense.

All I got was pain, numb lips, and uncontrolled shaking. My knees hurt and my hands were frozen and I was tired and just wanted to go to bed. Still, I felt good that I had done it.

At the chapel, Senóbio and don Juan offered me another handful of coca leaves. I chewed; they smiled; I smiled back. I handed them some carob-covered almonds that Karen had given me for the night. They each ate a small handful and put the rest in their pockets. I put my few remaining coca leaves in my pocket. We passed around the last beer. Don Juan rubbed his knees and laughed about how sore they were, saying it was worth it to please the souls of the dead.

We held each other as we walked slowly to the village below. About half way down I started singing a song from my early childhood, an off-key version of "Jesus Loves Me, This I Know." I don't know why I did it. Laughter and singing accompanied us all the way to the village.

Chapter 11

The Q'orpa at Irucancha

Larry

January 1999

The *yacho* bent over the llama and cut her again, this time a long downward slice from the left side of the throat going clear and clean to the middle of her black chest. He pulled the ribs apart with his hands, and with one more quick cut he held high the still-beating heart as an offering to his god. the Pachamama. Desperate arcs of blood squirted several feet into the air in erratic pulses, splattering on the *yacho*, the rocks, and the llama. The llama was still kicking, not knowing she was already dead.

"It is a good omen," the *yacho* said.

We chewed coca leaf in the wind on a grassy slope called Irucancha, just under 15,000 feet near the top of Cerro Jayula. A kilometer to the south lay the yellow-brown village, its roof tops glazed by thin blue smoke. To the north stretched the white expanse of the Uyuni salt flat, the largest in the world, shimmering to the far horizon where a shadowy silhouette of a sleeping volcano hovered in the distant haze. The wind blew fast across the flats below us then expanded and cooled as it rushed over the top of Jayula. Even though it was a clear, sunny mid-summer morning in the first week of January, we found ourselves bundled with many layers as we stood in a circle around the bloody llama. Between stamping our feet and breathing into our hands, we asked the gods for rain.

The *yacho*, Lucrecio Rivera, stood as straight as a U.S. Marine, and with his unusual height of six feet, he towered like a lightning rod above the group. Gray, sparse stubble covered a deeply creased face. His eyes, hidden below thick brows, flashed like two black opals in the morning sun. He dressed in western clothes like the other men, with a Cincinnati Reds cap and Vietnam-era military boots, complete with canvas sides. One boot was wrapped in duct tape to keep the sole in place; the shoe laces were roughly cut strips of leather.

"Pleading to the gods apparently doesn't require a uniform," I whispered to Karen.

"Shhhh." Plus a frown. "This is their religion. Be serious."

The *yacho* put the beating heart into a clay bowl and passed it to the nearest person in the circle. Each in turn held it up to the cloudless sky, made a short prayer for a season of sustained rains, then passed the bowl to the next in line. Soledad had the bowl now, her arms extended into the air, her eyes closed, praying softly. The bowl was getting closer; the heart throbbing feebly. When it reached me I lifted it high, tilting it too much, causing a stream of blood to pour down my outstretched arm and into my coat sleeve.

I almost retched. It must have been even worse for Karen; she's a vegetarian. "You deserved that," Karen said, laughing. "Your irreverence got you into trouble."

Senóbio was pleased I was so bloody. "The blood, it is a good thing. The black llama is in exchange for the black clouds that bring the rains, and we ask the Pachamama to send us many, many such clouds." He handed me a handkerchief, and added, "The Pachamama will be pleased."

I wiped off much of the blood, wondering how I had slipped so far back into the stone-age.

Senóbio had mentioned that only the *yacho* and the elderly *Cacique Principál*, don Juan de la Cruz, were permitted to conduct this ceremony. Unlike the *yacho*, don Juan wore a special poncho made of llama wool from the local area. Only he could carry *El Rey*, the staff of wood and iron, decorated with silver and colorful ribbons.

"With *El Rey*, don Juan can strike a rock and water will come forth, and if he strikes a rock and pleads for rain, then strong rains will come that year. *El Rey* has such powers. It can also bring earthquakes if asked." Senóbio told us this while nodding his head up and down.

"But if *El Rey* can do that, why do we need this ceremony?"

"Gods are certainly all powerful, but even they need a little help from time to time," he said, once again changing the definitions.

Lucrecio rang a bell over the body of the llama, then faced south, his head held high, and among other supplications, shouted, "We ask the Santa Maria, the saints, the spirits and the Pachamama to accept our offering and in return to give us strong rains. Oh, Pachamama, please recognize the respect we show by this, our *Q'orpa* gift to you." Karen set the video camera on a rock and I scribbled notes as Senóbio interpreted for us.

The sky was free of clouds; the wind had picked up a little. Don Juan held an apron-sized red cloth up high with both hands, and after watching the direction of the winds, informed the crowd, "The rains come from the southwest, from Chile and the sea. Today the winds are from the northeast, thus we must ask the Pachamama to change her mind." He turned to face south, the woven cloth again held high, his tiny semaphore message to his gods.

Without the rains there would be no harvest and no grasses. The animals would die; starvation would surely result, Senóbio said.

I mentioned that an anthropologist in La Paz had told me that some of the Quechua ceremonies called for human sacrifice.

"Is that true?" Karen asked.

Senóbio frowned a moment in thought. He didn't smile this time. He stared at the ground for a second then replied that few will speak of it, but on very special occasions during the deep of night, a group of village men would take someone, usually an alcoholic or an unpopular person, treat him to a fine meal and get him thoroughly drunk, and during a walk in the hills he would be sacrificed. "For the good of the village," he said, adding it was a traditional offering at the opening of a new mine, to ensure the vein would be rich and continuous—a guarantee the jobs would last for many years. The body would be buried beneath the concrete foundation of the head frame or the mill.

"You . . . now you use a llama instead?" Karen asked.

"Oh, yes, of course, only llama."

"Of course," Karen repeated.

"Never would we do that to a person . . . well . . . maybe sometimes," Senóbio said, holding his palms open to the sky as he walked away.

Karen looked at me. "*Maybe sometimes?* They're so connected to the earth. I can't imagine them killing randomly like this," she said, looking at the gore around her feet.

The *yacho* picked up his knife again. Senóbio led another llama, a white one, to the circle. She was blindfolded, her feet tied together, and gently laid on her side. One woman patted and stroked her neck, speaking soothing words.

Don Juan looked to the southern horizon, pleading in Quechua. Some words were repeated often: "Pachamama, Santa Maria, *todos los santos*" and "*espíritus.*"

Lucrecio listened for several minutes to don Juan's prayers, his head tilted slightly to the left. Like a skilled surgeon, he inserted the knife into the llama's throat and quickly cut the veins and main artery, repeatedly filling the bowls with the warm, thick blood. The prayers continued as he splashed the blood over the rocks, exchanged bowls, and splashed again, until the llama was dry. As Lucrecio wiped his hands on his pants, don Juan again rang the bell.

Both Karen and I were half in shock as we stood in blood all around us.

Senóbio whispered to us that the bell calls the soul of the dead animal to return to the herd, to guide and protect those that remain with the living.

He was interrupted by Lucrecio shouting to the sky, "The sacrifice of the two animals and the blood represents the seriousness of our desire for more rains. The blood calls for the rain to wash the stones clean."

My arm was beginning to itch. I looked down toward the town trying to figure how I could slip quietly away to take a long, warm shower. "Should we go now?" I asked Karen.

"I want to see what happens next."

"Let's go."

"Soon," she said.

Senóbio leaned closer to us. "Now we will see if the Pachamama has heard our prayers. We will look for her answer under the sacred stone." As instructed by don Juan, the *yacho* removed the blood-covered rocks until a hole about two feet deep was made in the center of the circle. Together the *yacho* and don Juan lifted a flat rock the size of a garbage can lid and peered underneath. The people leaned forward.

"They are looking for water. If it is damp, it will be a good year. If it is dry, there will be another year of drought," Senóbio whispered.

It was dry. The Pachamama was not impressed by the sacrifices. It would be another hungry year. The people were grumbling—some walked off to sit on the larger stones, some women cried, many were on their knees in prayer. Don Juan and the *yacho* shouted to the scattered group that sometimes the Pachamama will change her mind if people pray hard enough. With the *yacho* frantically waving the red *aguayo* to the south and don Juan hobbling about striking the rocks with *El Rey*, all in the crowd began to pray.

Karen and I got on our knees as well. I tucked my hands under my chin and looked down at the dirt. I cocked one eye up to look about me. I saw everyone praying—earnestly, openly, and deeply convinced their prayers would be heard. The woman next to me spoke repeatedly to the Pachamama and the spirits, meanwhile kissing her rosary.

I thought again of how strong were their beliefs, but so devoid of science. Rain is a phenomena based on atmospheric pressures, temperatures, topography, and humidity; on the laws of physics and chemistry. Prayer doesn't make it rain any more than prayer can cure illness or make people change their behavior. Begging to an imaginary god might make you feel better, but your crops will remain dry at the end of the day. My knees still hurt from my last exercise in spirituality.

But I was in their land, squatting amid their rocks, surrounded by their customs, so I folded my hands and pretended to pray. It was a charade, but if it made them feel good, I'd do it.

Senóbio walked out of the group and started a large fire. After about a half hour of everyone praying, or pretending to, the *yacho* announced it was time for the *comelona* portion of the ceremony to begin. Pieces of the llama were put on a grill over the fire, bowls of soup were handed out, and the people began to wash it all down with abundant beer and the clear alcohol called *cingani*. I watched the adults drinking and noted with concern that half of my drill crew was there. There would be no drilling tomorrow.

Lucrecio, his *yacho* duties apparently over, sat on a rock chewing some ribs.

"This *Q'orpa* ceremony," I asked, "Can anyone attend?"

"Yes, but it is not like the old days. Before, the entire village would come, now we have, how many?" He swept his arm in an arc taking in the small crowd. "Each year there are less. The people think they have no need to believe any more."

"Where do you study to become a *yacho*?" Karen asked.

He chuckled. "No study, only luck. It is the Pachamama, she chooses you by striking you with lightning. Three times she must strike you."

"And you must live through all three strikes," Senóbio said.

"Yes, it is very helpful to stay alive, very helpful," Lucrecio added. Everyone laughed.

I noticed a few clouds building up in the southwest as Lucrecio continued, "I was a young boy guarding the herds the first time it happened. I knew then that I had been given special powers. I could find lost animals for my neighbors just by looking at the positions of pebbles I would cast upon the ground. After the next two times, when I was still a boy, I discovered I had more powers. In my mind I could see the lost animals, even though they were far away. But my right ear no longer worked."

I looked up and saw the *yacho* staring at me with eyes focused several feet behind my head, probably reading my skepticism as if written on a blackboard.

Don Juan leaned on his grandson for support as he carried a large piece of meat over to our little group. His hands were scaly red from the dried blood. He handed some ribs to Karen and me. We noticed the meat was red and greasy, barely cooked. We thanked him for the luke-warm meat, paid our *saludos* to him, and asked, "They say, don Juan, you are the oldest man in the village."

"That is so."

"How old are you?"

He paused, then said, "I am 62." He looked to Senóbio for confirmation.

"No, I think more like 64."

"I think more like 70, isn't that so?" added Lucrecio.

"Well, I was born in 1930, so that makes me . . . ," don Juan wrinkled his brow, ". . . 59?"

Lucrecio corrected his math. "Almost. You were born in 1930 and I, in 1932. I am 67 so you must be 69."

"So old?" don Juan asked, and a grin spread across his face, "So many years?"

"Yes, *mi abuelito*, 69," offered Senóbio.

"Such an amazing thing. Almost time to rest." He rocked back on his seat and laughed.

Nobody spoke as we ate and drank. I looked over at Soledad who was busy stripping gristle from the bones with her teeth, her enjoyment evident from the grease smeared over her face. Karen handed her ribs to Soledad, who wrapped them in a cloth and tucked them inside her jacket.

Don Juan looked at Karen and me and said, more as a statement than a question, "You wish to tell the story of San Cristóbal."

"Yes, don Juan, we think it is important."

"Then you will need to know of our ancestors before the ancestors." He picked up a small rock, *a piece of dacite porphyry, unaltered, probably post-mineral*, and folded it into the palm of Karen's right hand. He patted her hand gently as he said, "This rock is the soul of our ancestors. Guard it forever, someday you will have need of its wisdom, I assure you."

Karen stared at don Juan as I turned the video camera on, mostly for its good sound recorder, happy to have an excuse to stop pretending to eat the nearly raw meat. I had no idea even what to ask him, but he needed no prompting.

"If you want to see the Pachamama, you must look around you. She is everything and she is everywhere and she is for all time. You see her hair—it is the *paja brava* grass. The hills and valleys are her bones, the rivers are her veins. Her blood fills the waters of the lakes. She is soft and loving and peaceful, but if you harm her she can be angry and harsh. I have seen her furious, oh, yes, but she prefers to be gentle. We are born of her and in her. She is mother to us all. Plants and crops are given birth by the earth, thus the Pachamama must be a woman. Nothing can live without having a mother. She is beautiful, but like any woman there are some days when man may not touch her, and it is prohibited to work on those days."

Don Juan stopped speaking. He stared off to the south, to the distant snow-capped Nuevo Mundo Range where clouds formed thin lenses at each white crest. The *pampa* stretched flat and yellow at our feet, scoured by a half-dozen dust devils rolling across the surface, blowing in from the northwest. He stared silently, for what seemed about five minutes. Nobody spoke. We were in a cathedral.

Our quiet was broken when don Juan resumed speaking, Almost as an afterthought, "All things are alive, all have a soul. The wind, the grass, the rocks, the waters. All are part of us, they are our ancestors, we are their descendants. They are intelligent and must be consulted."

Don Juan pulled a white handkerchief from his jacket pocket, unfolded it, smoothed it out on a flat rock and dropped upon it five cigarettes and several handfuls of coca leaf. He watched the leaves fall to the cloth, reached into the pile for more, and watched them fall again. He nodded his head in some unspoken agreement, arranged the handkerchief on a rock in the middle of our small group and motioned for us to help ourselves. We all did.

He stuffed many of the leaves into his mouth, then reached into his pocket for a small piece of hard, compressed, yellow-white ash. He put it inside his mouth and bit down. As he chewed the ash into powder, the abrasion on his remaining teeth sounded like fingernails on a blackboard.

Glancing at the bones of the animals, he continued his story. "Even the dead remain part of the Pachamama; they never leave this place as that would put them beyond her care. The dead are with us always; watching us, guiding us, guarding us, demanding only that we consult with them from time to time. And, demanding that we respect their souls."

Lucrecio continued to chew coca, smiling and listening, leaning over to hear, taking care to pop into his mouth the ashes from the tip of his cigarette.

Don Juan pulled another small rag from his pocket, unfolded it, coughed several times, folded and returned it. The rag was stiff with dried mucus and black from hardened blood. Senóbio lightly patted his grandfather's shoulder. "The rocks are our ancestors before the ancestors," don Juan continued. "They, too, were born of the Pachamama. They also have souls."

"That is why you honor the rocks, why you ask their permission to do things of importance?" Karen asked.

"Exactly. We speak to them and they speak to us, and they protect us by always giving good advice," he answered as Senóbio and Lucrecio nodded their heads in agreement.

"But, if they are your ancestors, why do the gods allow people to mine the rocks?" Karen asked.

"If the rocks have veins of gold and silver, it is because they want to give us a gift, so of course we must allow mining."

"But mining destroys them, removes them, tears up the countryside."

"That is as it must be. The gods may be generous, but only occasionally."

We all had cheeks stuffed with coca leaf by now, and even I was dribbling a bit of green sludge down my chin. I noticed that most people spit out their spent coca mulch into a pile, to be burned as another offering to the Pachamama, so I did the same. I then added new leaves and as much cigarette ash as possible to my mouth as the custom seemed to require. My mouth felt like I had been shot up with Novocaine, my lips fat and full. I felt energized.

The wind picked up, blowing strong and cold, scattering a few coca leaves across the rocky slope. Don Juan did nothing to stop them, only saying, "More for the Pachamama." Lucrecio looked northwest into the wind and added, "It will be a good year." Without another word, he got up and walked down the hill toward town. The sun was behind dark clouds. A dampness was in the air. Karen and I put our notes away and prepared to leave.

Don Juan pulled on his staff, *El Rey*, to help him rise and began his slow walk to the village, striking rocks with El Rey along the way as he chanted in Quechua. Just about everyone else had left, many carrying large pieces of meat. Senóbio gathered the llama bones and threw them into the fire. The wind whipped up the sparks and scattered them for a dozen yards down the slope of Irucancha.

Karen put an arm around me and pointed up into the sky. We were below the pregnant belly of a heavy, black cloud. Droplets of moisture flew in the air. The wind had shifted to come from the south.

"Well, mister scientist, what do you think of *that*?" she asked.

"Hmm. Interesting. Of course, it could be just a coincidence."

"You can't admit it might be the ceremony?" A look of victory was on her face: yeah, she had scored a touchdown.

"OK. I grant you it is pretty amazing. But in science we are trained that the right answer is often the simplest. Therefore, coincidence. Why not?"

"It seems just as simple to me to assume the Pachamama heard their prayers."

"Maybe. Now, if they did this ceremony ten times in a row, and it rained *each* time, then *perhaps* I could say there was something to it. But I bet it doesn't work that way."

That night it did not rain. The Pachamama meant what she had said. She gave exactly what the sacred stone had revealed. Although she teased us with the darkening sky, the extra prayers did not change her mind. Those black clouds were imposters with hearts full of wet promise but empty of intent, rewarding the faithful not with abundant rains but with the suffering of two years of sustained drought, a time when llama, vicuna, sheep and alpaca died by the thousands. Hunger stalked not only the isolated *estancias* huddled around their withering springs, but also crept inexorably like a death shroud to smother the smaller villages. Graveyards filled, villages were abandoned, and their gods, if they existed at all, either were too busy or simply didn't give a damn.

I suppose I was assured that my doubts about God and prayer were vindicated; that the people's foolish myths kept them poor and backward. I could have gone to their church and laughed in the face of their impotent *Patrón*. I could have urged Senóbio to finally escape his poverty by giving up his gods and superstitions and learning to adjust to the modern world. I could have laughed at them all.

I could have, but did not. There was no comfort in it. I wanted them to be right.

Chapter 12

Pen-pals

Karen

January 1999

"*Fotos! Fotos!*" the fifth graders chanted. They never seemed to tire of looking at the images of my hometown in Oregon: the park with its green trees, the pond with the ducks and swans, the plaza and the paved streets lined with shops. I shuffled through my backpack, but the photos were gone.

"*Fotos! Fotos!*"

I was puzzled. I'd shown them in the freshman high school class the afternoon before. Maybe I'd left them there. I sent one of the children to ask. He returned, pointing out the door and rattling off words in a frantic way, then took my hand and said, "*Venga.*" Come.

There was a sudden hush when we entered. As often happened with some classrooms, the teacher used my arrival as an excuse for a break, and left the room.

"Has anyone seen the photos of Ashland?" I asked.

I looked at the students and they stared back at me. No one raised their hand. No one said a word. Two girls in the back row looked at each other for a second, and then back at me with utterly blank expressions.

"Did I leave them here yesterday?"

You could hear the afternoon wind whistle outside.

"No one is in trouble," I said. "I will not punish you. I just want to show them to another class." The image of the long, wooden sticks some teachers carried as they lectured their classes passed through my mind.

A few students shifted in their seats. Others cleared their throats. Then as if in unison, all heads turned and eyes focused on a boy in the back seat. Fingers pointed.

"Juan," they all said.

I was shocked that a group of teenagers would tattle on a classmate. I studied Juan. His face and hands were smudged with dirt and his sweater and shirt, wrinkled. He reminded me of neglected children I worked with back home. Here amid a village where material poverty was the norm, another kind of poverty singled out this student, a poverty of not being cared for.

"Juan, do you have the photos?" I asked.

He looked down. The students continued to stare at him. One ventured, "He has them."

Juan stared at the floor.

I was getting nowhere. "Juan, bring them to me after lunch, will you?"

He nodded without looking up.

"Thank you for taking good care of them," I said, hoping to help him save face.

I commented on the incident as we sat once again in the *comedor* at lunch. By now the mining engineers eagerly awaited the next chapter of *La Gringa Profesora and the Village Students*.

One of the engineers said, "Remember these people have very little. Better lock up your stuff."

"It's not theft that concerns me," I responded. "I've left my hat, my camera, sunglasses, items of much more value in classrooms, and every time, some student chases me down to give them back."

Two of the engineers chuckled.

I ignored them and went on. "I'm more shocked that the other students ratted on him. They pointed their fingers at him. That would never happen in an American high school where your first loyalty is to your classmates."

"No, theft is not one of the problems here," said Iván Quíspe, biting into the huge kernels of a corn cob. "Quechua has three laws." He stopped to chew and swallow. "*Ama suwa*—do not steal; *ama llulla*—do not lie; and *ama k'alla*—do not be lazy."

"And why these?"

"In a Quechua village, if the members steal, lie, or are lazy, the villagers would die. It takes everyone to build houses, care for the animals, and grow the food."

"And if they break these laws?"

"They're shamed like this student was."

Juan never brought back the photos and I stopped asking, but the importance of them left an impression. They were prized items in a town where few owned cameras or could afford film. I promised myself that I would bring more photos of Ashland on my next trip.

I also wondered whether the children might enjoy sharing photos and letters, perhaps through a pen-pal program, an interchange between students in Ashland and those in San Cristóbal. Our students back home could learn so much from exposure to such a dramatically different culture. I had to confess an ulterior motive. I was hoping the village children might express their feelings in their letters about the upcoming destruction of their village.

The teachers were receptive to my ideas and the children were thrilled when they heard I would be the post-woman and hand-deliver each of their letters to a pen pal in my Ashland school. Not only had the students never written a letter, they'd never received one. The closest post office was two hours away.

"Let me give you some ideas," I said as I handed out paper to Rosa's class of fourth graders. "Tell your American friends your name, how old you are, who's in your family."

The children stared at me with rapt attention.

"Do you understand?" I asked.

They nodded in unison, pencil stubs held in hand as they continued to stare at me.

"You can tell them about your family—how many brothers and sisters you have, your house, your animals."

I paused, waiting for them to get started. Their eyes did not leave my face.

"I know," I said, the excitement in my voice growing. "I've seen you take old rubber sheets from the mining camp and slide down the hills. I know the American students would love to hear about that!"

They watched me more intently than ever.

"Oh, the students in my town play soccer. They'd want to know about the soccer games here."

Still no action.

"And your bicycles," I said thinking of the fragile Chinese bikes they rode up the steep terrain with no gears to come zooming down with no brakes.

"You can begin to write," I said, hoping that a direct instruction might produce some result. Still they watched with quiet expectancy.

I looked at the teacher in desperation.

"I will help them," she said. "You can go to your next classroom and we will have the letters for you tomorrow."

As I left I noticed she was writing on the board:

Querido amigo,
Mi nombre es Rosa Colque Quíspe. Yo tengo 32 anos.
Vivo en San Cristóbal. Vivo con mis seis hermanos.
Dear Friend, My name is Rosa Colque Quíspe. I have 32
years. I live in San Cristóbal. I live with my six brothers.

I could hear the children's pencils at work as I slipped out of the classroom.

The next morning, my hopes for letters portraying their colorful lives were dashed when I translated the first bunch.

Dear Friend,
My name is Ernesto Alí Muraña and I have ten years. I
live in San Cristóbal. I live with six sisters and brothers

and my mother and father. We have sheep and llamas.
Your friend, Ernesto.

After reading sixteen of these letters, all identical except for the name, and even four or five had written their name as Rosa Colque Quíspe, I began to wonder whether every child had six brothers and sisters and sheep and llamas. A few even said they had 32 years.

Some expressed a bit more individuality in their drawings depicting a variety of animals, adobe houses, and images of the rocks; Achupalla and Tres Gigantes appeared in almost every picture.

What did I expect from children who learned by rote memorization? With no books, no computers, no Internet, these teachers wrote the information on the board, and the students copied it into their tattered notebooks, memorized and regurgitated it—not exactly conducive to creative, independent expression.

Not only had the students never written or received a letter, they certainly never had seen such a thing as a school photo. They were excited at the thought of attaching one to each letter.

I received enthusiastic permission from the Director who requested that I also take photos of him that morning. "To be certain your equipment works," he said. In fact, he wanted several, over a dozen, each identical to the last, each of him sitting stiffly at his desk with the flag draped over the back wall and the photo of the President prominently displayed over his shoulder. The Director first gave me his left profile, then his right, then a stern face-on view. When I had taken shots of him in every conceivable position, he then stood, repeating the profiles and the stern stare.

The next day I lined up the children in alphabetical order, no small feat in itself, and the shooting began. I had written their names on cardboard tags and strung them about their necks so that I could match their photos with their letters once I returned home. Standing against the adobe wall in their school uniforms with their names in bold black letters and solemn, frightened expressions on their faces, they resembled mug shots from a police line-up. Some, including several of the teachers, refused to be photographed.

As I looked through the viewfinder, I realized the image I framed of each child matched the lifelessness of most of their letters. What had initially appeared to be a sea of shiny, smiling faces now differentiated itself into individuals. Some did sparkle, and some did smile, but there were many with unwashed hair, blackened hands and faces, green snot smeared on the backs of their hands and across their cheeks, smudged and wrinkled shirts and dresses.

But the filth was not as hard to stomach as were their vacant looks and slumped shoulders. Was this the protein deficiency that Octavio and the doctor were talking about? There were those who stood out because they lacked the medical care: the one with the club foot or the harelip or the child who couldn't speak but whose parents couldn't afford to bring him to La Paz where he might receive services. I captured their poverty on film.

I returned to our little adobe home near tears. My idealism which had served me well most of my life was waging a tug of war with reality.

Larry looked up from the maps he had spread out on the large table. "Hard day?"

The tears came. With a tender expression, he pulled me towards him and embraced me.

"Their lives will be so limited," I said.

"Yeah, but if the world's economy collapsed tomorrow, you and I would starve to death. These people would go on living just as they are right now."

I grabbed a tissue and blew my nose, suddenly so aware of every little luxury I had at my fingertips—even tissues. "A pen-pal program's not going to capture the gifts of these people. I wanted their letters to express their creativity, the vitality of their culture, their resourcefulness so that the students back home could learn something from them, but writing isn't their medium for expression. Quechua isn't even a written language."

"Honey, they have some things we don't have: extended family and community, and," he said with a twinkle in his eyes, inviting a reaction from me, "they really *do* have an interesting culture."

I smiled weakly.

"Look at the kids' playground." He waved both hands in the air. "They're outside climbing rocks and herding animals while our kids are getting fat sitting in front of televisions and computers. It's so different here. Kids here, in some ways, they're luckier."

Chapter 13

The Proper Yacho

Larry

February 1999

Company engineers had identified a canyon about six kilometers to the northeast, its sandy bottom protected from the winds by yellow and orange cliffs, as the perfect site to construct the new village. There were rocks for kids to climb on and secret little caves for *achachilas* to plan their mischief and for teenagers to fumble their first romantic lessons. The canyon had a spectacular natural beauty through which flowed a perennial stream, a small one to be sure, but one which did manage to stay wet during years of normal rainfall. Wilson Córdova, the CEO of the company subsidiary in charge of the project, felt the site offered the villagers such a familiar setting that the disruptions to their lives could be minimized. The engineers also appreciated the source of water which would make supplying the town a lot easier and cheaper.

As had been agreed to in a signed contract with the company, a committee of villagers formed to select the final site. Within three days, and against the recommendations of the engineers, the committee selected a *different* site eleven kilometers away on the edge of the pampa south of the San Cristóbal Range. It had no cliffs, no caves, no obvious source of water, and no rocks to guard the villagers. It was flat, cold, dry, windy and dusty, and unless you admired vast, empty expanses, it had absolutely nothing attractive in view. The committee assumed that as the existing road between Uyuni and the Chilean border passed through this site, any traffic would stop in the new town, generating additional opportunities for commerce. Plus, the company was planning to improve this road for its own use, thus insuring a larger traffic volume.

According to the agreement, the committee's decision was final. With grumbling reluctance, Wilson and his engineers began the long, expensive task of designing and surveying out a town site of sixty new houses, a school of eleven classrooms, a clinic, an indoor market, a gymnasium with concrete bleachers large enough to hold 500 people; electric, sewage, and water systems; a hotel, town offices, and more. Someone on the committee also insisted on a racquetball court. The church, long ago designated as a World Heritage site, would have to be dismantled and moved to the center of the new plaza, every stone, beam, and bundle of grass.

The company was about a million dollars into the design and initial construction of the new town when a group of village men entered the large Quonset hut holding the make-shift offices at the mining camp. The church-mouse, Santitos, held one arm to steady old don Juan de la Cruz; Senóbio, the other.

Geologists, engineers, accountants, draftsmen and secretaries all worked together, desks usually only a few feet apart with no partitions between working spaces. Wilson often worked late into the night, dressed in his usual three-piece suit, as sharp and precise as a New York banker. He held an advanced degree in geology from Cal Tech, a degree and school affording him a position of high respect in Bolivia. His oval face sported a well-trimmed, pencil-thin mustache. Though slightly balding on top, Wilson was a handsome man, looking a bit like Errol Flynn, possessing a bit of the romantic but quite capable when under fire. Wilson had class—there was no other word for it—a dignity that others could only envy. He was the consummate Grand Old Gentleman, and he was accustomed to being obeyed.

The boldness of the three villagers was a surprise. As they stood stiffly in front of Wilson's desk, Don Juan began, "After much thought and study, *ingeniero*, it appears the people are not certain the new site is acceptable. We fear disaster will follow unless the gods and spirits are also consulted for their approval. There is much concern."

"But, how can you say this? You selected the site your-selves. Construction has started, the new cemetery is nearly finished."

"Yes, that is true," Santitos said, hiding behind don Juan.

"But the town may be in the wrong place," don Juan said.

Senóbio, as was his way, did not hesitate to make eye contact with the *ingeniero*. "We must obtain the approval of the spirits, for if not, we will be punished. This is very important. Nobody will want to live in the new town."

Wilson straightened his tie, cleared his throat, took a slow, deep breath and said, "Gentlemen, gentlemen, do you real-ize how much we have spent so far? The priest from Uyuni blessed this site. The Bishop came from Potosí. *Even God is in agreement.*"

Santitos poked his head out from behind don Juan and replied in a voice higher pitched than normal, "Of course you are correct, *ingeniero*. The priest said that all of the saints, even our own *Patrón*, have approved of the site." Santitos tucked his arms in close to his side as he spoke. "Even the one true God is pleased, after all, that *is* what the Bishop said. The site must be adequate. So, of course—"

"Of course, of course," Senóbio cut off his frightened friend, "but *ingeniero*, there are *other* gods to consider—and they have not been consulted."

Wilson gritted his teeth. "The new town is in the right place. We can't—"

"Of course you are correct, *ingeniero*, the town certainly is in the right place," Senóbio was quick to say. "God and the saints have said so, there can be no mistake. But, the other gods and spirits—"

"And demons," interrupted don Juan.

"And souls," added Santitos.

"—demons and souls must be consulted. If they do not accept this site, then illness and accidents and all sorts of pain and anguish will haunt the new town," Senóbio said, finishing with a slight bow to Wilson's desk.

Wilson rested his chin in his hands, his elbows on the desk, and slowly shook his head back and forth. "May God protect me," he said, in a very tired voice. "What must we do to get approval of these gods?"

"And demons—"

"Yes, yes, yes, what must we do?"

The committee looked at each other and nudged don Juan to answer. "It is very simple, *ingeniero*, we need to have a ceremony, a special *ch'alla*, to beg the gods to grant their blessing."

"A *ch'alla*. Is that all?"

"A big *ch'alla, ingeniero*," Senóbio answered. "The entire village will be there. We will need food and drink to celebrate."

"That is acceptable."

"And a *yacho* to officiate. We need to find a proper *yacho*," Senóbio said.

"This is not a problem," Wilson agreed. "Call on your *yacho*, this . . . Lucrecio, I think he is called."

"Lucrecio Rivera. Yes, he is a *yacho*. There is also Agapato Mamani."

"Yes, let's get one, both, I don't care."

The committee members again looked at each other and hesitated to speak. Finally don Juan quit grinning long enough to venture, "But *ingeniero*, they are not suitable. It must be a special *yacho*, one who has experience in moving a town to a new site. We know there is such a man, but we do not know where he lives. I am sure we can find him, given enough time."

"Maybe a week or two at most," said Senóbio.

Thus it was that Senóbio, Santitos, and old don Juan de la Cruz set out as the official *Yacho* Search Committee on an all-expense paid trip, with Marcos as a private chauffeur, to all the hot spots in Bolivia where such a proper *yacho* might be found.

Nearly two weeks later, Karen and I were in the old town plaza, leaning against Marcos' still-warm vehicle, our backs to the wind. The *Yacho* Search Committee had just returned. Marcos was telling us of his trip.

"The *ch'alla* is a ceremony where the gods and spirits are consulted for their opinions, and where the people can ask them for special favors," Marcos said, hunched over with his collar turned up.

"There seems to be a lot of drinking," I said.

"Yes, and smoking, too. You drink and smoke with the spirits to show you respect them. To honor them. And you offer gifts: beer, coca leaf, cigarettes, things like that. We will have one this morning. You will see. They are big parties, but very important, very serious."

"So you found the *yacho*?" Karen asked.

"Yes, just yesterday, at the very end of a most interesting journey, *profesora*. I never ate so well or slept on such fine beds," Marcos said, jumping with excitement. "For the whole trip we slept in the finest hotels. Even the Radisson, can you imagine. The food—"

"But Marcos," I said, "a *yacho* doesn't go to fancy restaurants and hotels. They're hardly rich people."

"You are right, *ingeniero*, I know that, but the committee said you can never tell where a special *yacho* might be, so if a search must be conducted, you may as well look in the nicer places." He laughed and winked at Karen and me.

"But we found no *yacho*, so we drove to Copacabana on Lake Titicaca. It is the perfect place for a special *yacho*, or so the committee decided, a town of spirits and gods and many myths.

"The next morning the committee spoke to a spiritual healer, a *curandero*, at the foot of La Santísima Virgin de Candelaria. The *curandero* told them if they wished their search to succeed they must first eat a trout dinner with abundant wine, at the most expensive restaurant and if the fish bones were white they must drive to La Paz to the witches' market. There, they should find a particular blind old witch named 'Irena'. She would know of the *yacho* they were seeking.

"Well, you can imagine how we felt hours later after the excellent fish and the wine, oh, so sweet and smooth. And indeed, to our surprise, the bones of the fish were white, just as the *curandero* had said."

"Weren't the people in Wilson's office a bit concerned about how long this was taking, and the cost?" I asked.

"I had to phone the office every day. And yes, *ingeniero* Córdova was getting worried. The costs were not small and time was short. We had only one more week. The ceremonies were all prepared. 'Any *yacho*,' he said, 'just find one, soon.'

"In the La Paz witches' market it took no time at all to learn of this blind witch, Irena. Just buy a lot of their merchandise and people tell you everything they know.

"We found Irena sitting against a concrete wall facing the main cathedral. At her feet she had spread a small *aguayo* on which she placed three onions for sale. She was old, oh, so old, and wrinkled like the dried-up llama in the *pampa*. And about the same color.

"She looked at us with milky eyes, and said, '*Ah, hijitos*, you have found me at last. But such a long time it took you.'

"Senóbio told her we were looking for a special *yacho* to help move our village. Did she know of such a man?

"The old woman smiled. 'Buy a dozen of my onions and I can perhaps answer your question.'

"Senóbio said, 'But, *mi abuelita,* the onions, there are only three.'

"'Nonsense,' she said, as she leaned forward and felt for her onions. Her hand touched one, and then another, and finally the third. 'Three,' she said. She continued moving her hands around until she had felt the same three onions once again, saying 'Six'. Two more times she did this, feeling the same onions over and over, and finally said 'Twelve'. She leaned back against the concrete wall and said, 'So, how many onions do I have?'

"'Um . . . three?' Santitos guessed.

"But Senóbio was quick. He shouted, 'No, no, no, there are twelve. Twelve onions. Certainly.'

"'You would not try to trick an old woman would you?'

"'Oh, of course not. Never would we do such a thing,' Senóbio answered."

Marcos said he pulled out his wallet fat with company cash and paid for twelve onions, "She handed us one," he laughed, "and dropped it into Senóbio's hat, but then pulled it out again. Many times she handed the same onion to us, putting it in and then removing it again, over and over, each time counting 'one, two, three, four. . . .' She had three, we paid for twelve, and she left us only one. She may have been blind, but she knew we were at her mercy.

"The old witch sat back and smiled at us. She had no teeth at all but at that moment she was so beautiful. She said to us, 'Yes,

I can answer your question, *hijito*. I do know of such a *yacho*. At least one town he has moved, I know for a fact.'

"Senóbio asked her the name of this man.

"'His name? Oh, *that* is a *different* question. Let me think. My, that is difficult. It is one of those biblical names. His name could be Báltozar, but I don't think that is it. Or maybe Ezíquiel, but, no, that is not it either, but perhaps if you buy twelve more of my onions, it may help me to remember. You never know for certain how such things work out.'

"We all looked at each other and agreed that, yes, indeed, we certainly were in need of another dozen onions.

"After we paid once again for twelve, and again only receiving one, she said, 'Oh, yes, I do recall his name after all. He is Zacarías Copa. He is old like me, but very active, and he is not blind. He is a dear friend of many, many years. *Dios mío*, how could I have forgotten his name?'

"Well, you can probably guess the rest," Marcos said, "Her dear friend lived in a town whose name she had somehow forgotten, but after paying for yet *another* twelve onions, she told us he lived in San Vicente, my goodness, only about four hours from San Cristóbal.

"Everybody thanked her, shook her hand, patted gently on her shoulder, and turned to leave, when she shouted out, 'But señores, he is not at home in San Vicente.' She pulled a single egg from her apron pocket and said, 'But maybe I can remember where he is now.'"

We all laughed so hard there were tears in our eyes. "I tell you *ingeniero*, it was such fun," Marcos went on. "After packing away the 'three dozen onions and dozen eggs', we immediately headed to the small village she had named, Sevaruyo, near Huari, to seek out this Zacarías Copa. That was only yesterday, *profesora*. We had less than one day to return to San Cristóbal.

"After a few minutes in Sevaruyo we learned he slept in a house atop a small hill. The committee started to climb to his home but were met half way by an old man carrying a small bundle. The old man said, 'You have come seeking my help to move your town. I am ready. Let us go now.'"

"He knew you were coming? How could he know this? Did the blind woman phone him?" Karen asked.

"There are no phones in Sevaruyo. Nor electricity. There was no time for a message. We drove faster than the buses."

"But he knew, somehow."

"Well, he is a special *yacho*, after all," Marcos replied. He wiped his eyes with his handkerchief. "This *yacho*, Zacarías, will cleanse any evil spirits from the site of the new church. The site is already surveyed in, right in the center of the new plaza. It will be a great *ch'alla*."

The two Foundation dump trucks and company buses would carry everyone to the ceremonies at the new town site. Women handed large bundles of food wrapped in *aguayos* onto the trucks. Children were hoisted high to the waiting arms of relatives. The people packed themselves like cattle into the beds of the trucks, shoulder to shoulder. There was no room to sit. Older people boarded the more comfortable buses.

Karen was the first to notice Lourdes Alí standing on the street with a group of women and a few men. "Aren't you coming to the *ch'alla*?" Karen asked.

"No," Lourdes answered. There were no smiles; one woman wiped her eyes.

"We can take you down in our vehicle if you wish."

"*Gracias, pero no*. We do not want to celebrate this."

"Why?"

"We do not want to move."

Karen didn't know what to say. They turned and walked away to their little rock homes up the street. Some pulled reluctant children by the hand.

"She must be part of that original fifteen percent who voted against the move," I said.

"They are mostly women," she observed. "I'll bet their husbands forced them to change their votes."

Trucks and buses were pulling out. Marcos drove as we sat between bouncing and shifting stacks of dried llama fetuses, bags of incense, small boxes with dried frogs and birds. "Souvenirs of the search committee." He chuckled.

By the time we arrived, the site was already full of townspeople. Wilson Córdova and his engineers were there, and also many people from Uyuni and even a few reporters from La Paz. Many women dressed in bright red and yellow *aguayos* sat like clumps of colorful toadstools in the dust on the upwind side of the crowds, feeding their babies and chatting. Kids ran around chasing nothing in particular and wrestled each other to the ground. The military band from the Uyuni army post played their brassy hearts out. The trumpeters had to stop often to wipe the sand out of their eyes. Many cases of beer were being unloaded from large trucks. People were building fires and setting up pots of water to boil. It was obvious that a major party was about to begin.

A large group was sitting in the dirt at the site of the new church. I watched Zacarías, the *yacho*, at work near the body of two slaughtered llama; both were white, signifying the importance of the ceremony. The ground around the crowd was wet with sprayed beer and blood.

Zacarías had built a small fire and was burning a *k'oa*, a paper plate full of candy, incense, and icons as an offering to the gods. A large, square rock was beside the fire, also drenched in blood and beer. It was a *piña*, a piece of the old church wall, to be honored as the foundation stone for the new church to be built over the next year.

Two men, chosen to drink as much beer as fast as they could, squatted next to the fire. Only when they each had passed out could the others in the crowd begin to drink. Lucrecio Rivera, the local *yacho* assisting Zacarías, was busy breaking a knotted string into as many pieces as he could. "To break the ties of any angry spirit or demon who may be living here," he said to the crowd.

Zacarías studied small piles of la *hojita* on his *aguayo*. He grunted. He spread the leaves evenly on the *aguayo*, folded the corners to the center, then doubled it over twice. He shook the *aguayo* in the air while chanting in Quechua. I heard the words "*espíritus, espíritus*" repeated often. He then unfolded it to study the pattern of the leaves once more. Again he grunted.

Wilson and the engineers looked on, surrounded by over a hundred townspeople. Zacarías stood up, the crowd pulled back just a bit as he raised his arm and pointed far to the west, beyond the airstrip. "The gods do not approve of this place. Over there it is acceptable. The church must be built there," he said.

Wilson turned pale. He leaned over to Zacarías and said in a soft voice, "But Mr. Copa, surely there is some mistake."

"I am sorry. This is what *la hojita* has informed me. We are too far to the east. This place is not suitable for a new church."

Wilson brushed the outside of his suit, held his two hands together at his chest near his heart, bowed slightly to the *yacho*, and said in a tight voice, "Surely there is a way to ask the gods to accept this site. I would appreciate it *very much* if you would try. It would mean a lot to us. You are certainly the only man in all Bolivia who can do this." It appeared as if Wilson's jaw would snap or his teeth shatter. "Can you please read the leaves again?"

Zacarías nodded his head. The crowd was murmuring. The engineers frowned and were clearly concerned. Iván Quíspe already had his calculator out and was tabulating the cost of designing an entirely new town somewhere else.

Zacarías faced west, then east, then squatted next to his *aguayo* and dropped the leaves into the fire, saying, "*Es buena hora, es buena hora.*" He pulled fresh leaves from his bag and sprinkled them onto the cloth. Three times he repeated this, studying the pattern of the leaves as Lucrecio continued to break the strings while Wilson and the engineers looked anxiously on. As the leaves spiraled down, we all leaned forward. One small leaf got caught, standing nearly vertically, stuck by its stem on some loose fibers fraying from the body of the cloth.

Zacarías smiled, stood up, and said, "The leaves have spoken. The church must not be built here."

Wilson was frozen, his mouth slightly open. The engineers were beginning to complain about stupid superstitions and false *yachos*.

"I will show you where the church should be built," Zacarías said, waving his hands to part the crowd. He walked twenty paces to the west, stopped, nodded several times to the gods and spirits and said, "Here."

Wilson was finally able to breathe again. A shift of fifteen meters to the west was no problem. "Tell the surveyors to measure this site for the church, in accordance with this gentleman's instructions," he said to Iván. The church would be on the west side of the plaza, not in its center. Wilson walked up to

Zacarías and shook his hand, putting his arm around his shoulder. The reporters took photographs. Everyone was smiling as the party began.

Beer flowed, the soup boiled, and the llama were eaten. Wilson retreated to the quiet of the mining camp. The townspeople were singing and dancing as the band played well into the afternoon. Families pulled away from the crowds to walk along the lines of survey stakes and strings, trying to find the locations of their future homes.

Senóbio and Santitos walked the perimeter of the new church site, declaring it well-located. Don Juan de la Cruz sat happy by the fire, clutching a nearly empty bottle of Chilean wine, staring into the fire with the usual smile on his face.

The old blind witch had done her job well. Zacarías was indeed the proper yacho. Senóbio went to Marcos' truck, brought out three onions and an egg and dropped them into the boiling pot of soup.

Chapter 14

The Rock Stars

Karen

February 1999

I clutched the rough edges of the rocks and dared a glance down. If I fell, I wouldn't even bounce until I hit the sandstone about thirty feet below and would eventually ricochet off two or three jagged ledges to land in pieces on the road far below.

I looked up at Larry and Soledad now well above me. Thank goodness, Larry was carrying the video camera and Soledad, my pack. Ahead of them, five young men scampered up the slope, instruments in hand, darting from rock to rock, unmindful of the certain death should one of their footholds be loose.

Larry climbed back down and standing on the other side of the chasm, stretched his hand out to mine.

"Jump," he said. "I won't let go."

Soledad, too, came down, walking as if the broken rocks were a paved sidewalk. She also reached out and with both my hands now firmly grasped, I leapt. My heart raced as I landed on the narrow ledge opposite. Looking back, I felt embarrassed to see the crevice was a mere two feet across. I took a few deep breaths that did not fill my hungry lungs, and placed one foot in front of the other, Soledad still holding my hand.

By the time I reached the young men, they had already positioned themselves on a crumbling ledge of sandstone. Tuning their instruments, they looked over at me and flashed welcoming smiles as if there were nothing unusual about the scene.

The red rocks, some rounded, some pointed, some mushroom-shaped, each unique, contrasted with the broad blue backdrop of sky, and behind these rocks rose the Tres Gigantes. Peace and awe replaced my previous fear. God's country, Pachamama's country, call it what you would.

These dark-haired, bright-eyed, red-cheeked young men looked as if they'd sprouted from these rocks. Their white ponchos with embroidered black trim waved like condors' wings in the wind. Jorge strummed the rhythm on his ukulele-like *charango;* Esteban ran his lips along the seven bamboo tubes of his *zampoña*, each tube of varying lengths bound together by a woven string; Isidro, with his one good hand, struck a home-made drum, animal skins wrapped about the sides; Rudolfo blew into a *quena*, and Raúl, the most handsome of the group, played the melody upon his guitar. From time to time, all broke into song.

Their native instruments mimicked the sounds of the Altiplano: the *charango* and guitar reflected the changing rhythms of daily activities; the pan pipes with their hollow, sad melodies spiraled like whirlwinds across the dusty pampa; the flutes sang of life, loving and gentle, but fragile; and the deep, steady beating of the drum marked time like a metronome, measuring in seconds the radius of a condor's slow circle above our heads.

With each song, the group moved to a new location as if in a choreographed dance. They positioned themselves to showcase other rocks, each scene offering a different but stunning view. One boy sat cross-legged atop a mushroom rock, another a bit higher posed inside a small cave, yet another crowned a boulder below, each capturing a spot where he had spent his childhood.

It was clear that they wanted my video camera to preserve for posterity not only their talent, but also their land as they played and sang a song dedicated to their town.

San Cristóbal tierra mía
Donde ha nacido mi linda escuelita
Con sus riquezas minerales.
San Cristóbal tierra mía

Donde ha nacido mi linda escuelita
Con sus cerros y sus Tres Gigantes.

San Cristóbal, my land
Where my lovely, little school was born
With its mineral riches
San Cristóbal, my land
Where my lovely, little school was born
With its hills and its Tres Gigantes.

I recorded their music on tape and in my heart. They had asked us with such hopefulness. "Maybe you can show the video in the United States and they will invite us to make a disc."

By now, Larry and I were assumed to be magicians endowed with the ability to grant every villager's wish. They gave us lists of what we should bring back from the United States on our next trip: tapes of English so that the teachers could actually hear the language and practice speaking; a Polaroid camera for the director so that he could take his own photos; medicine for a teacher's epileptic seizures; a magical cure for warts that covered the hands and face of a timid little girl; and salvation for the tiny toddler whose alcoholic grandfather abused her, this one from the young mother who served us in the *comedor*. The wish list grew as did my sense of helplessness.

Maybe I couldn't promise a gig for these young musicians in the United States, but for now, I could capture their magic on video.

After many songs, we nestled ourselves among the rocks. We passed the bottles of water around along with granola bars from my backpack. Soledad and the boys ripped the paper covering, pulled out one of the two bars, and took a small bite while rewrapping the remaining bar and slipping it into their pockets.

"We're interested in your opinions," Larry said. "Do you mind if we ask what you think of the move to the new town?"

The question jolted the group. They looked at each other. No one said anything.

By now we had learned that this silence was not unusual. These young people were searching for the right answer to Larry's question, one that would please the *gringo ingeniero*.

Soledad, more confident than the others and more comfortable with us, began to lead the way. "There's a lot of wind in the new site."

The others nodded in agreement.

"And it's very cold," she added.

More nodding.

"There's a plan to plant many trees around the town to break the wind," Larry said, then after a pause, went on, "You do know that the townspeople chose that location? They wanted to be on the main road so that they'd have more business."

The serious expressions on their young faces remained unchanged.

"No one asked our opinions," said Soledad. "And we didn't get to vote."

More silence.

"We will have to leave our school," Soledad said after several moments.

"Our church, our football field. . . ." Rudolfo started listing the losses.

"The rocks, Tres Gigantes. . . ." Soledad again.

The others looked down, nibbling on their granola bars.

"Is there *anything* good about the move?" Larry asked.

They shifted their bodies as if seeking comfort.

"*Nothing* positive?" Larry's voice sounded incredulous. "What about new houses? Electricity in every home? Warm showers? A new school?"

"I guess that would be nice," Soledad said.

The boys avoided our eyes.

"Honey," I said in English, "It's probably hard for them to imagine something they've never experienced. They know and like what they have here."

Larry sighed. He couldn't quite understand why these young people didn't share his excitement. He tried again. "Your fathers and mothers will have jobs. For the first time in your lives, your fathers will not have to leave town to find work. When you finish school, there will be company jobs for you."

They did not seem impressed.

Soledad glanced at the boys. The boys gave slight nods as if to encourage her to continue. "Yes, that's true. But our people will have to walk a great distance just to get back to their *chacras*."

We were surrounded by those *chacras*, small rectangular patches of land bounded by stone walls that made a mosaic on the hillsides above the town. There would be eleven kilometers between the new town and their crops; that is, if they didn't have to move their *chacras* to even more distant places. Their current ones were planted in soils rich in minerals.

"What about all the land surrounding the new town?" I asked. "Can't you plant there?"

"Most of the land is so flat it's hard to grow potatoes. Maybe quinoa, yes, but potatoes—"

"What do you mean?" asked Larry.

Now Rudolfo spoke up. "We've always grown potatoes on the hills. My grandfather built those *chacras* over there," he said, pointing his flute in the direction of more stone walls. "My father and mother work them. Every year my brothers and sisters, we all help with the planting and the harvest."

"Planting on hills is important," Soledad explained. "The water runs downward."

"Dry-land farming," Larry said. "Your harvests must be small."

"Our potatoes are small, but they are very rich," Rudolfo said.

"No possibility of irrigation systems?" I asked.

"That costs lots of money," Soledad said. "Besides, it's our way here. Our people have grown potatoes on the hills for centuries."

The group fell silent again, their serious expressions, alarming.

Larry frowned. "There's nothing, *nothing* positive about this move?"

Finally, Soledad said almost as if to placate him, "A new school. Maybe we will have more opportunities for education."

Larry, relieved for a moment, continued, "And you know, there will be a paved highway throughout Bolivia that passes through San Cristóbal. That highway will continue on to Chile and to the ocean. You'll be able to get to the coast in six hours."

Larry was stretching here, trying to convince himself as much as these young people. They'd never left their village except to walk all day to another village or take a three hour bus ride to Uyuni. Larry was talking about a foreign country, oceans, sights unknown. Dreams such as these were not part of their lives.

All nodded *yes* with their customary politeness, but still devoid of their usual joy.

Soledad's thoughts had not left the old town. *"Ingeniero,"* she said, taking a deep breath, "the tractor knocked down an important rock on the north end of town. El Soldado guarded our village."

"I know," Larry said. "It was an accident."

I knew nothing of this. "What kind of accident?"

"The driver of the tractor didn't know it was a special rock when he was clearing a patch for a drill site. Once it was shattered, there was nothing he could do."

"Nothing he could do?" I repeated Larry's words, incredulous that the mining company hadn't been careful enough to mark off these special sites, at least until the people had moved to the new town.

"The company asked what the townspeople wanted as compensation and they said, 'A *cancha*, a football field,' so we built 'em one. It's the one on the edge of town."

"Oh," I said trying to understand the exchange. "A football field for an irreplaceable, sacred rock." I didn't mean to be sarcastic.

Soledad blinked back tears. Rudolfo was making a depression in the dusty earth with his toes. The others were staring out over the hills.

"But the other rocks," Soledad said, "they will be destroyed too?" She wiped her cheeks with her two thumbs.

Larry's eyes were moist. He looked at Soledad, then turned away. After what seemed like a long silence, he asked, "Soledad, isn't there a prophecy that El Tío gave this silver as a gift? Isn't this all supposed to be a good thing?"

I was surprised to hear Larry speak of El Tío. Until now, he had described the orebody as a scientific discovery, only occasionally slipping and calling it a gift.

Soledad spoke almost in a whisper, "*Ingeniero*, what if the gift is not in San Cristóbal? What if it is in another place like Nuevo Mundo and you destroy our town and our rocks for nothing?"

Larry looked stunned. "It's almost the year 2000 and so far, we've not found silver anywhere else."

I knew the company had been combing the area and that Larry spoke the truth. There were no other known possibilities, but he'd also told me that there were never guarantees that the silver existed. It was still possible some huge error had been made, or some key assumption was wrong. On occasion a big mine was put into production only to discover the orebodies were not the size or grade they had calculated. Entire projects were shut down leaving desolate holes in the earth.

Larry's eyes were closed. I felt sorry for him.

No one spoke. There was nothing more to say.

Chapter 15

The Worth of the Land

Larry

March 1999

The labor foreman, Iván Quíspe, was a man accustomed to hard work. You could see his muscular body even through the bulky coats that everyone wore. He always seemed to be running; had lots to do. He wasn't unfriendly, he just didn't smile much. He was a quiet, focused kind of labor foreman.

A wife and child waited for him in Cochabamba. He saw them about once every two months, and after a visit of a week to ten days, he returned to San Cristóbal. Schedules like this were common and were hard on family life. Many engineers at least *talked* about getting a local girl and starting a "camp family," I guess some did. I don't think Iván had, but he sure did have sad eyes.

He was born a city kid. In Cochabamba, the city of flowers squeezed into a green valley carved by a year-round river, at milder elevations on the eastern slopes of the Sierra Madre Oriental.

Some in camp said his Quechua parents had made an impressive but short-lived fortune placering gold out of the rivers of southern Peru, an amount just enough to send their children on to the university. They said Iván had a pretty easy life as a kid. It's true that Iván said he never worked as a herder, he never planted or harvested crops.

He was bright. He had to be to graduate as a civil engineer. He wanted to build great mines, and helped plan projects in cities far away. His abilities and failures would reflect on him, and on the Quechua in general.

A few engineers groused that he was hired as labor foreman only because his last name proved he was indigenous. As a successful Quechua man he was supposed to build trust and confidence with the workers better than an engineer from La Paz, a *Lapeño*. Besides, someone from a similar background would keep labor relations smooth during the development of the mine. Making the people like you and getting the job done were often at odds, certainly not always coincidental. Iván had a lot on his mind.

The workers called him "*El Jefe*," the "boss."

La Paz had given Iván another assignment. It would be relatively easy—measure the hills around the village to determine the value of the land owned by each person. Nobody knew how much land there was, who used it, or what it was worth.

Iván had never explored questions like these. But he had a plan.

Early one morning I was atop a hill called Colón to the west of Tesorera Ridge, mapping the lake bed sediments with their numerous layers of sulfide-bearing breccias. The shadowed rocks and *paja brava* grass were frosted with druses of sparkling ice crystals, all slowly sublimating in the warming air. I looked down into the canyon and saw Iván climbing up the western slope toward me. He picked a spot just opposite the Tres Gigantes, bringing with him the *Cacique Principal*, don Juan de la Cruz; the guard of the church, Santitos; and my old friend Senóbio, the teacher. They hiked very slowly, helping don Juan over the rocky, steeper parts. The men kept their silence. I traversed down the slope to greet them. Don Juan had a cold, made worse by a harsh wheeze. He sent out small clouds of frozen breath with each deep-throated cough. Senóbio wasn't even breathing hard.

We met about half way up the slope from the canyon floor, where a grassy area lay between piles of siliceous porphyry outcrops. Scattering like jackrabbits, *vizcacha* disappeared into the cracks as we approached each other. Iván stretched out a tape measure and with a few short stakes and string, laid out a square 100 meters on a side.

"There. You see it, do you not? One hectare," Iván said.

The men nodded in agreement. "Yes, one hectare, *mi jefe.*"

"How much is it worth?"

"Worth?" Senóbio asked.

"Yes, how much money would you sell this for?"

The three men looked at Iván in silence. Senóbio shook his head and looked down at his sandals; Santitos murmured something to himself and rubbed his ears; don Juan merely smiled at Iván, and his eyes seemed to twinkle a bit more than usual. None wanted to be the first to answer, but they all knew that if your boss asked a question, you had better come up with an answer that would satisfy him.

Had Iván not been an engineer and a person of "higher class," they would have answered him immediately. They would have told him that land is not measured in squares with string and stakes every hundred meters. If Iván had been a villager or a visiting relative, they would have explained that the land is not measured at all, that the amount of land a person uses is exactly how much he needs to feed his family. No more, no less. The land is divided by how many kilograms of potatoes are needed to feed his pack of children and his wife, or by how much a *quintal* of seed will cover, assuming, of course, the birds do not eat it all or the wind does not scatter them into the rocks.

They could have told him this, but they did not, for despite his family name, Iván Quíspe was an outsider, and he had, after all, asked them the question of the worth of the land in a rather unceremonious way. He had asked it directly, abruptly, in the way of La Paz, without the elegant hours of chewing coca and the sharing of beer and food. In spite of his Quechua blood, he simply didn't know how people do things in the Altiplano.

Everybody waited for somebody else to answer. Somebody had to do it. Iván was unsure what was wrong. He rubbed the top of his head as he waited.

It was don Juan, who during the drier years had worked in Chile and had more worldly experience than the others, who finally looked over the 100 meter square with the *paja* growing between the rocks and calculated to himself that one llama could eat about that much grass in a season. He said simply but without much conviction, "I know this land. I think it is worth one llama."

"One llama?" Iván was relieved to have an answer, but taken aback by a currency he did not expect.

"*Si, mi jefe*, one llama," don Juan de la Cruz repeated to the eager nods of Senóbio and Santitos.

"Well, tell me what one llama sells for."

Senóbio, who recently had sold a few animals from his herd of about 40 llama, stated, "About six hundred Bolívianos, *ingeniero*."

I made a quick calculation. About eighty-five U.S. dollars.

"Six hundred? Excellent," Iván said, as he jotted the number down in his field book.

"But that is after it is shorn for its wool," added Santitos. "The wool is worth about thirty Bolívianos, so maybe if the llama is not shorn it is . . . uh, maybe, umm . . . six hundred and . . . six hundred and . . . how much?"

"If it is not shorn it is worth about six hundred thirty," corrected Senóbio.

"Six hundred thirty. Good," said Iván, scratching out the "600" in his book.

Old don Juan held up his hand to comment. "Of course, a slaughtered llama has a different price than a live one."

"Well, that depends on who does the slaughtering," said Senóbio.

"Certainly. My cousin is a butcher. He can do it correctly, but many do not," Santitos said. "A good butcher is not easy to find. Did you know that my cousin can—"

"Slaughtered?" Iván blurted.

"What if it is a male llama? There are so few of them, but they are worth less than the females anyway," Senóbio added.

"So it is not six hundred thirty?" asked Iván.

"And, as you may see, this particular land is a bit more rocky than most, so maybe it would be worth a shorn llama, or a male, but certainly not a female, but maybe worth—maybe a male and one sheep?" volunteered don Juan, as he cocked a wink at me.

"And what if the land had been cleared already for potatoes, and has a ditch to it for irrigation, would that be worth a female?" asked Santitos.

"But—" protested Iván.

"We must also consider the age of the llama. Would it be young or old?"

"And its color—the color, that is important."

Iván looked from man to man, hoping for a simple number to put into his calculations. This is not the way an engineer is supposed to gather data. His plan falling apart, Iván resolved to return to camp and think about it. The men walked down the hill more quickly than they had climbed it while Santitos told them long stories of his cousin, the butcher.

After several nights of punching calculators in his little room in the camp dormitory, the multi-parameter permutations derived a figure which indicated that 1.27 llama would be equivalent to one hectare of land. Iván concluded this after taking into account the quantity of rocks, the status of any ditching, the age and gender of the llama. He also factored in just how often a llama is shorn in a year. He did not know what to do about the color of the llama so left that variable out, hoping nobody would notice.

Thus was set the value of the villager's land, at 1.27 average llama per average hectare. It more or less worked out to 715 Bolívianos per hectare, and the company put this magic number into all of their financial calculations.

When don Juan de la Cruz, Senóbio, and Santitos heard of Iván's calculations, they celebrated with coca leaf, beers and laughter all around. Friends were invited to share, and Octavio, the doctor, joined in, inviting me and a few others. After several hours, the unanimous conclusion was that all land was managed as a community trust. Nobody owned the land in a sense because everybody did. And since the land varied so much, they concluded it was impossible to calculate what constitutes an "average" hectare. Each one was so different, Don Juan said, and gave examples. Anybody who cleared the land and planted at least once every three years could maintain the plot for family use. That land becomes more valuable than uncleared hillsides and if seeded, its worth would rise. Boundaries of grazing areas may be diffuse, without fences or walls, but limits were long ago agreed to among the herders. Grassy parcels had more value than drier slopes, and proximity to springs was invaluable. There was no such place as "average."

The general consensus was that the company would pay something, but the people felt like the money was sorta unexpected, thus would be just more fat for the soup.

While Santitos talked long into the night about matters of importance, Senóbio sat alone in a corner calculating that he ought to get from 15.9 to 22.4 llama from the company this year, and maybe he could talk them into a few sheep as well. He bought drinks for the house.

Chapter 16

Too Many Deaths

Karen

March 1999

The two-year-old Clemente, whom I'd met at Civics Hour my first day at school, sat sandwiched between two high school boys, a tiny red plastic disc in each pudgy hand, as if it were the most natural thing to attend school. "BINGO! BINGO!" he chanted along with the students, his short legs dangling from the wooden bench. BINGO was their favorite activity. We practiced English words by playing BINGO with colors, BINGO with shapes, and today, BINGO with pictures of all sorts of objects: animals, household items, body parts.

Juan, forgiven for the missing photographs, was distributing the BINGO cards and red markers. He loved nothing more than to be my helper.

The students sat side by side, three to a desk, arms wrapped around each other. They counted the twenty-four markers Juan had placed in front of them. Gaiety filled the dark, dusty room.

I lifted a picture card from the box and called out "Pig," then waited a moment as the students scanned their cards. I walked around the room holding up the image for all to see.

As soon as he saw the picture, Juan shouted, "*Chancho.*" Sitting in the front row with a sweet smile upon his face, he was helping me learn Spanish. He came to class early, lingered afterward.

"Hammer," I called out.

Juan echoed, "*Martillo.*"

"*Martillo,*" I repeated.

"*Lo tengo! Lo tengo!*" shouted one student. I have it! I have it! Then others shouted as they discovered the picture of the hammer.

Clemente watched wide-eyed as the students next to him placed their markers on the open spaces of the cards and did his best to imitate them.

"Baby." I smiled in Clemente's direction.

"*Bebé,*" shouted Juan.

"*Bebé,*" I repeated, winking at him. This learning was indeed a two-way street.

More calls of "*Lo tengo,*" but as much as I tried to explain to the students that only a row or column needed to be filled before a *ganador*, or winner, was declared, they remained firm: winning meant filling the whole card, and not just one winner; here they played until everyone was a winner, every spot on every card had to be filled.

After many words, a student shouted "BINGO!" as he covered the last square on his card.

"*El primer ganador,*" several called out, acknowledging him as the "first" winner. The game continued.

"House," I said. I waited for Juan to say "*casa,*" but instead he said "*wasi*" as he stared at me with a serious expression.

"*Español?*" I asked, playing along.

"*Sí,*" he said. He made the sound again.

I tried to imitate him. "*Washi, washi.*"

The class laughed.

"You can't fool me." I laughed, too. "That's Quechua." I tried once again to imitate the sound.

Juan's face beamed, knowing he had one over on the teacher.

Later, Clemente giggled as the children played tag with him outside. The teenagers grabbed his arms and swung him back and forth, his legs high above the ground while he screamed with joy. Clemente was like a toy or a school mascot.

"You just don't see such caring and affection among kids at schools in the United States," I reported at lunch in the *comedor* to Larry and the mining engineers. "As a teacher, you'd never be able to bring your toddler with you to school."

"Well, there aren't a lot of alternatives," Iván Quíspe said. "That teacher has no family here and Clemente is an only child so he has to attend school while she and her husband work."

"Even if it's from necessity," I said, "it's a healthy start for a child to be next to his mama while she teaches, plants, harvests, or tends the animals." I pictured the Bolivian babies nestled in the cocoons their mother's created with the *aguayos* wrapped around their backs.

Doctor Islas and Iván looked at each other.

"If only it were as ideal as you wish it to be," the doctor said, "but unfortunately, most mothers leave their babies in the care of very young siblings, some as young as six or seven. It would be hard for the mothers to take the babies when they have so much to carry and so much to do in the *chacras*."

As was often the case these days, the doctor's words woke me up to a different reality, a reality I witnessed, but did not want to let in. I had seen it: most of the time, the mother's *aguayos* were filled with tools and provisions for their multi-day treks to their *chacras* or the distant hills where their llama and sheep grazed. The children left at home were barely big enough to lift, wrap the baby in an *aguayo*, and hoist the bundle onto their own backs. They'd lay the babies down on the street like discarded dolls while they played a game of hopscotch with a friend.

"Survival," the doctor said with an apologetic look as he watched my enthusiasm fade.

But I'd seen such excitement and genuine interest in the faces of my students that morning. "It has to be more than just survival here." I pleaded, "They're so helpful, cooperative, less competitive. I can't imagine our high-schoolers playing a game and not competing to win." I didn't say a sixteen-year-old back home wouldn't be caught dead playing BINGO with his buddies.

"Maybe so," the doctor said. "Cooperation is essential in these remote communities. But it doesn't help them improve their lives, at least not in the long run."

"Can't life be good enough just as it is?" I asked knowing full well how ridiculous I sounded to those at the table—and to myself.

I doubt anyone learned much English during those few months, but some things were changing. I'd hear a "*Gude morneen*" or "*Allo teacher*" as I walked the streets of town. The teachers' and students' enthusiasm was contagious.

The parents were more relaxed with us. Some women even began to talk with me. "If you love our children, you must be a good person," one said.

Larry and I were becoming accepted members of the community. I looked forward to each day.

Summer moved over for fall. The days grew shorter and chilly. One day in late March as we ate breakfast in the *comedor*, I noticed the doctor slumped in front of a bowl of untouched cereal. There were dark circles under his eyes. His head rested in his two palms, elbows leaning on the table. His usual well-groomed hair was disheveled and his chin, scruffy.

"*Se murió Clemente*," the doctor said as we sat down across from him.

"Clemente died?" I looked from the doctor to Larry. "Did he say that Clemente is dead? The teachers' son?"

Larry nodded.

"But he's not even three years old!" I said. "I saw him around town the other day. He looked fine. He couldn't be dead." My throat constricted, my eyes blinked.

"It doesn't take long," the doctor said. "Respiratory illness strikes these babies, and they usually die within six hours."

"Usually die," I repeated his words as if that would make them more believable.

"I tried to get them to the hospital in Uyuni in time, but they always call me too late. I drove as fast as I could, but you know the road. The mother tried breathing into the baby's mouth, but it did no good. He died on the edge of the *salar*. We were so close, we could see the lights of Uyuni." He paused, sat quiet for a moment, then continued, "Anyway, the hospital isn't equipped to save lives even if we did get there in time."

I thought of the endless ride on that bumpy road in the middle of the night with a dying toddler. "What about medicine?" I asked. "Don't these people have any medicine? Antibiotics?"

"That's just it," the doctor said. "I have antibiotics, but they have to let me know as soon as the child has a fever. Often, the family tosses eucalyptus branches in their adobe oven thinking the aromatic smoke will help the child breath. They don't realize this makes the symptoms worse."

I was having trouble following the doctor's words. Not because of his Spanish, but because I kept seeing Clemente. He was riding on the shoulders of a high school student; he was nursing on the lap of his mother during her moment's break from teaching; he was posing with two girls who tickled him so he would smile for the photo. I was bewildered and enraged.

"They call me when it's too late," the doctor said again.

"He was their only child," I said.

"Yes, that's the worst of it. These parents lost another child the same way, just three years ago."

"And they're both teachers, educated people. You'd think they'd understand how important antibiotics would be," I said.

"Karen," the doctor said, "all the teachers here are from small villages in the Altiplano. Their education is very poor."

Larry asked, "Do you think the classes you and Octavio offer will make any difference?"

"These people have had their ways of dealing with sickness for centuries. Medicine and doctors are new to them. It'll take time to build trust, a long time."

"Certainly the townspeople trust Octavio," Larry said.

"Yes," said the doctor, "but Octavio's learning too." He paused, then sighed. "Octavio's a good man. He helps a lot of people, but he still shares many of the old beliefs. Along with the few medicines he has, he still uses herbs and roots from the desert to try and cure diseases."

Larry and I sat speechless. The doctor closed his eyes.

Larry broke the silence. "Things will be better in the new town. The company is building a hospital, isn't it?"

The doctor nodded.

"There will be medicine and classes to help the people understand."

Again the doctor nodded.

"Then not so many children will die?" I asked.

The doctor looked at me with weary eyes and said in a quiet voice, "I hope so. Life is hard here. Two days ago, another baby died."

Another baby?" I hoped I didn't know this one. When they were faceless, their deaths seemed easier.

"María Luisa's. Apparently she rolled over on the baby while nursing and the baby suffocated."

"That's impossible!" I said. "Mothers don't suffocate their babies. Was she drunk?"

The doctor studied me a moment and then said, "Maybe, but I don't think so. I think she simply fell asleep. Mothers are so exhausted, they sleep through anything. She probably didn't realize her baby couldn't breathe."

"I can't begin to imagine being so tired I could suffocate my baby."

"No, I'm sure you can't," the doctor said, "but it does happen, and I am fearful that two more will die tonight. Yeni is in labor and struggling to birth twins. A complicated birth and we can't even move her to Uyuni—as if that would help."

Early the next morning, we parked the Toyota up the street. A young man carried a rectangular wooden box no more than two feet long out of one of the houses. The wood was aged and brittle as if he'd hammered some broken old crate he'd found into this tiny coffin. He slid the box into the back of our Toyota and returned to his house for the second box. His eyes spoke more than words ever could.

Octavio stood by the door. When the two rickety coffins were in the vehicle, he put his hands in his pockets and walked slowly down to his little clinic near the plaza. Larry and I sat in the Toyota. I looked back at the boxes holding the babies who never had a chance to survive their births. The doctor had warned us.

Having the only vehicle in town, we would transport the coffins down to the cemetery near the site of the new town. A *chola* climbed into the back seat with a little girl. Maybe she was the mother's mother; maybe the girl was a sibling of the twins. We didn't ask. The *chola* removed the *aguayo* from her broad shoulders and placed it over the two tiny coffins, carefully tucking the edges of the cloth under the corners. The father climbed in after them. The mother would remain at home to rest. She had lost lots of blood.

I didn't want to know anything more about this family. I didn't want to know whether there were more children. I didn't want any details about what the past twenty-four hours must have been like as they watched the mother struggle to bring new life into the world, only to fail. I didn't even want to know their names. I was numb.

No one spoke as Larry drove the eleven kilometers to the newly-completed cemetery near the site of the new town. The young girl looked eagerly at the dashboard dials and buttons, and twisted her head right and left as the scenery passed us by. The *chola* and the young father merely stared at their feet, their eyes often closed.

Our makeshift hearse bumped its way down the curving road past the cliffs and caves bordering Toldos Canyon. Under different circumstances, I would have explored for eyes and fangs hidden in the dark openings, but there was already enough darkness this day. I did not need to search for more. Although it was warm, I pulled my coat tight around my chest and put on woolen gloves. As we passed the construction site for the new town, the men stopped their efforts, removed their caps, and stood in silent respect. Word had already spread.

A deep, lonely whistle followed our truck as the wind sliced between the branches of the *th'ola*. Out on the *pampa*, llama stood with their tails tucked between their legs, their faces away from the blowing dust. The grass was gone, shriveled to a powder of dry carbon in the continuing drought. Even the olive green of the *th'ola* was now a pale yellow, but the llama ate it anyway, desperate for any nourishment. Across the vast *pampa*, a single dust devil, *Cola del Diablo*, swirled high into the air nearly to the clouds, but the top of the swirling vortex of dirty air collapsed, dropping its load of sand at its feet. You could see forever but there was nothing to see. It was vast and empty, dry and dead; even the salty lakes were shrinking, their migrating flamingos lost to wetter climates.

The new cemetery was alone to the east of town, on a flat bench of pediment gravel. You could see it from a distance, its tall walls of yellow flagstone mortared with concrete formed a square about 150 meters on each side. No *paja brava* grass capped its walls as in the old cemetery. But like the old cemetery, it had an arched entrance, only this one was at least fifteen feet high with new metal doors painted bright white. They blew back and forth without purpose in the wind, their hinges screeching a monotonous dirge.

The father pulled back the *aguayo* and with one hand carried one coffin inside the gate. Larry carried the other. Two newly dug pits awaited the bodies in the children's section.

The babies' father spoke a few words in Spanish as he shoveled dirt over the boxes. "From dust we come to dust we go; from ashes to ashes . . ." He hammered in two little wooden crosses, no more than two feet high, one at the head of each grave. From his pocket, he pulled a handful of candy wrapped in gold and silver paper and placed one on each cross, then he handed bottles of orange soda to the *chola* and the girl. They shook them, lifted the caps off, and sprayed the sticky liquid all over the freshly dug earth. Before leaving, the *chola* and the father lit two candles, placing each in a metal can by the crosses. The whole ceremony took maybe twenty minutes.

A deep-throated moan jolted me from my sleep. It was only the wind. Restless dreams and racing thoughts of death haunted me. My sorrow was unbearable.

Larry wrapped me in his arms and tried to soothe me with his words, "It's okay, it's okay."

But it wasn't okay. My body heaved with tears. I cried for all the mothers of San Cristóbal who had lost their babies; for the men, women and children of the village whose stomachs hurt from hunger; for those who were cold and didn't have warm clothing, those who were sick and didn't have medicine, and those who were so exhausted that they slept through the sound of their babies gasping for air. I couldn't stop.

Larry held me for a long time until I ran out of tears. "Do you want to go home?" he asked.

"I do and I don't," I said. "Well, maybe for a little while. Yes, I want to go home."

Chapter 17

Senóbio's Dream

Larry

June 1999

The eve of the birthday of Saint John falls on the 23rd of June. The people say he is the guardian of lost animals, a kindly man who spent his life searching the rugged hills and valleys to rescue stray sheep and cattle and, I suppose, the lost people of the world. At night he lit fires as a beacon for wanderers far from home, offering a sanctuary from the dangers of the dark. That's what they say.

The eve of Saint John is generally the coldest night of the year. The villagers celebrate it by climbing the high hills around their homes and setting fire to the clumps of *paja brava* grass. For a few hours the town wears a saintly halo of amber lights marking the tops of the surrounding black ridges. That perennial sparkle was soon to flicker and die. This year would be the last. The prophecy of El Tío demanded it.

A bitter wind that began at four in the afternoon felt like a pack of hungry wolves nipping and snapping at me as I retreated the three kilometers back to the shelter of our camp. I shook down to my bones, and I knew there was no way I'd go out again. Freezing in the dark was not worth it.

I was in my room in the mining camp getting undressed, looking forward to a long, hot shower and then my bed of heavy llama-wool blankets and a comforter. Like previous nights, I expected to lie there for an hour or so shaking in the dark, then gradually fall asleep. With luck my feet would thaw by dawn. I had been working at the project for about a week this time, and except for the shower and occasionally the bed, I never felt a warm moment. I wished Karen were here, but she needed her break. She would return again, but on this trip, I was to sleep alone.

But my plans were put on hold. Senóbio knocked at my door and shouted to me. I hadn't seen him for about a month. After the usual pleasantries about wife and children, he got down to business: did I have any suggestions how he might sell his new house soon to be built in the new village, what he called the *Nuevo* San Cristóbal?

"You want to leave the village?" I asked.

"I have five children," he said. "I must think of how to educate them. I may move my family to Uyuni, where I already have another house."

"You can't leave the village."

"The schools are better there. Education is life. My children will have more opportunities." The edges of Senóbio's chiseled face were in deep shadow.

I had no idea how one goes about selling a house in Bolivia, and told him so, then added, "If you leave, the village will lose a valuable man."

"I am just thinking about it," he said, putting his hand over his mouth, like hiding a secret. "I will be given two new houses in the new town because I owned two in the old. I only need one."

I felt sorry for Senóbio. Every day he was excited about some sure-fire way to escape his poverty. Each morning's idea held out the promise of success, allowing him to forget the long string of previous failures. His one big possession, a 1955 Dodge truck rusting on blocks in his back yard, remained a constant reminder of the reality of his life.

"But only you and don Juan de la Cruz know all of the customs. He is old, and if you leave—"

"I don't want to go. If I could sell one house maybe I could stay. But you are right, *ingeniero*, during a *ch'alla* a week ago a group of friends and I were talking about our ceremonies and customs. I was the only one who knew them all. I am the only one, except for *mi abuelito*, Juan de la Cruz."

I sensed he wanted to talk about more than houses, so in spite of the cold, I offered to buy him a beer. We had to drive to San Cristóbal as the Toldos camp was dry. We got into the Toyota, the one with a heater, thank God, and drove up the canyon to the village, where in a few weeks we would discover just how fast a D-10 dozer could level a thousand-year-old town. I parked in the little plaza beside the church. A few people milled about, well-bundled against the cold. Small yellow fires glowed on the ridge to the west, sending short-lived sparks high into the darkness.

Senóbio suggested the store of the Alí family, our former neighbor, about fifty yards up from the plaza. It was a single adobe room with a thatch roof like all the other buildings, lit by a hissing propane lamp, a slightly warmer place with two chairs and a rough-hewn table in front of a wooden counter. The room smelled of the years of grease used to fry the family meals. Everything was painted a lime-green: the table, the chairs, the walls, the counter. The monotony was broken by colorful calendars nailed on the walls, all years out of date, mostly displaying nude Germanic blondes or little cherubic kids with yellow curls, cuddling puppies and kittens. Nobody in this town looked like those pictures.

Leather goods and ropes of various diameters hung from the ceiling. Behind the counter were rough wooden shelves stacked with canned tuna, candles, toilet paper, candy, cooking oil, Chinese-made pots and pans—the exact wares in every other storefront in town. Everybody seemed to have a store now. Because of the company, there was money.

After a toast to each other's family, and a toast to the people of the old and new San Cristóbal, I asked him to tell me of his youth, his family history, and was surprised how full and detailed an account he gave.

"When I was born we were very poor, we didn't live in such a nice house as this," he said, waving his hands at the adobe walls around us. "My mother was blind so no man wanted her. I had no brothers or sisters. My father came and left. I don't know him. My mother and I lived alone down next to the Río Grande in a *ch'ujlla.*

"You do not know the *ch'ujlla*? It is a round shelter made of sticks covered with mud. Not much larger than this table. It was not high enough for my mother to stand upright, and she was not tall.

"We slept together on grass and llama skins. There was never enough to eat. Every day I would go out to guard the llama and sheep, and I would dig for roots and herbs. At night I carried back twigs for the fire. There were not many roots, so we were always hungry. *Por Dios*, I remember those days," he said as his head shook side to side, eyes focused on the table.

"Why didn't don Juan help you? He was your grandfather, your *abuelo*, no?"

"Oh, *compadre*, everybody older than us is our *abuelo* or *abuela*. It's an honor, to have lived so long."

"So, don Juan really *isn't* your grandfather?"

"Oh, yes, he is. One of many."

I felt frustrated. Senóbio's flexible meanings made it hard to understand him. I took another drink.

"My *abuela* knew that—"

"Now, this is your *real* grandmother?" I interrupted.

"Of course. What other could she be?" He looked surprised that I would ask. "She knew that most of the ceremonies included an offering to the gods, and that the people cook and eat the animal that is sacrificed. She took me to the ceremonies so we both could eat. For many years we went to every one. That is how I came to know all the ceremonies. *Mi abuelita*, she was so clever."

"You're amazing, Senóbio," I said. "From such a beginning you have become a teacher in the school, a respected man of the village."

"I fought life, *ingeniero*, I fought always. I still do. You must write the story of our lives. Let the people know how we lived."

I poured another round as Senóbio leaned forward and said, "Then Andovasa, the private company, came in and reopened the Toldos Mine. I helped the miners. I was a *chango*, only fourteen. I carried firewood and supplies for the miners. In 1980, when I was fifteen, I falsified some papers and joined the army. They sent me to Potosí. I didn't like it but I had a lot to eat, at least mostly. I got out and married and quickly started having children."

He leaned back and threw his hands up, "So young, and so many children." He laughed. "So of course I had to work. I went back to the mine. I shoveled all day. My God, how hard the work.

"And then when I was twenty-four and already had four children, I went for two years of teacher's school at Illca. That is how I became a teacher. I fought life all the time."

"You are an example for the children here."

"I hope so. I think so. That is why I stay."

We poured more beer in the fashion of the Altiplano, letting it flow slowly down the side of the glass to prevent too much foam from forming. I felt very small in comparison with this short, dark man sitting in front of me. I don't generally like people, but I did like Senóbio. Maybe it was the beer, maybe the cold, maybe I just needed to be close to someone to keep from shivering, but I felt good sitting with him.

A couple of kids came in to buy candles and a can of tuna. They stared at us, wiped the yellow-green snot from their noses, and walked off into the dark.

"And you, *ingeniero*, did you always live well, in a house like this?" he asked.

"Well, not like this. Our houses are made of wood—walls of wood, floors of wood, roofs of wood. We have many trees in my country. Even so, we were not rich. My father was a soldier in the army. In those days life was good. But one day when I was six he left with another woman, so like you I never did really know my father."

"Men do that. Sometimes," he said.

"Then my parents divorced—"

"No, *ingeniero*, no! Not a divorce. That is a sin!"

"Maybe," I said, "but if it is a sin, it's a common one."

"And the children suffer so. They are branded forever."

"Yes, of course." I hesitated, looked down at my beer and finally said, "I remember as a child I lay in bed every night listening long hours to my mother's sobs. I prayed for them to get back together. Every night for two years I begged God to bring my father back to our family. But he never came, not even for a visit, not a call, not a letter. Then one night in the middle of my prayers I suddenly felt angry. I knew then that he wasn't coming back, period. I realized that nobody was listening. There was no god. So I don't pray. From that day."

"A man cannot leave his gods," Senóbio said.

"I did. I relied only on myself. I went into science where gods are not needed. In mathematics there is always a right answer. You may not know what the answer is, but you can be certain there is one. There is comfort in that."

"You may try to leave, but the gods will always be with you, even if you do not welcome them. But a man with no god? How lonely you must be."

I nodded my head, "That is the price you pay."

At that moment the entire world was silent. Senóbio stared at me. His eyes were wide and his mouth open. He reached out and touched my shoulder. "I am so sorry, *ingeniero*."

"Yeah, me too," I said.

The hiss of the propane rose and fell, sputtering at times, the light glowing bright, then dimming, then bright again only to fall back into darkness once more, caught in a slowly dying sine wave of light and shadow. A moth beat itself frantic in erratic, meaningless circles around and around the scorching mantle, inevitably to fall into the fatal fire.

Senóbio ordered two more beers from señora Alí. I felt I had gone too far in my conversation. As we poured the beer into our glasses, he began to speak again, leaning forward so the señora couldn't overhear, "One time about ten years ago I had a dream. I think it was an important dream. Can I tell you about it? It happened a few months after I bought two cows. That was many years before you came to San Cristóbal. It was the time of the rains. My neighbors told me not to do it. They said I was mistaken."

"But even the Spanish never brought cattle here. Why did you?"

"To give milk to my children, and maybe to sell the extra if there was enough. One died right away. It was not accustomed to the cold, but the other lived. Oh, she was so *brava*. All of the children were afraid of her," he said, laughing. "One day she strayed. I looked and looked but couldn't find her. I hiked many hours to the east of San Cristóbal looking for her. But I could not find her.

"To the south over the whole horizon of the *pampa*, it was black, cut by thousands and thousands of lightning flashes. The rain was coming to me. It was nearly night and I was in the open *pampa* and the lightning was getting closer. There was no shelter. Where could I go? I walked and walked to the north, toward the mountains. I could hear the thunder getting closer and then the winds began to push on my back.

"And a curious thing, just before the rains fell I found before me on the edge of a gully a little cave. Not a big cave, just a little one, just enough for a man to lie in. *Gracias a Dios*, I could shelter myself from the rains.

"But I was so afraid. It was dark and the rain was blowing hard. Whoooo, whoooo, the wind screamed all night, and the noise and the cold were terrible. I huddled in the corner of the cave. Dangerous spirits live in these caves, maybe angry souls. Oh, I have never known such a night. I had only one small *aguayo* to wrap around me and I tried to sleep. I did not sleep much, only a little."

Senóbio looked around to be certain no one was close, and whispered, "That night I had the dream. I dreamed I awoke and at the entrance to the cave stood two men. I pulled the *aguayo* over my head. I was so afraid. They stood there and stared at me. They were very short, like a child, but they were full-grown, with orange beards. Small horns came from their heads, from the top, you know? One did not speak. The other told me he had come from Chúquicamata. Do you know 'Chúqui', *ingeniero*?"

"Yes, just over the border in Chile. One of the largest mines in the world."

"Ah, you do know. So much mineral, so much wealth. He walked up to me, the one from Chúqui, and said he came to bring me a gift. That's all he said. Then he smiled at me. They both left to the west, back toward San Cristóbal.

"I awoke. The rains had passed. I walked all day back to San Cristóbal. I arrived just before sunset and went to the *yacho* and told him of my dream."

"This *yacho* was Lucrecio Rivera?" I asked.

"Yes, 'Crecio. He was very interested in what I said, so he prepared a *mesa* and took out a bag of *la hojita*. He dropped a handful of leaves on the *mesa*, spread them around with his fingers, then picked them up and two more times let them fall again.

"*Oyé, ingeniero,*" Senóbio said as he bowed his head low to the table. "'Crecio put his head to the leaves, almost touching them with his nose. 'Crecio said they were 'All the same. All the same.' Three times he said this. When 'Crecio told me this he sat back in his chair and stared at me. His mouth was open and he just stared."

Senóbio placed both palms on the table. "Lucrecio said the two men were El Tío! Can you imagine, *compadre*? El Tío came to me! *Las hojitas* told 'Crecio that El Tío had brought minerals with him, silver, and zinc and many others, he brought them from Chúqui and he hid them here. Right here in San Cristóbal. Lucrecio then said that El Tío went to the south to Mesa de Plata on the slopes of Nuevo Mundo, and hid more minerals there, silver and others. And then El Tío went home, one to Chúqui, and ours back here to San Cristóbal."

"Two El Tíos?" I asked.

"There are thousands of Tíos, but they are all the same. He came to me in a dream that night and told me he was giving us a gift, a gift for San Cristóbal."

"But wait a minute, Senóbio. I have often heard of the prophecy of this gift from others, and you have as well. Your dream maybe was just a memory of what you have heard all your life."

"Yes, that is possible, but *ingeniero*, never before had we been told exactly where the gift is hidden. We always knew it was close, but to be here, exactly here, right beneath our own village, now that is exciting, that is important.

"I never did find my cow. I never again could find it. But it is such a small price to pay. It is true. The prophecy is true."

"Yes, maybe it is possible," I said, surprising myself. I reached out and patted his shoulder. "Senóbio, my friend, you must not leave the village. The village needs you."

"Yes, I know."

"Don Juan is getting old. When he dies there is no one except you to do the ceremonies." We had finally come full circle, back to what it was that brought us to this warm beer, talking in long shadows cast by the propane lamp.

"I know I can't leave. The children must learn of the old ways." He sounded resigned to a long and difficult task.

"And as I told you before," I said, "I truly believe someday you will be *Cacique Principal* of this village, like don Juan. Someday I will visit and you will be the one carrying *El Rey*. That will be a good day."

"Yes, what a day that will be. I have studied for this. It has been my dream all my life."

We finished our beers with a toast to his village. "The old and the new." I paid for the beers, a dollar each, a little higher than normal. We stepped outside onto the cobblestone street. Bright yellow fires lined the black horizon circling the town. It reminded me of golden beads on a broken chain, a shining rosary to guide the lost souls home.

"Maybe my cow is there," he said. He smiled, patted my shoulders and shook my hand, but he held onto it, lingering for a moment. "And you know, you do pray."

"No, I don't think so."

"Oh, yes. I know it. That night in the cemetery. You prayed. I heard you. Yes, you even sang to God. And at the *Q'orpa*, you prayed."

I laughed like a little kid caught in a lie. "Maybe so, my friend, but I must not have done a very good job of it. Maybe I didn't believe strongly enough. Your cemetery is gone and still it has not rained."

He pointed his finger at my chest and said, "But you prayed. You are not alone."

Senóbio walked to his little adobe house, home to his wife and five children. I drove down the canyon to my hot shower in the mining camp.

But halfway there, I stopped below the foot of the Tres Gigantes, got out of the truck, and lit some grass on fire.

Part II

The New Town
1999–2007

Chapter 18

The Move

Larry

July 1999

Over four hundred people gathered at the old church of San Cristóbal. After a special mass and a few hours of praying and singing, the church emptied of ladies dressed in their cleanest aprons over layered skirts, and the men in their dark suits.

The acolytes entered the street, the first holding a large brassy cross, followed closely by several more swinging censers with smoking incense. Behind them eight men carried two stout poles on their shoulders holding aloft the glass box containing *El Patrón*, Saint Christopher himself. This giant man of paint and gilded wood once again transported the son of God over a difficult path. It was the first time the *Patrón* and the child had seen sunlight in at least twenty years.

"The last time, he was not pleased," said Santitos to an acolyte. "Years ago we took the *Patrón* out of the church to wash the walls. A dark, swirling cloud formed, here, right above the town, nowhere else, and the wind began to blow. A rock fell off Tesorera Ridge and crushed several houses. He was so upset. We put him back immediately."

"That will not happen this time," the acolyte said. "The priest is here."

The Virgin Mary followed, then the golden cross with Jesus, all borne aloft on the eager shoulders of the younger men of the village. They were to be carried to the little chapel in the new town, a crowded but temporary home until the old church could be dismantled and rebuilt, stone by stone.

Villagers fell in a line behind the saints to begin the last walk down Toldos Canyon to their new homes shining in the sun.

All eyes turned west as they passed the graveyard on the side of Tesorera Ridge; gone now their family members and their souls, gone the broken toys, the shadow of the cross. Music from a brass band from Uyuni bounced off the canyon walls, making a hollow sound as it flowed back upon itself, returning a beat out of time.

The children ran and skipped, anticipating a big party at the other end of the walk. Many of the adults sang along with the priest, sang of hope and a better life. Many others cried. Never again would they enter their old church, and tomorrow, once the hangovers passed, they would salvage what they could from their adobe homes. Heavy company trucks would take their belongings to their new home on the edge of the *pampa*. In a few too-short days, except for the church itself, the bull-dozers would flatten whatever remained.

Four hours they meandered down the canyon, forming a line a half-kilometer long. The people remembered that although those years held their share of disease and hunger and pain, they were not all bad. They had memories to carry with them. They could tell the stories to their children. But they knew they would never be the same again.

"You see, Santitos," said the acolyte with a smile, "there is nothing to fear. There is no dark cloud forming to harm the town this time."

Santitos looked to the sky. "What? You do not see it?"

Chapter 19

Promises, Promises

Karen

July 1999

I was eager to return. Although the comforts of our simple Ashland home filled me daily with gratitude, the memories of the harshness of life in San Cristóbal had begun to fade, and I missed the enthusiastic faces of my Bolivian students. I boarded the plane, heading not to the San Cristóbal I had left four months earlier, but for the first time to the new town.

My suitcases were stuffed with letters and photos from Ashland pen pals along with pencils, crayons, books in Spanish and English, Bingo games and other miscellaneous school supplies. Back home, eight classes of elementary, middle, and high schools students had chosen to participate in our pen-pal program, beginning an exchange of hundreds of letters and photos with San Cristóbal.

Larry had mentioned that the government had implemented some state reforms in the schools during my absence. Fantasies took flight as my body was transported across the United States and South America. I saw reading circles with piles of plump pillows for children to sit upon; shelves of books with colorful covers; science areas with sea shells, rocks, and bird nests; maybe an art area with paints, colored pencils, fabrics, and glue.

Two days later, I stood in Rosa's classroom in the new town of San Cristóbal, my feet upon hard cement, not packed earth.

The white walls, both inside and out, gleamed like a toothpaste ad, not yet dirtied by the constant dust. The smooth green-boards awaited the teachers' chalk. Beyond the shiny window panes stretched the blacktop basketball court and the huge metal gymnasium.

From the ceiling in each of the four corners hung a sign, one said "*Matemática*," another "*Literatura*," a third, "*História*," and the fourth, "*Lectura*."

"You're introducing learning centers?" I asked.

Rosa's raspy voice said, "Yes, one of the new reforms is for us to help the children become more self-directed."

"And the resources?" I asked. "Books? The children will need educational materials to pursue independent study."

Rosa shrugged, pulled out a single worn book and showed it to me. "This is what we have."

She began to read. The children opened their ragged note-books and raced to capture the teacher's words on paper.

Dust gathered in the bare corners under the new signs. Other than this brand new sterile room, a new green-board, and four useless hanging signs, not much had changed. The broken-down wooden desks from the old school filled the empty space, and nothing more.

Fifteen eager fifth graders were waiting to see if I had kept my promise. Every eye was focused on me. They dared not breathe. For the moment, my love for these children erased my concerns.

From my backpack, I pulled out a large manila envelope and from it, the stack of letters and photographs. Each letter had a Spanish translation. Stapled to the left side was a photo of an American pen pal and to the right side, another photo of the Bolivian student I had taken on my last visit.

As I called each name and distributed the letters, a hush filled the room as if no one dared breathe until they held the precious gifts in their hands. Once they received their letters the excited chatter echoed off the barren walls. "*Qué bonita! Qué preciosa! Qué increible!*" Some children stared at their own picture, giggling nervously. Several had never even seen their own image in a mirror. They studied the photos of their pen pals.

Circulating the room, I helped the students read their letters and answered their questions. Then from my magic backpack, small zip-lock plastic bags emerged, one for each child. Inside each bag were three crayons, two pencils, two magic markers, a pencil sharpener and a few stickers. They studied their bags in awe. Eyes wide, they "oohed" and "ahhed" as they zipped them open and closed.

My throat constricted and my eyes watered at the sight of their happy faces. One thing was clear. These children didn't lack gratitude.

Larry and I agreed it would be dishonest to edit the letters from the Ashland students. Messages about swimming pools, computers, televisions, games of Nintendo, and ski trips all arrived in the hands of the Bolivian children, uncensored.

I sat with one student, wondering what he was thinking as I read the Spanish translation of the letter addressed to him:

Hello Eulalio,

My name is Sam. I am one of four children in my family. I have a cat. She's nice.

I got your letter. I liked the picture you drew of the Three Giants. Your school looks pretty neat in the video Karen showed us.

So I see you guys play soccer. My favorite sport is football.

Here in the U.S.A. we have gigantic cities. Have you ever heard of a mall? They are huge stores and they are really fun.

Have you ever been on a plane? I have. It is very fun. A plane is a huge thing that flies you places so we can fly over the ocean. I flew to Europe last summer.

I heard you guys are going to live in a new town. What is the new town like?

Your pen pal,
Sam

The students bubbled with excitement and couldn't wait to respond. Wiser from my first experience, I wrote very specific questions with a still-precious stub of chalk upon the brand new green-board to guide them. In addition to questions about their families, their hobbies, their pets, their favorite foods, I added, "What do you like about your new town? What don't you like about your new town?"

With great care the students chose one of their new pencils for writing and one of their new crayons for coloring and set to work. Eulalio was one of the more articulate students despite his lack of punctuation. He had no problem answering Sam's questions, nor mine:

> Hello Dear Friend,
> I call myself Eulalio Mamani Alí I am a good student I am in the 5th level. I live with my parents and siblings. I have a baby llama called Tac. I like soccer, basketball, volleyball I like music and I play the charango and zampoña I have twelve years now we live in the new town. I like the school. It is like in the big cities there are bathrooms and sinks in my school I miss the cliffs around the old town. I don't like the wind that races through the plains around the new town it is very cold in the houses. To answer your questions, I would be afraid to fly in a plane and I have never seen the ocean what is Europe?
> > I leave you friend,
> > Eulalio Mamani Alí

This honest response to Sam's questions touched me, but what appeared in Eulalio's letter as well as most other students' were their references to their discomfort. Letter after letter described the cold, the wind, and how they missed the rocks. Yes, they acknowledged that their new school was beautiful, at least in their eyes; that they now had indoor plumbing in their homes as well as their school; that the flat plain made for good bicycle riding; and that the electricity at night gave them street lamps to light their way. But their sadness and longing for their old town stood out as if written in bold ink.

By late afternoon, the wind was indeed whipping through my layers of clothing and stinging my eyes with sand as I made my way back to "our" new house.

Like a makeshift military barracks, the pre-fabricated white-walled houses with their shiny, metal roofs lined the parallel streets in perfect, straight rows. Everything seemed built at right angles, bounded on all sides by endless desert to the horizons. I no longer rested my eyes on the sheltering hills or the Tres Gigantes rising up in their splendor.

New trees, as promised, had been planted on each street corner. I peered over a sheet-metal enclosure that protected a tiny sprout from wandering llama and burros. No more than two feet high, the twig struggled to stay straight in the wind. "Please water me," read a sign attached to the sheet of metal. I poured a bit of water from my plastic bottle on the feeble plant. "Good luck," I murmured.

I plopped the letters and drawings the students were sending back to Ashland on the table. Larry was once again studying maps. The little propane burner hissed next to him.

A group of children who'd followed me home now gathered outside the curtainless picture window facing the street. Gone were the days of privacy when one's tiny windows opened only onto the courtyard. The children pressed their noses against the glass leaving streaks and smudges of spit, sand, and snot. They pointed at the company's plush sofa and two stuffed chairs that adorned our living room and jabbered with excitement. I walked into the bedroom seeking a moment alone. The same little faces pressed against the bedroom windows, now oohing and ahing over the king size bed, the bureaus, and the end tables the company thought we'd need.

I shouted through the glass, "*Vayan*." They jumped back with puzzled looks. Some ventured a *"chau"* before running down the street.

Larry called from the dining room table, "What's wrong?"

I stomped back to where he was working and glared at him. "Look at these."

His eyes widened. "What are they?"

"The next set of children's letters and drawings for the Ashland kids." I held up one of the drawings of Tres Gigantes. "They miss their old town."

"Of course they do," he said his brow knitted. "They've only been in the new town a few weeks."

"They're cold. There aren't any hills to protect them and these houses are shit. Not only do they lack any charm, look at these walls. Hardly insulated, nothing like the foot-thick walls of adobe bricks. At least those blocked the wind."

"Wow, what happened to you?"

"I want to know what happened to the model town *your* company was supposed to build."

"What are you talking about? The company built them modern houses with indoor plumbing, a new school, a gymnasium, and even a racquetball court."

"Look around," I ranted, pointing toward the kitchen furnished with just a sink. Electric outlets awaited appliances on empty walls. "The power is only on a few hours a day. Even if they do get more electricity, how will they know how to use appliances once they can afford them? They've cooked on open fires and adobe ovens all their lives. They've dried their food, not stored it in a refrigerator."

"People will figure these things out, Karen."

I ignored his comment. "I even saw women squatting in the desert this morning just like they did in the old town. Did anyone explain to them what an indoor toilet is for? Hello? A little bit of education might have helped here."

Larry threw his hands up in the air.

"I thought the company was supposed to bring in sociologists to help the people make the transition," I persisted.

He shrugged. "I don't know whether they did. I heard the people were just given the keys to their houses the day they moved down from the town."

"Nothing makes sense to me. What good is all this modernization if they can't even afford fuel for the generators? The company must know the people can't afford fuel."

Larry hesitated, then said, "The company doesn't want to make the people dependent on them for everything."

"Dependent?"

"Dammit all, Karen, you're going ninety miles an hour wanting everything to be nice with no obstacles for anybody."

My heart was pounding. "The least they could have done was make those classrooms a bit more inviting—some new desks? A book or two?"

"That's the government's job, not the company's."

"Then the Foundation should donate some books and supplies. Wilson Córdova said it was *their* Foundation and *their* money. Surely providing books and pencils would not be a big cost."

Larry banged his hand on the table. "In seventeen years the mine will be out of ore. There'll be no more jobs. The Foundation is supposed to make additional sources of work. It's not their responsibility to buy stuff that lasts only a few years."

I knew this argument was going nowhere, but I didn't care. "It isn't fair. These children, all children, deserve what the children in Ashland have."

"Honey, you've just run into the stone wall of reality."

"Screw you! If someone doesn't try to make things better then nothing will ever change and the poor will always be cheated."

"Why is it that you have to be the one to fix it all? Let them solve their own problems. It would be so much simpler for you."

"Because I'm a witness and it's hard for me to watch these people being uprooted from their land and . . . and . . . and plunked down in this god-forsaken place to fend for themselves. They were promised so much." I could feel my eyes getting hot and teary. Damn it all anyway.

Shivering with cold and anger, I pulled my chair closer to the heater. I sat silent and sullen for minutes, then said, "You have to admit, the houses here, they're crap. They're cold. Even the walls are freezing."

"Yeah, yeah, they are. Damned nepotism. I heard somebody's cousin probably got the contract."

"*Your* company basically lied to the people. You're more than a witness, Larry. You're an accomplice."

Larry looked up at me. "You know, you're acting as if this is all my fault. I'd love to go back to the old town. Damn, it was a neat little place. I feel bad already and you blaming me doesn't make it any better." He paused as if weighing the two sides for himself, then added, "And you know the people did choose these so-called modern materials themselves, prefab walls and metal roofs. They also picked the town site. It wasn't me, or the company."

This arguing exhausted me. Why did the company in Reno allow such low standards for this model town they bragged about? Larry was right. I wanted reality to be different. I wanted it to be kinder. What was wrong with that?

Relief flooded Larry's face when we heard a knock on the door. It was Senóbio, clutching several weathered folders containing a half inch of paper.

"*Ingeniero, profesora*, I would like your opinion on these documents."

He pulled out the papers from the yellowing folders, each a bit larger than legal size. Stamps and seals covered the black type on the front page; illegible signatures covered the back pages. Senóbio held them like they were a treasure.

Larry cleared his geology maps from the table and motioned for Senóbio to sit down. Taking the papers from him, Larry started to read. Senóbio leaned over the gas burner and rubbed his hands together.

I poured some hot water, dropped in a tea bag, and placed a cup in front of Senóbio, then dug a granola bar out of my pack and placed it next to the tea. Senóbio cast me a look of appreciation.

"This is the contract to set up the foundation," Larry said as he skimmed the pages.

"Yes, *ingeniero*. I was hoping you could tell me what you think of it. Is it a good contract?"

Larry continued reading to the end, then reread a page or two. He leaned back and looked at Senóbio as he pointed to a paragraph in the middle of the document. In a soft voice he said, "Do you see here that the decisions of the Foundation will be made by a committee, and that their vote is final?"

"Yes, a committee of five people."

"And all decisions are based on the majority. That means that if over half vote in favor of something, then that is what the Foundation will do."

"Yes, that is what they told us."

"That part is OK. That's normal in these kinds of agreements," Larry said. He read some more, glanced at me with sad eyes and muttered, "Oh, my god." He looked at Senóbio and said, "It says here that the committee will come from both the company and the townspeople, three from the company and two from the town."

"Yes, Santitos and I are on the committee."

"But it means that the villagers never really get to say what the Foundation should do. They can always be outvoted by the company representatives."

Senóbio sat back in his chair. "We can't say what the Foundation does? We never get a voice?"

"Well, you do get a voice. You just don't really have *much* of a voice. The company can always decide what is done and what isn't done."

"Did they trick us?"

"I don't know if it was a trick, but it is a legal document and it is binding. I think you guys needed to have a lawyer represent you before you signed."

I was thinking, *I told you so*, but kept quiet.

"We had a lawyer, a very good one from La Paz. His name is Roberto _____. The company said he was very capable, very responsible."

"I have heard of him. How did you find him? Was he expensive?"

"Oh, no, not expensive. The company paid for him. Can you help us, *ingeniero*? Can you talk with Reno?"

Chapter 20

Canuto and Esperanza

Larry

March 2000

Like most in the Altiplano, the dirt road started off as a single trail but gradually anastomosed into a hundred tracks leading off into nowhere.

Senóbio said, "Take whatever looks easiest. It doesn't matter. Each road knows where it is going."

I wasn't so sure.

"They all go to the same place, eventually," he said. He pointed the way across the low rises and shallow washes and then up into the canyons cut deep into sand and jagged rock. I ate a banana as I drove, Karen straddled the gearshift of the company pickup, and Senóbio sat to her right by the open window.

Senóbio was acting *cacique* this morning, substituting for don Juan whose bones ached too much to climb to the headwaters of Montes Claras Canyon. We were visiting Canuto and Esperanza, an old couple who had sold their water rights to the company for use in the new town. Senóbio came to ask if the promised payments had been received. He was worried about them.

It was March and moisture was sparse. Rain might be coming but nobody wanted to bet on it. The sun was high, warming my left elbow as it rested on the open window. I pointed out to Karen the ditch along the side of the hills leading

Canuto's water to the town. It was a gently sloping canal dug along the contours of the hills, changing to pipes and scaffolding to cross the numerous side gullies. Water leaked in a few spots, shooting up a growth of bright green grass. No pumps or wells were needed. Gravity is as cheap a way as possible to move water.

Karen was not impressed.

"The company planned to dig some wells in the *pampa* to pump the water to the town, but the people didn't want wells. They wanted water from a spring. There aren't that many springs around, you know. Canuto's was the only one even remotely feasible," I told her.

"Is this true?" Karen asked Senóbio.

"It always worked, water from a spring. We are accustomed to springs. They are reliable, usually, and pumps and pipes are expensive to maintain."

Karen paused, shook her head. "How can the old couple live if the company took their water?"

"*Bought* it, not *took* it. The deal guarantees a new house in town and a lifetime of income. Not a lot, but more than they ever made before," I said.

"But it makes almost nine months since we moved and yet Canuto has not left his home," Senóbio added.

Our branch of the road ended at a shallow canyon with its wide-bottomed bed of sand and gravel, lying about twenty feet below the bounding alluvial benches. A few twists of the wheel and we were driving north up the canyon, making it to second gear on some longer stretches. As we drove, the country became steeper, the walls of the canyon closed in tighter, and red cliffs of bedded rock hung above us, their skirting piles of talus stabilized by grass and *th'ola*.

After a few bends in the canyon floor, the untamed slopes of talus changed to multi-layered terraced fields marching shoulder to shoulder up the hillsides. Each field was a narrow, linear strip of land bordered by thick, rock walls, forming a series of parallel benches from the canyon floor halfway up the side of the hill. About ten acres of these terraces covered the east side of the canyon and extended as smaller rock-walled plots up into the tributaries. I guessed maybe three or four families could survive here but I saw no houses, people, llama, sheep, or dogs.

We pulled to a stop. Hiking east on a well-worn path, we noticed each terraced field had rock-lined ditches leading in from the field above and out to the one below. The design would allow every field to be watered by gravity through a complex system of ditches and narrow canals. But there was no water; the fields were brown or yellow, the soil, dry and hard.

A sun-bleached circle of three adobe houses shaded only by thatch squatted on the edge of a steep canyon. A ragged fence of crooked, thorny sticks tied together by strips of rawhide and bits of wire surrounded the one-room buildings, forming an enclosed patio about thirty feet across. No smoke seeped out of the thatch, no radio was blaring.

The gate was made of flattened, rusty cyanide drums from the old Toldos mine. Senóbio struck the metal with a stick, rattled it, and shouted out Canuto's name, adding something in Quechua.

I was careful not to lean on the fence. Too many thorns and sharp edges.

We waited. Senóbio shouted again. After several minutes, we heard a faint yell from inside one of the huts. A few seconds later an unpainted wooden door opened and an old man stooped out into the sun. He leaned one hand against the rock wall, straightened himself, and walked stiff-legged across the courtyard. He squinted through the holes in the fence, reluctant to let us enter. He was nearly my height.

Senóbio said something more in Quechua. The old man hesitated as he listened, then beamed, "Ah, Senóbio, Senóbio. . . ." The rawhide ropes were loosened, the gate swung open, and Canuto welcomed Senóbio with a pat on the shoulders, a shake of his hand, a second pat and another handshake, followed by yet a third, all the while laughing and talking in Quechua. He squinted at Karen and me but hesitated to shake our hands until properly introduced.

Although Canuto's face was as deeply creased as any old man's in this desert, it was paler than those I had seen before. Short, white hairs grew on his nose and longer ones in his ears. He actually had a sparse beard. I noticed his gray hair was full, long, and wavy—not the ubiquitous straight black of the Quechua—but what surprised me most were his eyes. They were pale blue and watery, transparent, under thin, arched eyebrows.

Senóbio presented Canuto with a bag of coca leaf which he stuffed into his pocket with a soft "*gracias*" and another shake of the hand.

Canuto's tattered shirt was bound by coarse, irregular stitches, fixing patch upon patch, mended so many times the original color was uncertain. His baggy wool pants were the same. Despite the increasing warmth of the day, he wore an old military hat with oversized ear flaps hanging to his shoulders.

The three adobe houses faced a cozy courtyard, protected by the wattle fence. On the fourth and uphill side, a rock wall and steps led to some terraced garden beds. Senóbio called them *parcelas*. Green lines of onions filled one *parcela* and the young shoots of potato another, but the rest lay fallow. Chickens wandered about the courtyard pecking at the ground, and in the far corner a dozen rabbits huddled inside a wire pen. The courtyard was swept clean. In a shady corner against an adobe hut lay a pile of dirty clothing and animal pelts. Slabs of raw meat were drying on a wire hung from hut to hut. Flies buzzed in furious circles, spreading the smell of hot blood.

Canuto placed a wooden bench for us, dusting it with a few quick blows from his hat. He seemed excited and talked nonstop in Quechua.

My attention was attracted by movement in the shady corner. The pile of dirty clothes and furs began to stir, expanding slowly as two spindly legs stretched out. Two eyes rose from the fur, embedded in a face the brown-black color of desert varnish. Wrapped in layers of cloth and rags, Esperanza sat up and squinted at us. She held a wooden spindle and on her lap was a pile of soft, fluffy llama fur. She had fallen asleep spinning yarn.

The edges of her sweater and shawl were shredded. Her outer skirt was covered by a stained apron. Two black braids reached down to a tiny waist from beneath a bowler hat that had seen much better days.

Esperanza rolled to all fours. Canuto went over and linked arms as she stood, and nearly carried her as she wobbled over to us. He lowered her cautiously to a stool. She reached down with one hand, trying to find the stool top, her eyes straight ahead, seeing nothing.

Esperanza, the oldest person I had seen in Bolivia, sat before us as fragile as spun glass and nearly as thin. Even straightened out she would be a foot shorter than Karen.

Canuto spoke to her as he introduced us. Esperanza leaned her head in his direction, the better to hear. Her thin lips broke into a smile revealing a toothless mouth. Wrinkles spread across her face. She mumbled something in Quechua as we shook hands.

I struggled to concentrate as Senóbio and Canuto spoke, hearing numerous Spanish words mixed with Quechua, but the thin air and the brilliant sun left me light-headed and a little sleepy. As they talked on, Esperanza would nod or whisper a word or two.

"How old are they?" I finally asked Senóbio.

My question was translated to Canuto. He paused for a moment or two, chuckled once, trying to figure out what the answer might be. Finally he decided, "Esperanza is one hundred and I am seventy." Senóbio was not satisfied. After a brief conversation, he told us Esperanza was probably more like eighty-five and Canuto not more than seventy-five. No records in these parts.

Karen pulled out several lunches from her backpack. She peeled the bruised skin of a banana halfway down and placed it in Esperanza's hand. Esperanza felt it with her other hand, then raised and sniffed it, and rubbed it against her cheek. She pulled the peel off, shoved the entire banana into her mouth, and gummed it into a mush. In seconds she had swallowed the last of it and had begun to scrape the inside of the peel with her gums, removing the last of the soft tissue.

"Oh, Honey . . . ," Karen whispered as she pulled a green pear out of the pack and placed it in Esperanza's hand. Esperanza bit into it, but it must have been too hard, as she let out a high-pitched squeal, folding into herself with her hands clasped tightly to her mouth. The pear fell to the ground, a little spot of spit and blood collecting dust as it rolled. She rocked back and forth in silence. We all stopped breathing.

Karen reached over to place another partially peeled banana on her lap, letting her hand rest a moment on the woman's arm.

Within seconds Esperanza had forgotten the pain in her mouth and had consumed the second banana, again scraping the inside of the skin with her gums.

Canuto shoved an entire sandwich in his mouth in a series of quick gulps, without slowing down to chew.

Senóbio spoke, almost in a whisper, "*Triste. Mucha hambre.*" Their hunger was obvious. I handed a pear to Canuto and a sandwich to Esperanza. They ate continuously as we spoke.

"Do you still have your llama and sheep?" Senóbio asked.

"The last," Canuto said, jerking his thumb over his shoulder to the drying meat.

"Have you received the payments from the company for the water?"

"*Nada*," the old man responded looking down at his feet, his mouth full of bread and cheese. "*Nada, nada.*"

"You received nothing?" I asked.

"No, no, no. They said they would give me a house in town, with a kitchen, and they would pay for my houses here and all the *parcelas* and the water." He waved his hand at the surrounding fields.

"But they promised you money. They have to pay you," Karen said.

"We have heard from no one for a long, long time. Many months ago a man named Iván visited us. He said he would come back, but he has not. We do not know what is happening."

Senóbio leaned forward, his hands on his knees. "Do you have enough water for yourselves?"

"Sufficient for those few *parcelas* above us, over there. We have some crops for ourselves, but nothing left over to sell. The water is too little to keep the other fields alive."

As we handed more food to the couple, he spoke of his fields and houses. He had worked all his life around this one spring. "Water is life," he said, "and this spring is reliable. My family has lived here since, *por Dios*, I don't know how long. At least since my grandfather." He wanted to show us his spring, the one he sold to the company.

Canuto took a second sandwich with him. Esperanza remained seated, cutting her pear into thin slices, swallowing them as fast as she could. We left through a second rickety gate also made of flattened drums, leading up a yellow hill behind their home.

Canuto stopped at a flat bench about the size of a kitchen table, turned and with an expansive sweep of arms presented his lifetime of work. The tonnes of rock this man's back had picked up and carried would constitute a major engineering feat, not to mention the many hundreds of cubic meters of llama dung he'd gathered for the fields.

"Each of these *parcelas*, like jungles they grew, every year they offered good harvests. Every one had a river flowing to them. Every one. Now there are none."

The increasing winds made it difficult to hear. "My neighbors have left. Their water is gone, too. They were given houses in the town already. We are alone here." He pointed to two spots in the canyon where dismantled houses lay in rubble.

"They said I would be paid immediately. 'In a half hour,' they said. Hmmph, some half hour. I walked to the offices after I signed the agreement. 'Not so fast,' they said. I had to come back later, maybe in a week or so."

"Did they pay you eventually?" I asked.

Canuto dismissed it with a wave of his hand, "How can you trust people like that? I never went back."

I was trying to figure out if I had heard him right when Karen asked, "And about the house in town? Your neighbors got theirs. Why not you?"

"We want to stay here. We think we can find enough water to maybe grow a few more crops."

"So you don't want the new house in town?" Karen asked.

Senóbio was quick to respond, "Oh, yes, *profesora*, they need the house in town. Certainly. It is a five-hour walk to sell their onions. If they try to return it would be too late, so the house in town is where they could spend the night. They need it. But they don't want to leave here."

"Maybe we can grow more onions," Canuto said again, pointing off toward the house.

I leaned over to Karen. "I'm beginning to think these folks don't understand. They have to do what the contract says. They have to move."

"It's their *home*. They just want to stay," Karen said.

"Oh, sure, but they can't have it both ways."

Canuto continued, "If the company lets me take more of the water, then maybe there will be sufficient." Senóbio nodded in agreement.

"And they never paid him," Karen persisted.

"But he only went once. C'mon, he's gotta at least *try*. The money's probably waiting for him. Canuto signed the deal. Hell, he could be living in town, buying all the food he wants."

"He wants to *grow* it, not *buy* it." Karen was angry. "He signed. Maybe he shouldn't have, but he did. Your company seems quite willing to get people to sign contracts they don't really understand. And then they forget all about paying them."

"OK. You're right. I bet he can't read. He may never have really understood what he was signing."

"It probably isn't even legal," she added.

"The spring is here," Canuto said as he pointed into a narrow side gully cutting down to bedrock. Water dribbled from several damp fractures in the rock, dropping crystal clear from rounded masses of green moss, finding its way to collect in a deep pool inside a concrete box. Canuto pointed out the new, large-diameter pipes at the base of the pool draining the water down to the canal that fed the town. He spoke without pause, always referring to the spring as "his," never acknowledging that he had sold it. He pointed south then north and spoke of ditches and rainfall and water flow, and how he planned to plug the town's pipes and send water to a new ditch he would construct, to feed his dry *parcelas*, especially those nearest the house.

"If I dig a new ditch from here, perhaps I can get a little more *aguita*," he said, pointing to a slope covered with boulders the size of bathtubs. Senóbio and Canuto started walking the route of this imaginary new ditch. "I will need help with these rocks, but we could maybe get enough for two more *parcelas*." Canuto and Senóbio were well advanced in planning their diversion of the town's water, all the while assuming the company and the town would somehow agree to give them extra water.

I felt such despair for this man facing his impossible task. I knew already the town was short of water, even with the canal from this spring. There was no way they would agree to give some back to Canuto. The company would likely demand that he take his money, move to town, and be done with it.

We hiked along the difficult route of the new ditch to the houses and courtyard, finding Esperanza had limped her way back to the pile of animal skins and to her spinning. Karen asked if Esperanza and Canuto would permit us to photograph them. They both nodded after we promised to give them a copy of the photo. Canuto asked us to wait as he helped his wife disappear into one of the huts.

Canuto reappeared wearing a light blue-checkered sports coat over his patched shirt. A gray felt hat replaced the cap with the oversized earflaps. A slightly cleaner shawl was wrapped around Esperanza's shoulders and a clean black bowler balanced upon her head. They wished to pose in the bed of onions.

Karen and Senóbio each held an arm while lifting the tiny woman above the rocky steps to place her by her husband. Facing the camera they stood stiffly together, touching along their sides but not holding hands. Esperanza smiled for the camera as Canuto gazed down on his little wife.

We thanked them for their hospitality with smiles and handshakes. Esperanza handed us the bag with the remainder of lunch. We explained through gesture that the food was for them.

Esperanza motioned for us to follow. With Canuto by her side, she hobbled into one of the huts and returned cradling six eggs. She placed one egg in each of our six hands, gifts for the three of us. She refused when we tried to hand the eggs back to her.

Chapter 21

Soledad's Home

Karen

May 2001

Soledad could not conceal her delight when she found us in the plaza. Time between our visits to San Cristóbal had grown longer as family needs kept us at home. A grin spread across her face, and as always, she hid her front teeth. The black rot had spread, now covering whatever was left of the stubs. Other than that, her appearance had not changed. The familiar cap with the NIKE logo still topped her disheveled, shoulder-length hair, and an over-sized black nylon jacket and sweat pants still concealed her now fully-formed, nineteen-year-old femininity.

Soledad spoke of her year of teacher's training in Illca, a town almost as remote as San Cristóbal. She confessed she still dreamt of being a chauffeur or even better, a mechanic. Not a teacher. Then with a twinkle in her eye, she said, "Come, I have a surprise to show you!" She led us through the town with a brisk step. We had trouble keeping up.

The houses had changed since our last trip. Shutters framed the windows of several; others were decorated with curtains. Bright red geraniums in tin cans nestled among blue morning glories climbing the walls. Fences defined territory—adobe bricks so high you could no longer see the little white houses behind them. For wealthier homes, flagstone walls rose a few feet high, topped with metal railings. Each design was unique.

Several trees planted that first year now reached three feet high. Many had not survived, leaving empty protective enclosures still with the sign's futile plea, "Please water me." Now they were used as trash receptacles.

Soledad found herself a half block ahead of us and looped back to where we had halted to peer over fences, surprised to see simple adobe structures with thatched roofs built in the backyards. Some people had cultivated small gardens in the lots behind the houses. Green, bushy plants relieved the drabness of the dusty soil. One woman knelt by her golden quinoa, shaking the seed into a bowl.

"Soledad, many people have gone back to building homes in the traditional way," I said.

"They are warmer. The winds do not pass through the walls." The smile never left her face. She shifted from foot to foot, bouncing like a child eager to move on.

On almost every block, a company-built house opened its front doors to reveal a store, converted from a former living room. Here, miscellaneous items were sold: a few pencils, clothes, aprons. Soda pop and beer lined the shelves. Even though the high-paying jobs of the mine had not yet begun, everyone was employed, and most were making better money than ever before. Many had been hired to construct dormitories in the mining camp for the thousands of workers who would arrive when construction began on the mill and rail spur.

At last we arrived at Soledad's parents' house. She motioned for us to enter the yard as she swung open a large gate of welded iron bars lined with chicken wire. She grabbed my hand and pulled me toward several attached adobe buildings behind the company-built house. The morning's wash hung on a line across the courtyard. Hens wandered about, scratching at the dirt.

Soledad stood in front of an adobe building about the same size as the houses in the old town, a replica of the ten-by-ten foot rooms that families had lived in for generations. Its adobe was so fresh the straw stuck out in all directions. Soledad opened a wooden door, paused, and took a deep breath. "*Profesora e ingeniero, bienvenidos a mi casa.*" She led us through the doorway and watched our expressions as we scanned the surroundings.

"I built it myself," she said, her face glowing.

"Incredible," I said as my eyes wandered.

Soledad sat on a small bed, the fuzzy llama wool blanket pulled tight, corners tucked in. It took up most of the room. The *charango* I had given her years ago leaned against a folding chair in the corner. She saw my eyes looking at the instrument. "Do you remember?"

"I remember. Do you still play?"

"A little. I don't have much time with my studies."

A short stack of papers and a few books sat neatly arranged on a wooden table under a window with real glass, admitting the afternoon sun. Recalling the dark adobe huts of the old village, I was struck by how light and comfortable the room felt. Yellow curtains added a feminine touch.

Larry put his hand against the smoothed mud covering the walls and asked, "Where did you buy the adobe bricks?"

Soledad jumped up from the bed and came over to pat the wall near Larry. "I made them myself."

"And the roof?" I looked up at the thatched grass forming the high ceiling.

"I cut them. I dried them."

The scent of the yellowed grass, like fresh mowed lawn, mingled with the earthy smell of clay.

"And the electricity?" I asked, noticing a cheap plastic radio and a small bedside lamp plugged into the wall.

Soledad clicked the lamp switch on and off. "It works when the electricity is on." She laughed. "I put the wires in myself."

"My God," Larry said, looking around the room. "I couldn't have done this."

A brown llama, still wobbly on its new legs, stumbled through the open door, followed by Soledad's nine-year-old sister, Ana. She carried a baby bottle filled with white liquid. Sitting on the bed, the little girl pulled the *llamita* close to her, allowing the animal's mouth to find the nipple and begin sucking vigorously. He seemed to belong in this room, a natural pet in the Altiplano.

As I stroked the soft fur, I noticed high up on the walls a border of a dozen calendar photos. Blue-eyed, light-skinned blond beauties baring overly large breasts looked down from their perch. I caught Larry gazing up at these sex goddesses, his mouth slightly agape.

Below the goddesses hung a large silver crucifix and a photo of Jesus looking sad-eyed on the cross. Next to Jesus, another calendar photo displayed four studly men in Levis and flannel shirts looking like dwarfs as they leaned against a 200-ton yellow Komatsu dump truck designed for hauling ore. Their hard hats barely reached the top of the tires.

"That's a helluva truck," Larry commented.

"Yeah, I'd love to drive one for the company," Soledad said.

"You know many companies in Peru and Chile prefer to hire women as drivers."

"Really?" Soledad's eyes widened.

"They don't drink as much as the men and therefore are more reliable." His eyes drifted back to the goddesses on the wall. "It's remarkable what you've done here."

The *llamita*, his belly full, scampered out the open door.

I wasn't sure how to approach the subject with Soledad, but I wanted to see the old town site and have Soledad tell me the legends behind each rock for the final time so that I could film them. Larry had warned me that the town had been leveled shortly after the people had left. The company had wanted to make sure that the people would not change their minds and try to return. They used a dozer. Everything was crushed. Took about three hours. I remember thinking, *This is progress?*

I hesitated, then asked, "Have you gone back to the old town?"

"No, not in a long time. I'm not sure I want to."

I was sorry I'd brought up the subject. Perhaps I was being selfish. I wanted Soledad to accompany me, and I knew she would never say no.

The next morning, Soledad, Larry, and I drove to the mining camp at Toldos where we parked the truck, then set out walking up the winding, dirt road that led to the old town. The jagged tops of the ridges to the west glowed yellow and orange in the slanting sunlight, leaving the road along the canyon floor deep in shadows.

Soledad trudged in silence, bent forward, eyes downward, hands clasped behind her back. Despite the warm fall air, I felt a chill from deep inside. *Why was I doing this?*

As we revisited El Caballo Blanco, the first important rock to greet us on our way up the hill, Soledad, as she had done so many years ago, repeated the stories she'd heard from childhood while I filmed. But today, instead of planting herself in front of each rock or climbing over them and jumping from ledge to ledge, she stood by my side and spoke without enthusiasm.

"Soledad," I urged, "stand in front of the rock so you are in the film."

"Please, *profesora*. It is better that I stand by you."

"But why, Soledad?"

"I don't want to be seen with *them* anymore." Her eyes glanced at the sacred rock in front of us and she gave a little nod in its direction.

We stopped at various rocks along the way: The Tres Gigantes, El Sapo, El Soldado. Soledad repeated how these stone friends protected the village, how they have been here forever, how they were the people's ancestors. Her expressionless face and monotone contrasted sharply with her excitement the day before when she showed us her room. Her voice, even and controlled, concealed what?

As we approached the old town site at the top of the winding canyon, we hesitated, barely moving; perhaps because there was so little oxygen in our lungs or maybe heavy emotion slowed our feet, I didn't know. I wanted to postpone seeing it for as long as possible.

But then we reached the top and rounded the corner. I stopped cold and my heart jumped. No town. Nothing. Just a broad dozer scratch on the colorful earth covered by a thin scab of dust and broken adobe. The dirt roads still zigzagged through the hills and the pattern of rectangular patches of flat drilling platforms spotted the countryside. But the town was gone. Not just gone, obliterated. There was nothing to suggest buildings had once been here. No life. No children laughing in the gully, no gossiping women filling their buckets in the

plaza, no shouts of men and boys kicking balls across the soccer field.

Larry must have seen the horror on my face. "I told you it
would be a shock," he said, his voice defensive.

Soledad stood still, expressionless, staring at the lifeless
valley in front of her. Then, as if to comfort me, Soledad said
flatly, "Look, Achupalla is still here. Come, you must film this
rock since it is so important."

Like some joke made in bad taste, the huge mushroom at the
entrance of the town still greeted us with its engraved sign,
"Welcome to San Cristóbal, 4100 meters above sea level."

Soledad was talking, but nothing made any sense to me,
". . . the most loved . . . on the 28th of July engaged couples
are married . . . not a real marriage. . . ." I heard the words, but
I couldn't focus. "They marry a year later . . . a big party. Don't
you want to film this one?"

Mechanically, I raised the camera and filmed the Achupalla.
I wanted to scream at Larry, *Look what you've done! An entire
culture destroyed. For what?* But when I looked at him, his eyes
were watering. He held his hand to his heart.

Soledad had walked away. She climbed up into the small cave
within the Achupalla and sat looking away from us. I could see
her body shuddering.

Chapter 22

The Condemnados

Larry

May 2001

Our shoes squeaked as we walked down the empty hallway of the new hospital, a sprawling, flat building of ten
rooms, each with a linoleum floor and large, open windows.
Echoes reverberated back and forth between the angular,
hard surfaces.

We found Octavio and a nurse cleaning up from helping
Cirilia de Calcina give birth to her third. There was a new deliv-
ery bed and some tables holding a few supplies, but otherwise
the entire hospital was empty except for two wire-spring beds,
Octavio's little desk, and four or five chairs. He had petitioned
the government for supplies but had not heard back. The company had been mulling over helping out a bit for community
relations purposes, but so far, nothing had been given.

We asked Octavio if the general health of the villagers had
changed over the past year.

"There are some good things and some not so good," he
replied. "The good is that nutrition is greatly improved. The
Foundation's greenhouse assures us cheap vegetables in an
amazing variety. The people here are not used to vegetables.
It has taken all this time for them to appreciate the greens and
tomatoes and squash, but they are slowly adjusting." He put
away a couple of fancy new stainless-steel instruments I could
not even begin to identify.

"There is more money in town now. I see children carrying fruit to school every day, oranges and apples from Chile. Such a luxury." He added that more readily-available antibiotics had cut the death rate to about half of what it was before. "But also we have money now for candy and sodas. We seem to have exchanged malnutrition for anemia."

The drinking though, that worried Octavio. "Just go out at night and you can see them. They know a job is waiting for them at the mine so many do not study. They just lie around and get drunk." He was shocked that the men did it right in public. "I suspect they learned it from television. You have seen the antennae in town?"

"Yes, a pity," Karen said.

"All we get are Peruvian channels, and one from Chile. You cannot imagine how horrible an influence it is, full of sex and violence, drugs and depravity of all sorts. It gives the young people such a negative view of life. That Wide World of Wrestling, it has already led to several injuries as boys practice jumping on their younger sisters and brothers. And those novellas, those so-called love stories are nothing except extra-marital affairs, sex, and abortion and lack of moral strength. Such perversions."

Octavio continued, "We have even had two suicides, just a few months ago. Two young men. Such a strange event. Never before, maybe once in twenty years did we have a suicide. Now these two. They hung themselves on the same night right in their parents' homes. What a tragedy for the families. It is the television, of this I am certain."

"Were they locals?" Karen asked.

Octavio sat down on a new office chair behind a badly-stained desk. We pulled up two chairs as he spoke.

"Both local boys, Raúl Quíspe and Hérnan Condori. You probably taught them, *profesora*."

"Raúl? Raúl Quíspe? Was he a musician?"

"Yes, I think he played the guitar, and sang."

Karen whispered, "Raúl . . ."

"It is such a pity, such a waste of young life," Octavio went on, "and over a girl, of all things. Now our village has two *condemnados* to worry about." He shook his head slowly.

"*Condemnados*?" I asked.

"It is a mortal sin to kill yourself. You condemn your soul to wander for eternity seeking peace, but never finding it. *Condemnados* scream throughout the night. You hear it often in the village."

"Some of these Quechua beliefs are so harsh," Karen said.

"I think it came from the Catholics to discourage suicides," I said. "But people don't believe it much anymore."

"Oh, but it is true, *ingeniero*, we have all seen them. They roam the province everywhere. I myself was nearly killed by one, on a bus from Uyuni."

"You met a *condemnado*?" I asked, trying not to appear too skeptical.

"Everybody has. We stopped to pick up a man by the side of the road. His clothes were rags, ripped and soiled, we opened the door but before he could step in we saw blood all over his head and face, worms were crawling out of his nose. His hair also had worms dropping to the ground from wounds on his head. He smelled like rotting flesh. We shouted for the driver to shut the door before he could climb in. *Gracias a Dios*, we left him there. We all could have been killed."

Was he serious? I looked at Octavio closely. "But Octavio, you are a professional. You are educated. You believe this?"

"I saw him, *ingeniero*, I saw him, and others, too. He was trying to get across the Río Colorado. They cannot touch water, you know. Across the river he could then wander far to the south, nearly to Argentina. They say there is a place there for *condemnados* to finally rest, to find the peace they seek. He would have killed us all and taken our bus to get across the river."

He meant it. He believed it.

"You really believe your lives were threatened?" Karen asked.

"Oh yes. Many have been killed by them. They will approach a young person all alone tending the sheep. The only protection is to hold up a mirror. His image frightens him so much the *condemnado* will run away."

"Wait a minute, Octavio," I said, "you mean all the young kids carry a mirror around with them?"

"No, of course not, we have also found that *condemnados* are afraid of llama. For some reason they cannot see the llama.

Even if they walk into the middle of a herd, they cannot see them. So all the young herder has to do is shout 'llama' and the *condemnado* will run away."

While I stood there with my mouth open, Karen asked, "You knew the two young men who killed themselves. They were your neighbors, they played with your children."

"Yes, in fact I even helped birth them."

"And now you think they are wandering around lost and screaming all night?" Karen apparently found this hard to believe as well.

"I know it is difficult to understand this, *profesora*. You rely so much on your education. It can easily make a person a skeptic. I once was myself. But right after they killed themselves, we started hearing the screams. People hid in fear for many nights; they locked tight the doors of their homes, afraid of any knock or any sound in the courtyards. The *condemnados*, they crave human comfort and human blood to keep themselves warm. We heard them, we all heard them."

I was curious how Octavio managed to believe in his medicine and science yet still accept the demons and spirits of his ancestors. His education allowed him to function quite well to bring life and health to the hundreds living in the area, dispensing medicines and performing on-the-spot surgery. But at the same time, on his visits to share these wonders of the new world, he also collected wild herbs and roots and spoke of faith-healing, the power of the cross, the miracles of the *Patrón.*

I tried to find the words that would not insult him. "Octavio, my friend, I am surprised that you don't trust in the education from your medical school. I am certain they don't teach you such things as *condemnados* there. Your professors would not believe in them."

Octavio looked down at his desk top, then stood to face the curtainless window, staring across the *pampa* to the distant Nuevo Mundo Range. He took a deep breath, and spoke toward the snowcapped peaks. "When I was younger, just beginning my work, I did not believe in such things. On the contrary, I had complete confidence that the answer to death and disease was education and modern medicines and that the old myths of my parents had no value. But as I entered the third age of life, I gradually began to understand that medicines and education did not explain everything, that some diseases should not be prevented and not everything needs to be treated. In fact, what some medicines promise us is really only destructive: they make our lives worse than before. Not always, of course, but at times."

"How do you mean, Octavio?" Karen asked.

"I have a daughter. Beautiful she is. There is no one like her on this earth. She is married to a good man—lives here in San Cristóbal. She has two children. The eldest a boy of eleven. He was born fat and healthy and ready for life."

Octavio took another slow, deep breath, shut his eyes and continued. "Now, he is crippled, his arms and hands twisted in pain, his legs shrunken to the size of sticks. He cannot speak or hear. My daughter must care for him for the rest of his life."

"What happened to him?" Karen asked.

"He had an infection of some sort. We never knew what it was. Fever, weakness. My daughter tried some *wira wira* and several other herbs. He did not get worse but not better either. I injected him with penicillin. He had a reaction."

"*Dios mío*," I said.

Octavio continued to stare out the window into the haze. "At first I felt . . . I felt . . . horrible. Of course, at first . . . of course."

I remained seated in my chair, staring at his back. I heard Karen's voice from a distance, "*Lo siento mucho.*" She stood beside him.

"I have learned to accept that it was one of those accidents of our modern medicines, one of those statistical events that we spoke about in our classes as so rare that we could just ignore it. You have heard of that one-in-a-million reaction so unlikely that we dismiss the chance of it happening. We push that inconvenient number from our minds, erase it from our notes, and go on studying our textbooks, forgetting forever the thought that our modern methods are far from perfect."

He paused, then said, "The truth is that somewhere, some day, those odds will catch up with somebody."

I sat enveloped in heavy silence. Karen finally had the strength to say what I felt, "*Qué difícil. Qué terrible.*"

She raised her hand to place it on his shoulder, hesitated, then lowered it again.

Life is hard, it's just harder for some.

Octavio turned from the window and sat at his desk, fiddled with some papers for a moment, and after a pause, leaned back in his chair. "I continue to believe in my pills, I still give injections, but I know that nothing is perfect; there are other possibilities as well. The herbs, the *ch'allas*, the prayers, they are just like the medicines. They are often helpful, but sometimes not. You can trust them, but not always."

"Like the *condemnados*?" I asked, "You can believe in science but also believe in them?"

"Why not? What is important is that the people believe. This new world has such uncertainty; following our ancestors gives us a few answers to at least some of the questions. Not all are mathematically proven, but they remain worthy of belief."

"It must be comforting to believe in something, even if not perfect," I said.

"Yes. Comforting, and for that, so very necessary," Octavio said.

Chapter 23

No Mine?

Karen

September 2002

Larry, usually so calm and patient, slammed down the receiver in his office in our Ashland home. "That was Reno. They're shutting down the project."

"What do you mean?"

"They say they're postponing it, putting it on hold, but it probably means everyone's going to be laid off."

"They destroy a whole town and then three years later just stop the project? How could they?"

Larry leaned on his desk, head in hands. "With the drop in silver prices, the bean counters say it would cost more to get the silver out of the rock than it's worth."

"My God," I said, stunned. "They can't."

Larry went on, "A mine right now would lose money. If they're right, they have to protect themselves by not going into production until metal prices are higher."

I didn't want to believe what he was saying. "Who's making these decisions? Reno? La Paz?"

"Neither, it's the board of directors and the bankers. They have the power to keep the project frozen, even permanently halt all operations. They control the money."

"So David, for all his wealth and prestigious position as President, doesn't have the last say?"

"Not really. He answers to the board. Apparently, the banks and stockholders who control the board are scared."

"So, there's a possibility that the mine will *never* get built?" I could barely get the words out of my mouth. "What will happen to the people?"

"I don't know. It depends on the metal prices. It might be months. It might be years. It might be never. Some fuckin' gift this El Tío gave."

The company started laying off people from the Reno office: secretaries, accountants, even engineers. Somehow it managed to keep Larry employed with the hope of his finding another orebody, one rich enough in metal that it could withstand the low prices. He fought to keep his team of Bolivian geologists, but several were let go. Mines closed all over the world leaving tens of thousands of miners and engineers unemployed. Geologists were driving taxis or selling real estate.

Images of my last visit with Soledad to the old town haunted me. Only the earth was left—no trace of the village that had existed there for centuries. If there were no mine, what would happen to the people? Confused and worried, I wanted to blame someone, but whom?

I had succeeded in fostering an exchange between Ashland and Bolivian students for four years and I wasn't going to give that up now. I tucked away my worries and once again helped the Ashland students prepare letters for me to bring to their friends. I gathered books for the library we had started in San Cristóbal, and waited for an opportunity to return to Bolivia.

Four months later, in January, the company asked Larry to explore other properties throughout the Altiplano. I grabbed the chance to fly south with him. Since he would be working many days away from the village, this would be the first time I would stay alone in San Cristóbal, but I felt comfortable. My Spanish was now passable and the townspeople, even the engineers, always looked out for me. Larry would join me in ten days. After completing his exploration, he would fly to San Cristóbal from La Paz on the private plane with the "important" people: the company President, a new board member, and some bankers.

After the ten-hour drive from La Paz to Uyuni, Larry and I parted ways, Larry to the old mining camp in Pulacayo and I to San Cristóbal. Marcos, still our chauffeur, greeted me in Uyuni with a royal welcome. "Everyone is waiting for the arrival of *La Reina*," he said with one of his mischievous smiles.

"*La Reina*?" I asked. "Me, the queen? And to what do I owe this honor?"

"Your subjects love you," he said, and we both laughed.

Marcos grabbed my huge beat-up suitcases filled with pen-pal letters, photos, and books. He hoisted them into the back of the jeep and slammed the door, releasing a cloud of dust.

"And how many subjects do I now have in the camp?"

Marcos' smile faded. "There are only about eight of us from La Paz and not a lot of work to do. The men's morale is pretty low right now."

On previous visits before the recession, the camp bustled with over four hundred workers or more, many of them townspeople. They had been constructing the mill foundation. Four hundred plus jobs lost, just like that.

Marcos stared straight ahead, biting his lip, a nervous gesture I'd never seen before. He steered the jeep onto the embanked road that cut across the *salar*, leaving a contrail of salty dust.

"How bad is it?" I asked.

"The future is so uncertain. I can be optimistic because I know that if the company lets me go, I have other goals in life."

"What would you do?"

"I would return to school. Maybe teach. But the others are so scared. They don't know how they and their families will survive without the company's work."

Marcos continued, "And Iván Quíspe. He just doesn't trust us. The eight of us have worked in the mining camp for a long time, many years. We know very well how to do our jobs. But Iván has to tell us everything. He has to know everyone's whereabouts twenty-four hours a day. I feel like I have to tell him when I go to the bathroom. Everyone is so nervous about the President's visit. There's a big push to clean up the mining camp and the town."

"Does that mean jobs?" I asked.

"Some. We're tearing down abandoned buildings and removing piles of rusty scrap iron."

"That doesn't employ many people, does it?"

Marcos swerved the jeep to avoid a deep pothole and took off on a dirt track leading out onto the salt flats. We sped along on the relative smoothness of the dried surface. The sun reflected bright off the white salt. I put on sunglasses. I remembered that Marcos said he never used them, but even he was squinting now.

"I'd be pretty pissed if I were you and the others," I said. "Aren't you mad, Marcos? They made all these promises and now they're not going to keep any of them."

"*Profesora*, the company is doing its best to keep the townspeople employed."

"Well. . . ."

"Only a few are working at the mining site, but many more have jobs in the town. The company has hired men and women to build roads. Also to fix the doors of the houses so the dust doesn't pile up inside."

I was surprised to hear this. At least one problem of the houses was being addressed.

Marcos went on, "They're also building a road from the town to their *chacras*, one which will bypass the old town and the future mine."

"So they'll have to walk even farther to get to their *chacras*?"

"Yes. They can't go through the old town anymore, especially once the mine is built."

"*That* must bother them."

"Some more than others. They are happy to have work. But, *profesora*, do not worry. The people can take care of themselves."

I took a deep breath. Marcos was right. They didn't need me to save them.

Marcos smiled. "It's remarkable what the people are doing. They are building the road, maybe as much as thirty kilometers, by hand, all picks and shovels. You should see it. It's a good road." He shook his head in disbelief.

"Well, I guess that's one way for the company to create work. But what will happen, Marcos, when the cobblestone streets and the road are finished?"

"That depends on what the important people say next week. Let's just hope this recession doesn't last too long."

I pulled a bag of gorp from my backpack and lay it between us, offering food as consolation as I so often did. Neither of us touched it. Staring out at the familiar monotony of the landscape, I reflected on the company's effort to fulfill their promise of employment for the townspeople even though the professional engineers and others in La Paz and Reno were now unemployed. I had expected a lot worse.

We arrived late. I awoke early the next day, eager to see for myself the townspeople's reactions to what felt to me like impending disaster. Noisy, rumbling trucks full of rounded rocks, probably from the bed of the Rio Grande, dumped piles every fifty meters or so along the streets. With picks and shovels, men and women dug trenches while others worked on their hands and knees, placing the rocks in patterns that formed the cobblestone paving. The people went about their work humming and conversing with each other. The town was getting into shape.

The church was fast becoming a replica of the church in the old town, the same size, layout, and thatched roof, and constructed with the very rocks that had been in the walls of its precursor. The only change at the request of the townspeople was the new flagstone that covered the rock and adobe walls. Built slightly off center in the central plaza as decreed by the proper *yacho*, it remained the focal point of the village. Its two bell towers, one still missing a bell, rose above the houses. The total cost for the company would be over six million dollars for the move and reconstruction.

Since it was a registered historic site, the government insisted that its own highly-trained technicians and artists do the interior restoration of the church. During the dismantling of the old church, five layers of paintings, some over 300 years old, were discovered on the interior walls, each separated by a layer of whitewash. With painstaking care, they were photographed and registered; then some were restored and transferred to the walls of the new church. The townspeople hoped this unique historic structure would draw tourists. Santitos would be happy.

In the central plaza, townspeople were planting saplings in large wooden boxes. A small group of teenagers gathered, chatting on the steps of a recently constructed gazebo.

The school children spent most of their days preparing for the President's visit, practicing traditional Bolivian songs and dances. Their excitement felt tangible. Everyone was so busy, I could barely find a time to distribute the pen-pal letters and help the children write back.

The mood in the town contrasted with that in the mining camp. Both bustled with activity, but the mining camp was glum. Iván barked orders, demanding the men work from sunrise well into the night, destroying the old buildings and cleaning up the accumulated garbage of a hundred years of past mining. The place looked like a tornado had whipped through it.

Iván didn't look much better. He hadn't slept in days, his clothes wrinkled and stained, his hair disheveled. Behind his back, the men complained and the women cried. I wondered how the camp would ever be cleaned up in time for the President's arrival in seven days.

One day, as I sat on a plaza bench my eyes were drawn to an elderly *chola* carrying rocks on the road to the school. The bent-over woman cradled a rounded boulder the size of a watermelon. She shuffled along dragging her left leg. Her face strained and her muscles tensed as she dropped the boulder onto the sandy earth. As if in slow motion, she lowered herself to arrange it to line up with the others, then rose from her knees and stood lopsided. She rubbed her hip before returning to the pile of rock for another load. I went over to talk with her.

"*Profesora*, it makes me happy to see you," she said, welcoming me with a pat on my shoulders and a toothless smile.

My impression that she was elderly faded when she said her school-aged children looked forward to my return with messages from their American friends. She was probably younger than I. Thick, black, braids hung down her back, no gray yet in sight, but wrinkles and the absence of teeth added years to her appearance.

"How are things in the town?" I asked.

"Oh, *profesora*, they are good."

"But I see it is hard work you have."

"Oh, yes, *pero gracias a Dios* I can send my oldest son to school in Illca. He wants to be a teacher." She winced as she rubbed her hip.

"Does it hurt a lot?"

"*Torcionada.*" She explained that she'd broken her hip years ago and it had twisted as the bones fused. It pained her constantly.

"*Lo siento.* I'm sorry," I said softly. "Is there no other job you could do?"

She shook her head and said, "I am so happy to have this one."

"Can you have surgery to fix your hip?"

She smiled as if wanting to take the concerned look away from me. "That is not possible. That would cost so much."

"Do you have medicine?"

"No," she said shaking her head, "too expensive."

She now tried to comfort me. "Do not worry," she said.

Quickly scouring my backpack I removed a small bottle of aspirin and put it in her hands. "Please," I said. "For pain."

"*Gracias,*" she said and then as if reading my mind added, "This work—it is good for me."

Close to the plaza, a new building had been constructed since our last visit. Built in the quaint style of the old town, its mud walls were painted red and its roof made of *paja* grasses. I took a second look. On top of the thatch lay three solar panels soaking up the afternoon sun. This was the Foundation's latest project, a hotel, which would generate income immune to the whims of metal prices.

From the big glass door of the new hotel, the manager recognized me and waved me over to take a tour. He could not stop smiling as he spilled out the latest news. The hotel had already hosted more than a thousand tourists in its first six months, mostly young backpackers from Europe and Israel.

I marveled at this modern facility, such comfort and conveniences we'd not experienced even in the large city of Uyuni: a well-equipped kitchen, a restaurant with its large television, and bedrooms with private bathrooms. A generator provided electricity twenty-four hours a day. Solar panels perched on the roof ensured hot water whenever water was available, the springs of Canuto and Esperanza never having supplied sufficient water to the growing town. The first telephone system, set up for reservations, was fast becoming the center for the townspeople to connect with loved ones out of town.

Marcos continued to treat me like *La Reina*, catering to my desires to see what was going on. Having been impressed by the hotel, I asked him to visit the greenhouse the Foundation had built.

Tucked between two small hills about two kilometers from town, the greenhouse was a mirage in this yellow-brown desert. Rows of lettuce, leafy greens, onions, tomatoes and other delectable treats such as watermelons brought back images of my lush Northwest home.

Walking amid the greenery, I took in the rich oxygen and felt the warmth of the Altiplano sun. I suggested they create a place for Larry and me to stay inside the greenhouse during our visits to the town so we could breathe better. The men working there laughed. They thought I was joking.

They boasted that the greenhouse was already providing vegetables for the local people as well as the market in Uyuni. *When*—they never said *if*—the mine went into operation, it would become the major supplier for the company cooks. I was impressed.

As we drove back to town, Marcos shared other dreams for the Foundation money that he'd heard expressed by the townspeople. A main highway was to be built through the Altiplano to facilitate getting supplies to the mine. There was talk of building a gas station, raising new strains of quinoa and breeding llama for export, and creating more tourist facilities—restaurants, an internet café, souvenir shops, even a cross-country bicycle tour down the 15,000 foot Mount Jayula.

I realized the townspeople and La Paz representatives on the Foundation committee must be agreeing on projects. Several years had passed since Senóbio had shown us the original Foundation contract. Perhaps our worries about fair representation were for naught. Things were getting done and this restored my hope, but still, I couldn't help wondering whether or not the townspeople had any idea of the larger picture, of just how precarious was their future.

Chapter 24

The Meeting of the Caciques

Karen

September 2002

"Listen, you can hear the plane coming," Iván said.

I turned my ear to the sky. "I don't hear anything."

After a few minutes Iván started barking orders for the men to start the engine of the fire truck. Then I heard the plane far to the south, the silvery fuselage dipping lower. It came in for a perfect landing. At last the dust settled, the propellers slowed and stopped. The noise ceased.

We were quite the welcoming committee: the little red fire truck with *Fire Department of Keokuk, Iowa* in bold black print on the side; four company jeeps, washed and waxed for the occasion; Iván with dark circles under his eyes; I, so eager to see my husband after our ten day separation; and all eight company employees, Marcos among them, dressed in blue coveralls with serious expressions holding their mandatory yellow mining hardhats under their right arm, obeying a rule even though no mining was going on.

The doors of the plane opened and the stairs were lowered. One by one, the men ducked their heads as they passed through the plane's tiny door and stepped down the three steps. First came the familiar faces.

Wilson appeared as dapper as always. Our previous encounters had been brief, just the usual handshakes and words about the weather, but always cordial and polite.

People from the Reno office followed Wilson. Then came my husband, his eyes searching until he saw me. He blew me a kiss. A new face appeared next, a white-haired man, casual but meticulous. I guessed he was the new board member. Three men in their early thirties stepped down, all dressed in identical black pin-striped suits with thin, black ties. Those had to be the analysts from the banks.

David, the company President, finally emerged. He flashed a big smile and waved. His entourage in tow, he strode across the landing strip shaking hands with everybody from the highest paid engineer to the lowest-paid laborer, spending a moment with each to share a greeting in his faltering Spanish. "*Cómo está? Mucho gusto.*"

Most noteworthy was David's youthful appearance for a man approaching middle-age. His step had a bounce to it as he walked across the landing strip. He was only a few inches taller and not much heavier than the small, thin Bolivian men awaiting his arrival, but he appeared so much larger, taking over the tarmac with his energy. A brightness in his quick, green eyes spoke of a *joie de vivre.* The blue cashmere sweater complemented his red curls. He could have been a model who just finished a photo shoot for Armani's.

I took no time to find my husband's arms. Then David hugged me warmly. Merely being married to the man who had found him this billion-dollar deposit put me in his good graces.

Larry seemed distracted. His eyes were on the other men who accompanied David, particularly the older man whose skin was almost as white as his thinning hair. He was a bit stout and carried himself as a man accustomed to commanding respect.

"Who's he?" I asked.

"Remington Bronson," Larry answered. "He's the new board member from England who initiated this whole trip. He's one of the guys who will decide when to reopen the project." Larry paused. "I have to get him excited about it. David wants me to send him home with a nice sample of silver core, told me to make it good and rich."

The group sorted itself into the waiting vehicles, much as school children on a field trip.

"We have to keep our eyes on the clock," David said, looking at his Rolex. "We have meetings in La Paz this afternoon."

If they wanted to return to La Paz the same day, they needed to leave before the afternoon winds picked up or the plane would be grounded. Their trip would be short. So much energy went into preparing for this visit, so many hopes and, of course, plenty of fears. I wanted David to take the time to appreciate all the efforts.

Larry jumped into one of the Toyotas with David and Mr. Bronson so he could point out the mining potential. Our romantic reunion would have to wait.

Wilson surprised me with an invitation to ride with him. After the customary chit chat, he turned around to look at me from the front seat and smiled weakly, the usual energy in his eyes gone. Pausing as if uncertain where to begin, he said, "You know, the employees we have hired are good and now with the budget cuts, we may have to let many go. The board of directors doesn't understand how hard it will be if we do. We've trained them. They're loyal and committed. They'll go to other mining companies and we'll never get them back."

I glanced at Marcos. He kept his eyes straight ahead as we drove up the canyon. I wasn't sure how to respond. Wilson's confiding in me caught me off guard.

Wilson loosened his tie a little, just enough to breathe a bit easier but not enough for anyone to notice that it wasn't tight against his throat. "I must also convince the board that we have to keep the people of San Cristóbal employed. We don't know how long it'll be before the mine opens and the people must not lose trust in the company."

Wilson stared past me to the back of the truck. He stroked his mustache slowly, without purpose, as if collecting his thoughts. Usually confident and in charge, he now appeared vulnerable knowing that the next fax could cancel his whole program. He was just another player caught in a very complex web, doing the precarious act of balancing San Cristóbal villagers, the La Paz mining employees, Reno, the board, and the banks. And now, low metal prices.

In a wistful voice, Wilson recounted the dreams he had had for San Cristóbal. The town was to be colonial-style: white adobe houses with red tiled roofs, the winds blocked by a perimeter of hundreds of green leafy trees, and the people living there, happier than they had ever been in their old village.

The wistfulness left his voice as he went on sounding more exhausted than angry. "But the people chose the metal roofs because it was more modern, and only a few of the little trees that we gave them managed to survive. The people didn't water them. And now the entire sewage system of the town is blocked. People are using the toilets to flush down their garbage."

"What about educating the people?" I asked the question I had been harboring so long. "Weren't there supposed to be anthropologists, sociologists, professionals who could prepare the people for the changes?"

He confessed his surprise that the people didn't know how to live in the modern houses. So many of the men had lived in big cities. They should know. But yes, he agreed with me, the company had sent some experts to help them, but he realized more should have been done to prepare the people. Wilson sounded like a frustrated father who loved his "adolescent" town.

"But you know," he said, "we didn't have much time. We had to move the people quickly once they voted, because if they changed their minds, we could never construct the mine."

He paused and rubbed his hand through what remained of his thinning hair. With a deep sigh, he said, "It was such a nice dream. And now?"

"Wilson," I said, "you must be doing something right." As I heard my own words, I was surprised. "The people seem so much more content than on my previous visits. They're happy to have work. They're proud of the hotel and the greenhouse."

I felt sorry for Wilson, sorry that his good intentions for the people and the new town had not been realized and that now he had the additional pressures of keeping the people employed. I also felt a growing respect.

The Toyotas drove to a viewpoint overlooking the orebody where Larry waved his arms to suggest its enormous size. A few comments on geology, a few questions answered, and the men jumped back into the two Toyotas and descended into the canyon for a quick stop at the core shed where one hundred thousand meters of drill core samples were logged and carefully studied. Larry stood near the long lines of boxes containing samples from each hole and explained the meaning of textures and minerals, from the rusty red and orange colors near the weathered surface to the black and white sparkling crystals in the veins and breccias from deeper in the earth.

Remington Bronson looked closely at the samples, often borrowing Larry's hand lens to study the crystal forms up close. They shared their excitement like old prospectors on an outcropping vein.

One of the men held his watch up for others to see and declared they'd better hustle if they were going to get a glimpse of the town before they left.

The first stop in the new town was the school. Children jumped to attention when they heard the vehicles and began waving Bolivian flags to welcome their guests. The tiniest students recited poems with the usual dramatic gestures and gracious bows, and the high school students performed several folkloric songs with traditional instruments. It was hard to know if the visitors appreciated the performances because each of them kept sneaking peeks at their watches. I knew their minds were on their appointments in La Paz. They scurried out of the schoolyard for a very quick tour of the church and the hotel.

The government offices sat diagonally across from the hotel. Newly painted in bold black letters, not yet dry, read *La Oficina del Gobierno.*

The crowds had already gathered as the men approached. A shower of colorful confetti fell upon them as the people parted to let them pass. A brass band trumpeted an enthusiastic welcome, the discordant notes reminiscent of the middle school bands my children had played in many years ago.

The visitors shook hands with the government officials standing at attention in their suits and ties. The men blew harder on their trumpets and tubas and clashed their cymbals with force as David and his retinue took their seats at a table facing the crowd. More than a hundred townspeople, dressed in their best outfits, pushed their way forward to get a better view of these powerful men who had come from so far away. Freshly scrubbed toddlers peered from behind their mothers' skirts to see what the commotion was about.

The band stopped. The people applauded. The crowd pressed forward, encircling the seated dignitaries. Men and women whispered among themselves. An occasional laugh bubbled up. They waited, expectant, staring at these men whose decisions would determine the future of their village. The men stared back, smiling. They may as well have been from two different planets.

The *Corregidor*, the mayor, began his speech with effusive hand waving and gestures, as dramatic as the poems of the students. "We, the people of San Cristóbal, thank you, most esteemed President for all that you and the company have done for our town."

More applause. Wilson translated as the *Corregidor* went on.

The midday sun beat directly on us. The sweat rolled into my eyes and made them burn. Remington's fair-skinned, balding head grew bright red; finally, Wilson handed him a tube of sun block. Remington's attention was focused on something other than the sun or the crowd. He fingered a cylindrical slab of rock, a sample of the core from deep in the earth, proof that the silver, zinc and lead existed. Light sparkled from it as he rotated it in the sun.

As the *Corregidor* finished his speech, a murmur spread through the crowd. A man appeared wheeling a large llama folded into the confines of a bright red wheelbarrow, its front and back legs bound with rope and its eyes covered with a gray cloth.

"Uh oh," Larry said. "It's white."

Four men lifted the llama and placed it firmly on its side on the ground. Larry and I held our breath, but they removed the ropes and blindfold and lifted the confused animal to its feet. They turned it about so it faced the men at the table.

David looked as befuddled as the llama. Wilson came to his rescue whispering for him to stand by the llama and shake the man's hand. The llama was a gift for David.

"Who will care for the President's llama while he is not here?" Wilson asked the crowd.

A *chola* stepped forward and volunteered. She took the rope tied to the llama's muzzle and moved away. The llama seemed content to stand by her side, much as a faithful dog.

David looked caught off guard for a man usually ready with a witty remark. After a moment to regroup, he smiled, and shaking the hand of the man who had wheeled in the llama and the hand of the *chola* who now stood holding the leash, he began to thank the crowd.

Before he could say much, the murmuring intensified once again. The mass of bodies parted, creating a passageway for a tiny man. Stooped over as if his poncho weighed him down, he limped forward in slow motion. The crowd hushed. Long strands of thin gray hair straggled down from his wool cap and hung about his weathered face. His cracked and dirty toe nails peeked out from worn sandals. In his shriveled hands, he held a carved wooden staff decorated with iron and silver bands, ribbons and feathers. He had to walk only about five meters, but it seemed to take all morning.

"Don Juan," Larry whispered with surprise in his voice.

"The *Cacique*?" I asked.

I didn't recognize the old keeper of the customs at first, he'd shrunken so. His face resembled one of those dried apple dolls. He nodded feebly as he passed us, his cheeks still bulging with coca pulp. He looked miniscule as he took his place beside David, a mischievous smile on his face.

He removed his wool cap with ear flaps and standing on tiptoes, reached up to place it upon David's head. David bent over to receive it. David's curls stuck out from under the cap, accentuating his youthful appearance. Don Juan then removed his hand-woven gray and white poncho with the help of the *Corregidor* and the two men placed it over David. David smiled, fingered the woven wool of the poncho as if to test the quality, and turned about modeling his new attire.

A hush came over the crowd as don Juan picked up his sacred staff, the ribbons blowing gently. Like the scepter of a king, *El Rey* was the symbol of the ultimate power of the *Cacique*. This was the magic wand which could bring forth water from the rocks. No one but a *cacique* could touch it.

Again I held my breath.

Don Juan lifted *El Rey* in the air and in slow motion, placed it in David's hands. These two kings held the rod for a brief moment, their eyes locking.

Don Juan winked.

David looked surprised and jerked his head back a bit. Then they both smiled.

"From one *cacique* to another," don Juan said, his face beaming.

The crowd burst forth with applause.

I heard Larry gasp. He took my hand and squeezed it.

A pleased look upon his face, David began once again to thank the people. "*Gracias a todos los oficiales aquí por su. . . .*" He looked to Wilson for help.

"*Recepción tan cariñosa,*" Wilson whispered.

"*Recepción tan car . . . car . . .*"

Wilson stood by David's side, spoke in his ear, then announced that the President had a strong desire to speak from his heart to properly thank the people of the village for their many years of support and good will, but his heart speaks a language that is not Spanish, and certainly not Quechua. A ripple of laughter passed over the crowd. "So to find the words that truly express the gratitude he feels for the people of San Cristóbal, I will translate as the President speaks in his native tongue."

David looked grateful. He then looked out into the crowd, "Mayor, city officials, and people of San Cristóbal, I cannot express enough the pleasure I feel at the warm welcome you have given me and my colleagues. I am, how can I say, deeply, profoundly touched." David paused to let Wilson catch up.

"You have sacrificed. You have worked long hours to make the dream of the mine and your new city become a reality. You have welcomed us into your community and together we have proved that dreams can come true. You have made a new future and a new life.

"But dreams can be shattered. Outside forces can prevent us from enjoying the fruits of our labor. All your work has been put in jeopardy. You know that the price of silver has dropped this year. But not just silver. The price of lead and zinc are also down to historic lows. I would not be honest with you if I said that all was well with the project. Mines throughout Bolivia and the world are struggling to operate with these low prices; indeed, many have closed and thousands of your countrymen are out of work.

"A mine that produces silver and zinc but cannot sell it on the market will die. If that were to happen, the mine would shut down and all the people would lose their jobs, everyone would be without work, from Reno to La Paz to San Cristóbal.

"But these low prices are only temporary. I can state with certainty that the price of silver will someday return to a level where the mine can open and we will finally see our dream realized. I do not know how long this will take. It may be only months, it may be years, but that day will come when we will all benefit from this fabulous silver deposit that you have lived with for so long."

The crowd seemed hyped up by the poetic words of the President. Their faces reflected fear at what might be coming, but also glowed with the hopeful dream articulated by this pale young man standing before them.

"My friends and colleagues, we must be patient. Our mine will see the light of day, it will come, but in the meantime, we all must sacrifice yet a bit longer.

"And so it brings us to today. Our company has signed a contract with the people of San Cristóbal. We promised you work in the mine to ensure your family's future. We cannot give you the jobs in the mine, at least not yet, but we will do all we can to keep the entire town employed here in your new city, beautifying it, adding parks and sidewalks and streets, making it a city you will be proud of. We have not forgotten your contribution to this project, and in these difficult times, we will not abandon you."

The crowd applauded again, this time even louder.

Larry's eyes never left *El Rey* as David leaned it against the table.

The men were soon back in the jeeps. After the handshakes and thank yous, these important people boarded the little plane; David still dressed in the gifts of don Juan's garb and holding *El Rey* in his hand. Remington carried the silver-laden core that Larry had given him. The propellers hummed, the cloud of dust rose as the plane took off and once again became a silver speck that disappeared into the vast blue.

Iván Quíspe sighed with relief.

Larry took my hand as we walked back toward town.

I said, "I sure hope David understands the significance of *El Rey*. I would hate to see it end up in his closet along with some umbrellas and golf clubs."

"No," Larry said. "He's a *Cacique* now. Maybe he can use *El Rey* to raise the price of silver on the world market."

Chapter 25

Markawi

Larry

November 2003

The drought was over. Rains began falling a month ahead of schedule. Puddles from last night were drying around our feet as we sat on a rock in the sun in the middle of the new plaza. Karen and I were enjoying the warm spring days as a refuge from our arthritic northern winter.

Even better, the mining recession had ended. The prices of metals crept up late in 2002 and by the end of 2003, silver had risen fifty percent, zinc about thirty percent, and the price of lead had nearly doubled. The company immediately initiated construction of the railroad, bridges, housing facilities, and other infrastructure to open the mine. High-priced contracts were let to purchase trucks and loaders, ball mills and crushers. Another $200 million was committed in the space of a year.

The healthy, the eager, the strong worked at the mine and mill sites. The older, the ill, the feeble of mind or body were hired to continue working in the village.

In the plaza, four men, looking skinny and tired, arranged the stones into a mosaic between the chalk lines marking the eventual walkways. They moved slowly; their hearts weren't in it, or maybe their bodies just didn't have a lot of stamina.

I had expected everything to be finished by now. Years ago road work had left piles of stones and gravel on the streets of the new town, and similar piles still lay scattered about. Why did things take so long? Even after four years of reconstruction the church remained unfinished, filled daily with government and NGO artists and craftsmen.

We watched Soledad pick her way around the rocks and mud puddles. She had grown in the last couple of years, becoming a full, young woman, attractive actually, now in her final year at teacher's school in Illca. Unfortunately, the black rot had finally corroded her front teeth down to the gums. I could only imagine the pain.

After the usual greetings, I asked, "What do you think of all this?"

She looked around. "All what?"

"The streets are torn up, the plaza is full of rocks, the church still unfinished. Things are a bit of a mess right now."

"Yes," she said, glancing around at the broken slabs of rock. "But it is temporary, it will get better. Everyone has a job with high salaries now. Even my mother is working at the *comedor*. This is better than before. Look, I already have new shoes and a jacket."

Her hiking boots were certainly an improvement over the sandals of old tires and rawhide, and although her new jacket probably was another pirated Chinese imitation, at least it looked warm and modern with its North Face logo on the front.

Soledad's optimism was contagious. "Do not be concerned, *ingeniero*, I am convinced the first part of El Tío's prophecy is coming true. We can all see it. The mine is opening soon. There will be jobs for everyone."

"The first part of the prophecy?" Karen repeated. "What did you mean by that?"

"Did I say that? No, I don't think so."

"Yes, you said 'the first part'. Is there more?"

Soledad looked down at the ground, turned her head to see if anyone was standing close, and spoke softly, "You did not know? You have not heard the rest of the prophecy?"

"There's more than just the gift?" I asked.

"Yes, the gift at first, there is that, but then the rest happens . . . the other part."

"And what is that?"

"I do not know."

"Aw, c'mon, Soledad."

"Well, I can't say. Not here. Not in the plaza. I should not tell you this."

"Who can? Don Juan de la Cruz? The *yacho*, Lucrecio?"

"Them, yes, and others. I must go now. I will talk with them about this. It is possible they may not speak of it," she said as she kissed Karen's cheek, shook my hand, and walked quickly away.

I did not sleep well that night in our little room in the San Cristóbal Hotel.

"There's a second half. Damn. What could it be?" I said to Karen well past midnight. I turned on the heater again.

"Probably just more gifts, maybe a sacrifice of a llama or something."

"It can't be good. Soledad would have told us if it were something good."

"Try not to worry. We'll find out tomorrow."

Light rain fell on and off all night. The room was too cold, the bed too hard. I could not get comfortable and cursed the human body with its limited choices of positions for sleep. After many hours my dull and heavy head was greeted by light coming in the window from a pastel blue sky with pale pink clouds.

Soledad got us out of bed with a tapping on our hotel window. "Nobody will discuss the prophecy here in the village. Only at Markawi should we speak of this, but don Juan is too feeble to make the journey."

"Markawi? What's that?" Karen asked.

"A city. Near, in the hills," Soledad said. "Don Juan gave permission to Senóbio. We start today, this morning, now. It is a good hour."

We shoved health food bars and bottles of water into our backpacks and headed out the door, Toyota keys in hand.

"No, we walk," Soledad said.

With Senóbio leading and Soledad at the rear, we traversed northwesterly, climbing the pediment slope of the San Cristóbal Range, up the alluvial fans and down into the incising canyons, all still wet from the rains. *Th'ola* and grass were sparse in spite of the early wet season; areas of sheet wash left rock-strewn fields. This was sprained-ankle country. The pink clouds of the morning puffed up into fluffy white cumulus balls with flat bottoms of purple-grey.

Senóbio chose a straight-line course gradually climbing in elevation, passing folded and faulted blocks of red, clay-rich sediments displaying their bedded stratigraphy along steep canyon walls. We hiked for three hours, speaking only rarely about the fine weather, the paucity of grass, and how much drier the Altiplano had become since Senóbio was a boy.

The bottom of a canyon deeper than most blocked our path. We turned abruptly to the north, then climbed uphill parallel to the canyon floor. Collapsed rock walls lined both flanks along the base of the canyon, as if long ago someone had tried to channel the course of the stream. The climb was steep.

Two parallel rock walls about thirty feet apart wound their way up the slope. Senóbio spoke as if a tour guide, saying it marked what they called the "boulevard," the entrance to the city of Markawi. Karen and I clasped our hands behind our backs, leaned forward, and trudged on, carefully picking each foot-fall in the rocky path.

After ten minutes or so, we heard Senóbio singing in Quechua. We could not see him, the sound apparently coming from all directions at the same time.

"We are there," Soledad shouted to us as she bounded up the hill and disappeared beyond a ledge. Senóbio's singing was louder, now joined by Soledad's.

As we circled around the ledge, we saw our two friends jumping from rock to rock amid the jumbled ruins of an enormous, deserted city. Houses, streets, walls, towers now spread out in front of us on a flat bench, completely hidden from view only a few footsteps before. All was in disrepair: multi-room structures with doorways and windows, streets lined with walls and houses, everything overgrown with the tallest *th'ola* and *paja* I had ever seen. None of the houses had roofs and most of the walls had collapsed. The village covered about ten acres.

"My God, an archaeologist's dream," Karen said as she gasped for breath.

Entering the maze of buildings, we separated as we explored the ruins, each picking a path over and around the rock walls, ducking into low doorways and peering out from rock windows. Surrounding the village in seemingly random positions were a dozen circular towers up to fifteen feet high and about ten feet in diameter, each hollow in the center with enough room for maybe two or three men to stand upright close together. Flat stones roofed a few of the towers; most were open to the sky. Shards of painted pottery crunched everywhere underfoot, forming a colorful rug upon which numerous rounded and smoothed rocks lay scattered, obviously used by human hands. Some had holes drilled through them, for reasons unknown to us.

I saw Soledad stretched out on a flat, smooth boulder and wondered how many of her ancestors soaked up the sun at that very spot, how many adolescents climbed over the walls and to the tower tops—were they lookouts for danger, storage bins for grain? Senóbio didn't know.

This was once a city full of men and their families. Children played in the streets, young boys and girls tended the flocks, and old women wandered afar collecting firewood. Wives and husbands planted their fields and made love in the cool evenings comforted by the warm furs from their llama. These were our friends' ancestors, the forefathers of all the Quíspe and Mamani and Colque who now lived in the modern town of San Cristóbal.

Senóbio asked us to sit. He stood before us, spread his arms, and said, "This is Markawi, built in the time of darkness before the birth of the sun, from the time when Pachamama took Wiracocha as a lover. He was an old man with a beard. He emerged from the waters of Lake Titicaca, gave his seed to the Pachamama, and satisfied, he returned to his beloved waters. The babies born from this union lived by fishing on the shores of Titicaca. Their lives were perfect: no pain, no death, no worries. It was paradise for them; with the condors they could fly. So many were the powers they had, but in time corruption infected them. They became evil. So the Pachamama turned them into rocks because they did not obey the three laws."

"Do not lie, do not steal, and do not be lazy?" Karen asked.

"Yes," Senóbio agreed, "three very simple laws but without them, their community could not survive. When she turned them into rocks, their anger was so great they became the *achachilas*. They are with us still, dangerous, mischievous always, and to this day they make their perversions."

Soledad added, "They not only live in the rocks, but they are the rocks themselves. At night they change their form and come out to wander amid the living."

Senóbio continued. "Later, Wiracocha returned and slept again with the Pachamama. She gave birth to new men, our ancestors before the ancestors, but this time as a precaution they were born first as rocks. Wiracocha hid them in caves and rivers and around springs. Often he put them beneath the soil. They could not grow crops, as anything that penetrated the Pachamama, like a furrow or a hole, was a violation of Wiracocha's right. Only he could penetrate her. The places where they were hidden are called *samiris*, and they remain to this day as places of refuge, where only certain people are allowed to go, and there they find rest, calmness, food and a place to reproduce."

"Are there any *samiris* around here?" I asked.

"Of course, several. You will know when you step into one. Oh, yes, you will feel it. They are very special places." Senóbio stopped long enough to shove coca leaf into his mouth. "One day Wiracocha called together the ancestors before the ancestors to form villages with their children. He turned them all into humans, in a form like ours. These we call our ancestors.

"But everything was dark; there was no sun. They lived by the light of the moon in cold houses made of rock, in cities made of rock. Markawi is one such city. It is a powerful place. They were cold all the time. There was little food. It was so dark they could not find salt; they ate no salt their entire lives.

"Then one day God made the sun. The ancestors were overjoyed. It was warm and beautiful, food could grow, and they could find salt at last. That day there was much happiness, but then the glorious sun went down in the west and the people feared it would never return. So that night they prepared a special ceremony to beg God to bring the sun back." Senóbio reached into his pouch for even more coca leaves, filling his already swollen cheek. "This ceremony they called *pij'char*, it was the chewing of coca leaf, our *la hojita*. The people of every city had to *pij'char* and *pij'char* all night and they begged the marvelous warm light to return. Even to this day we still perform it."

"This coca chewing," I asked Senóbio, "so it is more than just to stave off hunger?"

"Oh, yes, much more. The entire community partakes. If we did not, our world would die."

"Everyone must believe, everyone must *pij'char* to assure the return of the sun?"

"Yes," he said, spreading his arms out wide, "and look, the sun does come back." He sat looking at the city around us. "This is a very special place. It is here our ancestors learned that to survive they must honor the customs of all those who came before."

I knew the story of the life before the sun was just a myth, one I would have scorned as nonsense back in my less superstitious North American home. But here in the Altiplano where myth and reality are the same, where truth and rumor, demons and saints, fact and subjectivity are indistinguishable, somehow these blurred definitions no longer seemed to matter. These myths of ancestors and gods shielded the community from change by the outside forces. These stories became true, were true, simply because they were so desperately needed.

"It's funny, isn't it," I said to Karen, "that these myths seem so real."

"You are becoming Quechua," Karen said with a hint of approval in her smile.

"I don't think so. But while I'm here in Bolivia on the side of this range of mountains, right here where these stories were born, I think they make a hell of a lot of sense."

While we were speaking to each other, Senóbio and Soledad were watching us intently, listening to every word even though we spoke in English. Like detectives, their eyes darted from Karen and back to me, apparently trying to decipher the meaning above our words. At last Senóbio spoke, "*Es buena hora.*"

"*Es buena hora,*" Soledad repeated.

I got up thinking they meant it was time to leave. We would be lucky to get back to town before dark, but Senóbio remained seated and began to speak once again.

"Life was good here in this city. The people had all they could wish: water, *llamitas*, the sun, good soil for their potatoes, rocks for their homes; they had their customs and they showed respect for their Gods. They had their community. They were wealthy beyond our comprehension and lived long lives. Do you not agree, *ingeniero*?"

"Absolutely," I said, "I'm sure a man who was willing to work could raise a happy family here; probably still could if the outside world would just leave him alone."

"Yes, if he worked hard and obeyed the three laws and if the outside world did not destroy his faith in his Gods and his respect for his ancestors. This is much like in San Cristóbal, no? Your company is from the outside world."

"Well, yes. Yes, that is so."

"And it is bringing many changes to our way of life."

"That's true, but wasn't it the gift from El Tío that brought these changes to your village? It's almost as if our company were invited in."

"You are correct, it is the gift of El Tío that brought you and your company to the village. The changes are many and so powerful that the village can never be the same."

"Isn't that what the prophecy is all about? Wealth and a new and better life for you all?" Karen asked.

"Yes, to the wealth and yes, to the new life, and to the silver in our bright white homes with their shining roofs. But El Tío never promised a 'better' life for us. Maybe here," he spread his arms wide, "maybe here there was a better life. You said so yourself, *ingeniero*, that life was good here. Our ancestors maintained a faith in their ancestors before the ancestors, they showed respect for the gods, they continued to practice their customs."

"But you still follow your customs as before when you lived in the old village, don't you?" I asked.

"Some of us do, but more changes are coming, too powerful to resist. El Tío told us that our new lives will be so easy that we will forget our ancestors and stop respecting our gods. We will be so rich we will have no need to work the *chacras* and we will stop caring for the animals. We will no longer consult the rocks or touch the earth. We will lose all of our customs.

We will be like the rest of the world—we will be rich and comfortable but we will be hollow like the towers you see here in Markawi."

"As we have become," Karen whispered to herself.

"You won't forget all your gods? Not all of them?" I asked.

"The changes are too powerful. We cannot stop them. We will lose touch with our past, we will forget our ancestors," Senóbio replied.

"As we have," I tried to say. My chest tightened and my eyes felt hot. I looked down at the soil at my feet.

"But it is worse," Soledad added.

"Yes, much worse," said Senóbio.

Soledad continued, "We will have so much money we will not even bother to count our change in the markets. Nobody will grow food, nobody will tend the animals or work the *chacras*, and although we will be rich, there will be nothing to eat. Hunger will then invade our world. There will be starvation throughout our lands to the point of cannibalism."

"My God. Is this all part of the prophecy?" Karen asked.

"Yes, it is the second half, the part you wanted to hear," Senóbio said.

"Does it have to end this way?"

"It is part of the gift. If we accept the silver, we must accept it all, the good and the bad. All we can do is try to postpone the payment of this heavy price."

I wanted to lie on the ground and beat my fists and scream, *No, I did not want this. I did not ask for this. I never should have found the silver.* Their words were crushing me. I finally spoke, "I did not know. I am so sorry."

I walked a few dozen yards away. I sat down against one of the stone towers and through blurred eyes looked before me at the ruined home of the ancestors and then up and away to the gentle slopes covered with *th'ola* and *paja*, then to the flat expanse of the *pampa* disappearing in the distance. I could see someday this plain would be crossed by power lines, paved highways, and railroads. It would be green with irrigated fields fed by canals and pipelines. Extensive herds of cattle, llama and sheep would graze between new cities with large universities and hospitals, every bit of it paid for by the loss of customs, myths, and memories of their ancestors.

Without their history, the citizens of this exciting new world will be stalked by constant shadows of confusion, loneliness, and alienation; plagued by a vague sense of being out of touch with the land, their roots. This is the price my discovery would make them pay, this is what I did to them. *They will be just like we have become.*

I owed them a debt, one I thought I could never repay.

Chapter 26

Price of the Gift

Karen

January 2007

Three years passed. Events conspired to prevent our return to Bolivia. Larry had retired from the company but after a few months of rest, he helped form a new one, which sent him to different parts of the world: Africa, Asia, and the western United States.

Yet the people of San Cristóbal were always in our thoughts. We conducted *ch'allas* in our garden asking for rain when Bolivia was dry, for sunshine when it flooded, and always for good crops. Our own garden, having received these blessings of beer, wine, sweets, and whatever substitutes we could find for coca leaf and *cingani*, amazed us with lush crops and spectacular flowers. Larry developed a passion for composting and proclaimed every kitchen scrap a grateful contribution to the Pachamama.

The infrequency of our trips made the continuation of the pen-pal program unrealistic, so after four years, the interchange ended. But from time to time I encountered a former Ashland student who asked about his or her friend in Bolivia.

In March 2006, Larry was nominated for the Thayer Lindsley Award, arguably the most prestigious honor of his profession. It was soon confirmed. The Prospectors and Developers Association of Canada recognized San Cristóbal as the most significant discovery of silver made in the past century.

Donning our finest clothes, we headed for Toronto to attend the conference and awards ceremony. Nearly fifteen thousand geologists, miners, and promoters from around the world showed up. Larry whispered to me how uncomfortable he was as speakers gave long-winded paeans outlining his geological service, bestowing upon him an almost supernatural ability to find ore deposits.

When he delivered his speech, he joked about anal-retentive engineers in general and made light of his own skills, attributing his success to luck and the help of others, especially his old partner, Jon Gelvin. The crowd laughed, and I was pleased with the mixture of humility and pride in his voice, but I was also shocked when he made no mention of El Tío.

Alone in our hotel room afterwards, Larry removed from around his neck the green ribbon and its bronze medallion engraved with a bust of Thayer Lindsley, one of the greatest mine discoverers of all time. He rubbed his fingers over the metal disc.

"They probably would have thought I was nuts to thank a cannibalistic, beer-drinking god," he said, as if reading my mind.

I didn't say anything.

"I thought about it. I feel like I let him down."

I sat on the bed beside him.

"I could have at least mentioned the prophecy or something. El Tío deserves some honor here. I should've done it."

I agreed, but didn't need to add to Larry's guilt. "There'll be other chances to honor El Tío."

Almost a year passed before we finally returned to Bolivia for the sole purpose of seeing how "our" town was doing. We were zipping along at eighty kilometers an hour past the salt and *th'ola* flats toward San Cristóbal. A graded, double-lane road had replaced the narrow, rutted dirt of the past. Stretching from Uyuni to San Cristóbal and to Chile beyond, it cut driving time by two-thirds, but our speed wasn't fast enough for me. My eyes were wide and my senses alert as we sped along.

Concrete and steel bridges now spanned the Colorado and Río Grande rivers. Frequent summer rains had hindered crossing so many times in the past, but we'd always made it across thanks to Marcos. He'd wrap our distributor cap in plastic and plunge forward into the racing waters. I'd hold my breath as if doing so would help us get to the other side unharmed despite the water lapping at our windows.

Posted signs now whizzed by indicating our distance from San Cristóbal: ninety kilometers, then sixty, then twelve. They advertised the town's conveniences with images of a red cross, a bed, and a phone.

The low San Cristóbal Range rose before us. The village finally appeared as a mass of brilliant reflections off the metal roofs of the houses. The familiar bell towers and the gray metal gymnasium stood out above the shimmering town.

A mushroom-shaped boulder sitting atop a slender column greeted us as we arrived.

"My god, the company actually moved it." I spoke in a whisper.

The Achupalla was guarding the new town, still displaying its sign, "Welcome to San Cristóbal *4100 meters above sea level.*" It now stood in an empty field, probably a site for a future park. The cap, twenty feet across, was indeed the original rock, but the company apparently could not rescue the stem. They built the new one out of concrete and placed metal girders, like shiny braces, to support it. They'd worked hard to replicate the original, even etching the concrete to look like stratified layers of conglomerates and sandstone, but up close, the concrete copy was clear; it was not the real thing. It was out of place here, plunked down, the old superimposed on the new.

Across the road a gas station had sprouted. A sign in red and yellow letters proclaimed "*Gasolinera Tres Gigantes.*" I didn't know whether to laugh or cry.

We skirted large puddles as we walked toward the center from the outskirts of town, our boots now coated in sticky mud. The sun slipped behind gray clouds promising the customary summer afternoon rains. The moisture made it easier to breathe the thin air.

When the village first moved to this site, it seemed misplaced, remote, almost fragile, as if the winds could blow it into dust.

But back then, the same people who had walked the old village streets were walking on the new. The community had maintained its original sense of smallness; everybody knew everybody else.

Now the streets were full of strangers. Adobe houses had multiplied on all sides of the company-built dwellings, some with thatched roofs, some with metal, some not yet completed. A true housing boom was occurring as outsiders moved into the area to take advantage of the jobs the mine offered. The town had tripled in size, expanding outward like a halo of brown mud homes surrounding the core of original white houses, the church not quite in the center.

A sign on a corner, *Sonya's Restaurante*, drew us into an adobe structure facing the street. Brightly-patterned Bolivian weavings covered the four rectangular tables. The dirt floor was swept clean, the place immaculate. Posters of Alpine scenes, bubbling brooks surrounded by green trees, adorned the mud walls. In the courtyard, a woman was baking bread in a traditional clay oven. Another pulled wet clothing out of a washing machine to hang on a clothesline. Several attached adobe rooms encircled the yard.

Fausto Condori Condori entered the restaurant from the courtyard opening his arms to greet us with a Bolivian welcome. He'd always been one of the most enthusiastic teachers, supporting my classes and the pen-pal program as well as attending my English lessons at night.

"'Allo, 'allo, *profesora, ingeniero*, 'ow are you?"

Over quinoa soup and warm bread, Fausto told us that although teacher's salaries were still low, he was doing well. He was still teaching, but many others had left the school for better paying company jobs. He rented his company-built house to the mining employees, and his family now lived in the adobe buildings out back. With the extra income, he and his family ran this restaurant. Business was good.

Fausto spread his arms to show off the fruits of his efforts. "The best of all worlds," he said. "We live with the old, the familiar, but with more comfort. We're warmer in our adobe *and* we have the modern conveniences, electricity and indoor plumbing."

"And you make good soup," I added.

"And money," Fausto said, laughing.

Old friends and acquaintances greeted us with warm welcomes, speaking with genuine appreciation for the jobs the mine had brought and for Larry's part in the discovery. Two young men approached us.

"*Profesora*, I'm Esteban."

"And I'm Rudolfo."

I recognized them as two of the musicians I'd filmed on the rocks. They boasted of the education they were receiving in Chile. Promises of employment at the mine awaited them when they completed their training in mechanical engineering. They confessed they had no time for music these days. Their talented music teacher was now working in the mine.

"I'd hate to see the community lose your music," I said.

Rudolfo comforted me. "Don't worry, *profesora*. There's a new music teacher. I think he is teaching students how to play traditional instruments." He grinned and added, "As well as electronic music."

Esteban and Rudolfo couldn't wait to share what was happening to their friends. Jorge was studying agronomy in Cochabamba, learning how to help the mine with reclamation. Ignacio was studying medicine in Cuba. Interrupting each other in their excitement, they rattled off names of their friends availing themselves of remarkable educational opportunities. The list included women. Even the woman with the crooked hip had a desk job with the Foundation.

Life appeared good. The future was theirs. Everything seemed perfect, perhaps too perfect.

Days passed, each one filled with new discoveries. Marina and Victoria, young women I had known as adolescents, managed an internet cafe for the Foundation. Marina told me about her three children, all under five years of age.

"We have a day care," she said. "It makes it possible for the women to work for the Foundation or the mine."

"Do you think things will be better for your children?"

"Yes," Victoria answered quickly, then paused, her eyes looking past me as she recalled her own childhood. "Well, it is different now," she added. "I remember when I grew up we all helped our mama. When it was time to bake bread two of us would fetch *th'ola* for the fire, another would start the fire and keep it going. Mama would shape the little breads while yet another of us would watch them bake. We spent the entire day working together. Those were fun times, we talked and we laughed."

"Remember," Marina said, "how our mothers would whisper stories of the *achachilas* and El Tío? We'd listen and be so scared, but we loved it."

"And how we knew everyone in town in those days," added Victoria.

The young women relived the images of their youths, a smile on their lips but a hint of sadness in their eyes.

"What about your *chacras* and animals?" Larry asked. "If everyone is working long shifts, how do you have time?"

"Some of us still plant *chacras* and some raise animals. The company provides a bus to take us to our *chacras* since they are far away. But now we also have the *mercado* and with jobs, we're able to buy our meat and vegetables."

"Life is easier," Victoria said. "Though our childhoods were good, our children's lives will be different."

Different, yes. Better? I wasn't sure.

Five or six schoolboys monopolized a computer in one corner of the café. Their shouting echoed off the concrete walls as one manipulated the mouse trying to gun down the evil guys while the others huddled around and noisily advised him. Their attire hadn't changed much nor their dirt-smudged faces and hands, dusty sweat-shirts, and ripped pants. One even exuded a nasty odor. Another wore shoes with torn soles and his bare toes pushed their way through the tips. These children were captivated by cyberspace. No more climbing the rocks. No more hunting *vizcacha*.

The mine and Foundation did not rob all families of their time together. Three children, ranging in ages from four to fourteen, worked alongside their parents, laying a foundation for a small house. The father poured water into holes dug into the tops of conical-shaped piles of coarse sand, then added cement and slowly blended it with a shovel blade. The older boy carried buckets of wet concrete to the house walls, laying it among rocks to form a solid foundation while the two younger children helped their mother mix mud and straw to pack into wooden molds. Lines of adobe bricks were drying in the sun.

We introduced ourselves, asking if we might watch.

"So you're the *profesora*," the man said.

He wiped his sandy hands on his cement-spattered jeans before shaking hands with us. Though we had no idea who he was, he clearly had heard of us. He introduced himself as the new director of the secondary school.

"We still have photos of your town in the United States," he said, referring to a poster I had left many years ago. Eager to share, he spoke of how good life was here in San Cristóbal, using words like "swollen, rich, and fat" because of all the opportunities. "Look, look at this," he said as he pointed to construction that covered the area of a soccer field just a short distance from his new home.

"That is the new secondary school. We have so many students, perhaps as many as eight hundred, we needed a new building—seventeen classrooms. We will become a model school with many resources: computers, physics labs, chemistry labs, all new things."

I shook my head in disbelief.

"Impressive," Larry said, then asked, "You're new to town. Do you think the changes are overall for the good or the bad?"

"Oh, *ingeniero*, for the good, mostly. But, now that there is money, there are also vehicles. Just last week one of our young men, his wife and child were killed in an accident. He had been celebrating at a party here in San Cristóbal, drank too much, then drove to Uyuni. Spun off the road, horrible accident. And that's not all. People are forgetting our traditions. For weeks, there has been talk of having the *Q'orpa* ceremony, but no one seems to have time to make it happen." He shrugged. "This is life, no?"

On the street, we passed two boys, probably in their late teens. One had passed out in the dirt behind a house; the other, his face quite green, leaned on a wall. In the past, such drinking was common, but usually only during *ch'allas* or other ceremonies. Octavio had warned us.

The next morning we noticed a partially completed adobe house. Triple the size of most and decked with picture windows, it was large enough for a hotel or restaurant.

A young man jumped down from the metal roof he was pounding in place. I guessed him to be in his twenties.

"*Profesora, profesora*, do you remember me? I'm Rafael," he said.

Somewhere among the hundreds of photos of children taken over the years, there must have been a younger version of this face before me. Unlike the frightened and uncertain stares of those first photos, this face glowed with confidence and excitement.

"Are you building another hotel?" Larry asked.

Rafael laughed. "No, this is a home for my wife and baby."

He described his job with the mine, driving one of the enormous front-end loaders and earning a good wage.

"Do you like your work?" Larry asked.

"Yes, it's a wonderful job." Rafael beamed. He held himself straight and tall.

"They treat you well?" Larry asked.

"Except for the twelve hour shifts, I have no complaints. Please wait here," he said, and ran into the nearly completed house returning with a glossy 11" x 17" color photo of a bright yellow Komatsu front-end loader, explaining that it was capable of twelve tonnes per load.

"You operate this?" Larry asked.

"Twelve hours a day."

"And El Tío? Where did they put El Tío in the mine?"

Rafael looked puzzled.

"El Tío, the *diablito* of the mine. Where is his cave?" Larry asked again.

"We don't have a Tío. At least not one that I know of."

"No Tío?" Larry persisted. "This is Bolivia. How can there be a mine without El Tío?

"Does the company forbid it?" I asked.

"I guess nobody thought of it."

Larry shook his head. We stood in silence. Rafael shifted from foot to foot glancing back at the roof, apparently eager to return to his work. We wished him well and went on our way.

Larry was muttering as we ambled on, "No El Tío? How can they do that?"

"It isn't right. But, remember, the prophecy said the people would forget him."

The wife of the music teacher, Regina, stopped us on the street, inviting us into her home for a visit. Larry responded with politeness, but I guessed from his quiet and serious expression that he was still mulling over Rafael's words: "*I guess nobody thought of it.*"

Regina had been a lovely adolescent, snatched up and impregnated in her teens by her handsome teacher. Now she had three children. As we sunk into her comfortable sofa, I glanced about her living room. A stereo system occupied one corner, a computer in the other. The house was unlike any other I had entered. Attention had been paid to details: door and window trims and baseboard gave the house a sense of completion lacking in those of her neighbors. The linoleum in the kitchen shone, a brightly-colored rug covered the living room floor, and ornate curtains adorned the windows. A hallway led to bedrooms, hinting that the family had planned to give privacy to its growing numbers.

"Did you build this house yourselves?" I asked.

"No, we had an architect."

My face registered shock.

"The times are different, *profesora*," Regina explained. "My husband works long hours. So do most of our neighbors. It's not like the old town where we helped each other build houses. With all the new people in town, we live amid strangers. We've lost our community."

"Surely you are happy that your children will have more opportunities," I said.

"No, I would exchange this life in a moment if I could go back to the old town and our old way of life."

Larry and I made the hotel our home during this trip. The hotel was now leased by the company and run by foreigners. Paint was peeling from the walls and part of the ceiling in the bathroom hung down, revealing shabby construction. The cost had risen from forty Bolivianos, or six dollars a night, to three hundred, or forty-five dollars.

Many mornings we awoke to no water and were greeted by shrugs when we questioned the situation. The townspeople informed us that Canuto and Esperanza's spring had dried up. The company had constructed a concrete tank up on the hill where huge trucks filled it with water fetched from wells down near the Rio Grande. Now with the summer rains, muddy paths made it impossible for the trucks to climb the steep incline and their wheels sank down into the saturated earth.

Days passed without the tanks being refilled. No wonder the boys captivated by the computers looked and smelled so rank. I started to feel that way myself.

Years ago I would have ranted and raved at how the company had screwed the people. Larry would have told me the townspeople could have built wells but didn't want the cost of the electric pumps. I would have argued that since the company did things half-assed, they should pay for the electricity. And Larry would have aborted the argument as always, saying that the company should not be *patrones*, making the people dependent.

Those arguments seemed pointless now. The townspeople were not complaining as they might have in the past, at least not to us. Perhaps they were accustomed to water always being an issue in their desert lives, or perhaps because the promise of jobs had been kept, they trusted the future would also correct the water problem. They spoke of the electric lines operating at the mine, how they would be extended to the town, replacing the need for generators. Then they would install the electric pumps necessary for wells.

Morning walks brought us to the top of the one hill overlooking the town where a flat summit afforded a three-hundred-sixty degree view. Looking down upon the town, I felt a time warp as though I had returned to San Cristóbal and landed in the future. A part of me wanted to travel back in time to the old San Cristóbal, to that sleepy little village nestled amid the hills and surrounded by majestic rock formations.

Or perhaps if I were honest with myself, I would have admitted my longing to return to the way I saw the world when I first arrived in the old town: my romantic image of rural, indigenous living, pastoral and peaceful, but one which omitted the harsh realities of daily life.

Chapter 27

Of Almas and Ancianos

Larry

January 2007

If anybody could explain the lack of interest in the gods, it would be the *cacique*, old don Juan de la Cruz. People on the street told us he was living with his grandson in a house across from the hotel. After stopping in the market for gifts, we hurried to the house, finding a pickup truck parked on one side and the front yard surrounded by a picket fence. A man and a woman in their thirties led us into the living room. A couch and a couple of wooden chairs were in the center. A new stereo system covered with plastic sheeting lay on a small table in a corner. On the walls hung a few crooked pictures of snowy mountain scenes of either Switzerland or Banff, and the usual crucifix dangled from a nail.

Don Juan was sleeping, they said, but it was time for him to get up. They asked us to sit. The house smelled faintly of urine and disinfectant. A toddler walked around in a tee shirt, probably don Juan's great-grandson. The couple was talking in the bedroom, but we couldn't make out what they were saying.

They returned after a few minutes, one on each side of an even smaller don Juan than I had remembered. They lowered him to the couch. His hair looked brittle to the touch. His mouth was shrunken, lips turned inward. Wrinkles radiated out from the cavity where his teeth used to be. As the couple spoke to him about us, he turned his head but stared right past us with an empty, uncomprehending look. I don't think he even saw us sitting there.

"Don Juan, it's Karen and Larry," I said, "*La profesora* and *el ingeniero*, do you remember?"

Don Juan looked to his grandson for a second, then stared straight ahead, his face a blank. The young man put his hand on don Juan's shoulder and patted it gently, then looked at Karen and me with a face showing how hopeless it was.

"Don Juan, we met years ago, in the old village. Do you remember the cemetery, the *Q'orpa*, the ceremonies? The Tres Gigantes?"

The half-naked child kicked a small plastic ball across the living room, then went over and sat on it, falling backwards on the floor. He didn't cry.

"We came to ask you of El Tío, don Juan. El Tío is not in the mine," I said. Don Juan's blank face stared past the walls, fast asleep with eyes open. My shoulders slumped, my head fell. Nobody was there to hear me.

Karen placed some bananas on his lap, along with a small bag of coca leaf. We thanked the couple, said goodbye, and walked to the door.

We were about to leave when we heard, "I remember you. I remember you. I remember. . . ."

We turned back to don Juan. He held a banana in both hands and smiled at us; again that mischievous twinkle of long ago flickered in his eyes, but the spark weakened and died even before we could sit down next to him, again his face blank as he slipped back into his shadows. We patted his shoulder. There were changes to be explained all right, but our old friend could give no answers.

As we left, his grandson told us about two years ago a stroke, or old age, or something had happened, they were not sure, but don Juan never again left the house. "The new *cacique* is a man from Q'illu Q'illu."

"Q'illu Q'illu? That's a town of cantinas," I said.

"Yes, more bars than people. Chilean smugglers pay for sex and alcohol." He said goodbye and shut the door.

"Senóbio must be devastated," Karen said as we wandered aimlessly. Such an understatement. No Tío, no *Q'orpa*, the empty face of don Juan . . . now Senóbio's shattered dream. I held tight to her hand; I needed an anchor.

Karen asked some people we met about Lucrecio, the *yacho*. "No, not here anymore," they said. He worked in Cochabamba now. He had abandoned his *estación* on the *pampa* and went to greener climates.

We walked past the government buildings and turned east into an alley. In one back yard music blasted from a transistor radio hung on a thin pole holding clothes lines stretched between two adobe and grass huts. Karen pointed out a narrow gate made of flattened cyanide drums.

Straight rows of raised beds nearly twenty meters long had been dug from one end of the lot to the other, nearly reaching a courtyard beside the two adobe huts. The beds were filled with onions, chard, potatoes, cabbage, and some plants we didn't recognize.

Tin cans served as pots for flowers. Narrow paths of flagstone gave access to the harvests, leading from a rock-lined well with a hand crank attached to a rope and bucket.

It was a garden as green and lush as those in the Foundation's new greenhouse.

Fenced off from the garden were a few square meters of barren earth where chickens scratched for grit and rabbits huddled together in a wire cage. Pots and pans lay about in the smoldering ashes of a raised fireplace.

A tall, thin, old man with blue eyes stood washing clothes in a metal basin. We shouted to him, "Canuto?"

He did not hear us. Perhaps the radio was too loud. We shouted again and pounded on the gate. Puzzled by the two gringo faces, he shuffled over and before reaching us, broke into a smile. "You have not forgotten me," he said, his arm around my shoulder.

"That would be impossible," Karen answered.

He cleared away some coils of rope and wire from a bench and had us sit. Karen gave him a small bag of coca leaf from her backpack; he gave us some llama jerky. Karen put hers into her pocket. He spoke softly. The radio was too loud. We could not hear him.

"Yes, yes, please forgive me, I forget that not everybody has my ears," he said. "They do not work as well as before."

Karen asked of Esperanza.

"She stayed as long as she could, but in the end she could not wait for me. *Me dejó solo*," he said. The arched eyebrows that showed such a love of life turned down, but only for a moment before he smiled and pulled from one of the huts the framed old photo we had taken of them standing stiff beside each other in their little *parcela* behind their house in Montes Claras. "This is my memory of her, but I have others," he said, tapping his head with one hand and touching his heart with the other.

"You must miss her, terribly," Karen said.

"Yes, but we do talk from time to time, so it is not as bad as you might think."

"What does she say to you?"

"It is her *alma*. She is calling me. To join her."

"Does that frighten you?"

He paused for a moment in thought. "I have fallen, several times. Sometimes I find myself lying in the middle of the garden. I do not know how I got there. I am afraid I have hurt some of the plants so for them I give extra water. On many cold mornings my legs fail me until the sun brings the warmth. It is then I rise to feed the animals. No, I am not afraid. I will be happy to be with Esperanza again. But, I must stay until after the harvest." He pointed with his head to the field of green before us and added, "It will not be long; maybe this fall."

The sky was clouding over again; probably more rain was coming. We all seemed absorbed with our own thoughts. Canuto started washing the pans by the dead fire.

"All the *ancianos* are dying off, don Canuto," I said. "Your secrets are going with them. Then nobody will be able to speak with the gods or ask the *almas* for a bit more time."

"Yes, *ingeniero*, things are changing in the village. The ways of life are not the same. The youth are so in a hurry all the time. The fathers are gone to the mine and the mothers, some of them, are gone, too. The children are left alone with teachers or relatives. I do not like this. It is too fast."

I told him I was concerned about the mine not having a Tío and how nobody seemed to care.

He patted my shoulder. "I also worry. If they do not take time to listen to the ancestors . . . well, then they will never know the powers of the *almas* or the cards or *la hojita*. My prayers are that at least some of the young continue to respect the gods and honor the ways of the ancestors. But I am afraid they have come to think this is unimportant."

"We can only hope your prayers are heard."

"Oh, they will be. Don't you know the saints and the gods always listen? This I know. The *Patrón* and the spirits will keep the old ways alive. But I will not be here to witness it."

Chapter 28

Senóbio's Farewell

Larry

January 2007

I had no idea what to do about El Tío. Don Juan and Lucrecio were gone, and Canuto wasn't long for this world. El Tío had been forgotten, and the others like Pachamama and probably *El Patrón* were being rapidly booted out the door, too. The gods were being abandoned, and fast.

Senóbio would know what to do. He was the last remaining authority of the old ways, the last *piña* preserved from the decomposing rock wall that once formed the foundation of the world.

His home stood on the last street before the *pampa's* edge. As in years past, the same metal gate squeaked in the shifting winds, slowly grinding its pair of rusty hinges into little piles of red powder.

We crossed to his front door through the narrow yard, avoiding stepping on plastic bags and bottles. The old village hadn't been rich enough to afford trash, but here in the new one, it lay in abundance. Piles of possibly useful rocks and *paja* lay against the inside walls. Sharp-edged shards of window glass mixed with pebbles at our feet. Along the left side was Senóbio's rusty Dodge truck. He had constructed a new adobe house in the back and a clothes line was strung up, but unlike many of his neighbors, he had no flower bed, no clean curtains in the windows, no pastel painted walls, no yard raked smooth and clean.

We knocked on his front door and saw a child push aside a tired curtain and peer at us through the glass.

Senóbio opened the door raising both arms to the sky. "*Compadre, profesora*, you have come back to us, your home has awaited you," he shouted as he laughed and shook our hands repeatedly. It was good to see him. Smaller, maybe even thinner, he still had a warm complexion and his usual quick laughter.

With arms around us he led us into his front room, pulled three chairs from somewhere, and had us sit at the same old cracked Formica table. He had hung up a yellowing sheet between the kitchen and the table, cutting the room almost in half. From behind the sheet came the crying of a baby.

"A new child?" Karen asked.

"Yes, it is a gift from Tito. My eldest son. He is sixteen now and has a baby girl," Senóbio said. "I am now in the third age."

The third age. "Me, too," I said, thinking of our two grandkids.

"Tito is trying to get a job at the mine but they say he is too young."

"And your wife, is Vañia well?"

Senóbio leaned forward, placed his hands on his knees, and nodded his head up and down as he said, "She is working in the mine. She cleans the dormitories."

"That must help."

"Yes, she works. A woman should not do that, you know, *compadre*? She brings in money, but she is gone all the time and when she comes home, she is tired. I need to care for the children during the day." He leaned back in his chair and spread his arms, and began laughing. "And there are so many to care for."

"So that would be . . . about eight in your house?" I asked.

"Yes, more or less."

"And you still teach?" Karen asked.

"Oh, yes, I can never stop. Someone has to teach the little ones. Our wages are the same as before, so, of course, I remain poor."

"They have not risen? Still about . . . $100 a month?" Karen asked.

"*Ni un centavo más*," he said. To demonstrate his poverty, he spread his hands to motion toward the walls and floor of his house, leading our eyes to the accumulations of sand and hairballs in the corners. The white interior walls were stained by overlapping muddy and greasy streaks and hand prints up to about five feet high.

"You have a new refrigerator," Karen remarked, after seeing a white box sitting in the middle of the room.

"Yes, Vañia bought it. It doesn't work." He laughed again.

The hind quarter of a llama lay drooped over the top of the refrigerator, its drops of dried blood now nearly black. Burlap bags of quinoa rested against one wall. A chicken walked around the room. I noticed someone had taped to the wall a half dozen crayon drawings and several pages of beginner math problems.

"There are so many changes now," I said. "I hear there is no *Q'orpa* ceremony."

"They can't leave work long enough to respect the gods."

The new baby cried from behind the curtain. We heard the shuffling of clothing as the mother apparently tried to comfort it with her breast.

"So many changes, *compadre*. Did you know they do not even burn the grasses around the village to honor San Juan?"

"Even that is forgotten?"

"Not forgotten exactly. The hills here have only *th'ola*; there is no grass to burn. And we are barred from climbing to Jayula. The company fences keep everybody out, so we can't burn the grass up there."

"I do not like the changes, my friend," I said.

Senóbio looked down at his floor. "Do you know that Santitos Colque Colque has died?"

"Santitos, the little man from the church?" Karen asked.

"The same. He died in the church; that is where it happened. He went late at night. They say he was drunk and fell and hit his head against a stone wall. He died right there, right at the feet of the *Patrón*. As it should be, no?"

"Poor Santitos," Karen said.

"Poor, yes," Senóbio laughed, leaning back in his chair. "He was the only one in town more poor than me."

"We went to visit don Juan de la Cruz. Do you know of his illness?"

"It is sad, his age has caught up with him."

"They have selected a man from Q'illu Q'illu to be the new *cacique*," I said.

"Yes."

"I'm sorry. I had hoped it would be you. It would be logical."

"It was a surprise," Senóbio said as his eyes avoided ours.

"And a mistake."

"Certainly."

"Have you heard, *compadre*, there is no Tío at the mine?" I asked.

"A shame, a shame," he answered, looking down and shaking his head.

"Is there anything we can do?"

"That is for the new *cacique* to determine. But he is . . . well, nothing will happen. It is not up to me."

I did not know how to take what he was saying. His resignation hit me hard.

Senóbio went on, "I could do it, *ingeniero*. If I were the *cacique* I could find El Tío for us. I know I could. But . . . things have changed. So many people have money now, at least most of them do. And the new *cacique*, from Q'illu Q'illu, how can that be? You know Q'illu, the people there . . . they are . . . well, you know."

"Yes, you could do it, *compadre*. I know you could." I paused a moment. "But no Tío. How can there be a mine without a Tío?"

"Of course it is not right. Already there are accidents. Already some strikes. The new *cacique* should do something. They should have . . . he was not the right choice."

Only the chicken scratching at the floor broke the silence. We sat uncomfortable for a minute or two, until Senóbio leaned across the table and spoke almost in a whisper, as if revealing a conspiracy that even his children should not hear. "*Ingeniero*, I have come up with an idea how to make a lot of money."

"Oh?"

"I want to start a tourism business. I could teach and also run the business at the same time. I will buy four or five burros and lead the young tourists on hikes into the hills. The burros would carry lunches and drinks and I could guide the tourists and show them all I know of the old ways."

"Great idea. I hope it works for you," I said, not at all convinced.

"I would take them to Markawi. They could learn how the ancestors lived. I could sell them pottery shards for souvenirs, and at lunch they would pay us for the drinks and food. Do you think they would pay for such a thing?"

It was tough to fake any kind of approval. "Well . . . yes, I guess they would, they would find that very exciting, I'm sure. But . . . Markawi?"

Senóbio moved up and down in his chair with excitement while explaining his plan. "Yes, and in time I could build a small shelter there amid the ruins, they could even sleep overnight and then hike back to town the next day."

"But isn't that a sacred site? Perhaps even a *samiri*?"

"Of course, but that is why it would be so exciting for them. It is so different. They would pay for the burros, the food, the pottery, and then pay me for guiding them," he said leaning back, with a grin as large as his outstretched arms, ready to receive a shower of money. "What do you think?"

"Well . . . I think it would work, yes, but," I said this as gently as I could, "wouldn't it lead to the destruction of Markawi? In time the place would be stripped of all they could carry away. Other people would learn of it and excavate the ruins, the graves. The place would be robbed and you would have nothing left."

Senóbio paused as he rubbed the top of his head. "You think so? No, I think we can keep it a secret and still make money from there. No, I do not think it would be destroyed. How could they destroy something as powerful as Markawi?"

"Well, El Tío is powerful and look what happened. The same with the *Q'orpa*, already forgotten. Almost no crops, no animals. These were once powerful. I am afraid Markawi could be next."

We all stared at the table. Senóbio was slow as he stood up. He looked at the five or six little faces staring at him from around the corners, and said to me, "*Compadre*, could you come with me to the back of the house? Just you?"

I looked at Karen. We both shrugged. I went out with him to sit against the shaded east wall of his new adobe house.

"I need to do this. There are so many children and I cannot feed them all. I do not work at the mine like the others. A man cannot live off his wife. All I need is money for the burros and a bit of advertising in Uyuni." Senóbio leaned forward to conspire with me. "Could you loan me the money? We could be partners. I will do all the work and we can split the income."

"But it's Markawi; that's a special place. I think it may be the wrong thing to do."

"Look around you *compadre*," he said, motioning to the houses next to his. "Everyone is improving their lives and I cannot. People are buying cars and trucks and new furniture and television sets. I have nothing. Nothing. Like when I was a child, back then. This may be my only chance. I must take it."

Senóbio looked down at the dust as two children ran past, both barefoot. I pushed some of the broken glass to one side, closer to the adobe wall. I felt very uncomfortable. Things were not going the way I had hoped, not for El Tío, not for Senóbio, not for the Quechua community. For the first time since I had known him, Senóbio's arms and hands were still. He leaned against the adobe wall in the shade, without energy, arms dangling by his sides. He looked empty.

He turned his head away from me and said, "*Ingeniero*, I must also contribute. It is not right that a married woman should be a worker. I must do something, but what? I am only a teacher. I am not even the *cacique*. I must do something." He got up and walked a few paces away and stood with his back to me.

"I am sorry, my friend," I said, looking down at the dirt.

"How could they have done that? Didn't they know I was the right one?"

I said nothing.

"A man from Q'illu Q'illu."

"I am sorry," I said.

"Well, it is a responsibility for others now. The customs, the ceremonies, El Tío, they are in someone else's hands."

I looked over at the walls of the neighbors' new homes. I stared at his yard, at the plastic bags swirling in hopeless circles. I stared at anything, anything but Senóbio.

A half hour later, Karen and I bid farewell to him and his gaggle of kids, leaving the usual gifts of health food bars, bags of nuts, and dried fruit.

We walked silently to the hotel. About half way there, Karen asked, "What did you talk about behind the house? Will he help with El Tío?"

"No, he won't. I didn't even ask him again. I know he won't."

"How can that be? This is *Senóbio*, of all people."

"Yes. It must be hard enough to be poor, especially by Bolivian standards, but to have been dishonored like he was. Some guy in Q'illu Q'illu, for God's sake. He thinks he'll never lead the ceremonies, never be *cacique*. It took all his energy away."

"Do you think he will go ahead with this idea to exploit Markawi?"

"Yes he'll try. But I wouldn't worry about it too much. He has always been a dreamer, in a way."

"He doesn't even have the money to do it, I suppose."

"I gave him three hundred dollars to buy the burros," I said. I pulled my collar up around my neck and shoved my hands into my coat pockets. I was glad Karen was quiet after that.

Chapter 29

The Color When the Earth Bleeds

Karen

January 2007

A mist suddenly opened like a curtain and revealed the towering mass of the Tres Gigantes. All other familiar landmarks had been destroyed.

Two young geologists waved their arms while pointing out the mineral deposits now made visible by the exposed earth. They were at most in their late twenties; she with auburn hair and a fair complexion, round face, and freckles as if an Irish engineer had left a souvenir of his time in the mines of Potosí; he, more typically Bolivian, a handsome, well-built mix of Spanish and Indian.

They introduced themselves as Mayda and Tomás. As we stood sinking into the mucky earth next to our jeep, they could not express enough gratitude and awe as they shook hands with *the* Dr. Larry Buchanan. "Is it true you won the Thayer Lindsley Award?" they asked.

Larry acknowledged their question politely, but his attention was elsewhere. After more than eleven years, the orebody, *his* orebody, was finally exposed by dozer cuts in the side of Cerro Jayula. Like a kid exploring a new playground, Larry couldn't wait to crawl over the pile of broken rocks. He picked up samples and shoved them into his backpack. "Look at this!" he shouted. "My god, it's beautiful!"

Mayda and Tomás laughed at Larry's excitement. They watched his face as they told him that more recent drilling indicated the discovery was twice the size that Larry had calculated.

"That would double the life of the mine," I heard Larry say. "It could mean jobs for thirty-four years . . . thirty-four."

"All because of your discovery," Mayda said.

"Well, I had some help," Larry responded. "El Tío had a hand in this."

I caught a look of surprise on Mayda's face as if she weren't sure she'd heard right, but she rushed on to point out a thick pile of black rock waiting to be sent to the mill. "That's the sulfide ore stockpile that will be hauled down to the crusher when it's operating."

I couldn't share their excitement about the geology—or even the prospect of jobs for years beyond the seventeen initially estimated. I had never visited an open pit mine before and was not prepared for the overwhelming scale of destruction. As I stared in shock at the scene before me, I felt as if my own core were slashed open.

The souls of those sheltering rocks had been ripped apart by two-hundred tonne trucks and front-end loaders. All those landmarks such as *El Soldado* and *El Sapo* had been bulldozed over or covered by piles of black ore, dust and mud. The surrounding mountains had been sliced by a gigantic knife into dozens of horizontal layers, the upper layers pulled back and removed, bench by bench.

First, no town; now, no landmarks; just a huge hole in the ground with trucks spiraling their way up and down the endless horizontal benches.

"You okay?" Larry broke into my sorrow. The two geologists and he had stopped talking. They must have been staring at me for a while.

"You okay?" Larry repeated, moving to my side and putting an arm around me.

"Yeah, I'm okay." I tried to take a deep breath. "I just feel such loss. I can't begin to imagine what this must be like for the townspeople working here."

"It's ugly, isn't it?" he said. "These hills will never be the same. But it's also beautiful in a way. Imagine the wealth it's creating." He placed a light kiss on the top of my head. It provided little comfort.

Larry had no trouble reconciling his excitement and pride about the mine with his sadness and concern about the effects it had on the land and people. I envied him. Regardless of my feelings, I was staggered by his influence, the magnitude of his discovery that could change the whole economy of this impoverished country.

We drove above the destroyed town site to the west and arrived at a spot I didn't recognize. Larry pointed out that this flattened bench was once Tesorera Ridge, where Soledad had taken us so often to look at the rocks or to play music.

A monstrous, yellow, front-end loader was chewing up the ridge and dumping mouthfuls of broken rock into an equally monstrous dump truck. Suddenly our vehicle which had felt so large for four people seemed like a vulnerable toy. Its top didn't even reach the height of the tires on those gigantic trucks.

A tiny figure waved to us from the cab of the front-end loader.

"Soledad Quíspe?"

The person in baggy blue coveralls climbed down a ladder from the cab and jumped to the ground, then ran toward us. I almost didn't recognize her. Under the yellow hardhat, a smile spread across her face revealing a full set of perfect, bright, white teeth; no hand rose to cover black stubs. Her face was thinner than I remembered; her high cheekbones now accented her sparkling, dark eyes. No traditional greeting by tapping of shoulders. We embraced.

"I've dreamt of you," she said.

"And I often think of you. It's been a long time and look, you've become a lovely lady."

She accepted my compliment with a shy smile.

"What's this like for you, Soledad?" I had to ask. "Your dream of driving a front-end loader has come true, but you've had to destroy the land that was once your beloved town."

"*Muy triste*," she said looking out at the decimated hills. "Every day I feel such deep sadness when I come to work. But at the same time, it's okay for me. I love the work. I earn two hundred dollars a month now and can earn up to one thousand dollars in a few years. Who would ever have thought this could happen?"

"But the land? The customs?" I asked.

"That is hard, but not as hard for me as for others since I have a future. The *ancianos* suffer horribly. They had such dignity and integrity. Now they have nothing. Their past is gone."

Soledad bent down, picked up a broken piece of sandy rock and handed it to me. Its interior revealed a swirling pattern of whites and muted purples.

"Take this home with you and guard it. It is your *piña*. It still has its soul." Soledad embraced me once again. "I must get back to work, but I will see you at lunch," she called as she dashed back to the front-end loader.

We got into the vehicle and drove along a spiraling road down from the bench. I turned to take one more look at the enormous wound that cut across the red and yellow hillside.

"Is that the color when the earth bleeds?" I asked.

"No, señora," said Tomás. "That's the color of El Tío's gift."

Two lines extended around the building as the company attempted to feed some three thousand workers. We waited in front of *Comedor A*; the other line headed in an opposite direction toward the side of *Comedor B*. The *comedores* were ten times their previous size.

In addition to these, rows of dormitories, small stores, and a hall for movies and entertainment lined the streets. The former Toldos mining camp had become a city of its own.

The mine, now under the management of some Australian engineers, did not permit non-employees to pass through the gates. Without Mayda and Tomás, we'd never have been allowed to enter. They'd convinced the contracted guards that Larry and I had come to share geological information. It didn't matter to the guards that Larry's discovery made their jobs possible. They'd checked all our papers with a critical eye and rummaged through our backpacks to ensure we weren't sneaking cameras into the site. With much reluctance, they had let us pass.

Soledad arrived to the *comedor*, talking and joking with the other workers, mostly men, as she searched the line to find us. She had shed the navy blue coveralls and yellow helmet and was now dressed in a black form-fitting turtleneck and slacks revealing a womanly form and a professional appearance. I wondered if the girly pin-ups still adorned her walls. Her black hair was pulled back into a braid and a navy cap with the company logo covered her head.

After finding us, Soledad and I stood smiling at each other with that embarrassment that comes from long separations between friends.

We were speaking of family and homes when Soledad said, "I couldn't have done this without you," referring to a small gift of money we had given her to get a chauffeur's license. "I not only am learning to drive the larger trucks, but I also chauffeur the geologists and other company employees." She was quiet a moment, then looked directly into my eyes, and said, "*Tía*. From now on, I will call you *Tía*. When someone is close to our heart, it is as if they are related."

"*Gracias*," I said, delighted that our love was mutual.

I watched the lines move forward, slowly, but continuously, in opposite directions toward the two *comedores*. Soledad was quick to explain, "That is *Comedor* B for the workers, those who are not professionals. They are served different food from us and that has caused many problems. They've already gone on strike twice."

Soledad frowned as she spoke about the discrimination, perhaps remembering the day when she had been allowed to eat a meal only if she went to the back door of the kitchen. Other stories spilled out of her. The Peruvians working in the mine started many fights with the locals. Stealing occurred. People from other countries seemed to look upon Bolivians as inferior. There was a Brazilian in charge of cooking last year. He was heard to call the Bolivians *llamitas*, animals. Nobody did anything about it, but then later he said to someone that Bolivians like to urinate in their soup; it's hotter that way. One of the Americans heard him and the cook was gone by morning.

By now we had reached the food servers and the usual Altiplano fare of starches: potatoes, rice, corn, noodles, and bread with some unappealing chunks of beef. Soledad, carrying her own plate of food piled high, beckoned me to follow her to a refrigerator. As if reading my mind, she pointed to a cabbage salad sitting amid a variety of deserts.

At the table we settled in near Mayda and Tomás who were eager to speak more with Larry about how he had discovered the orebody. They both looked around the table to see if anyone else had been listening. Then Tomás asked in a low voice, "What did you mean when you said you had help with this discovery?"

"Well, I was not alone when I first came here. There were other geologists. And El Tío.

"Please, go on."

"I believe it was El Tío who led me here to find this mine. I didn't do it alone."

"Of course, *ingeniero*," Mayda said.

Soledad's eyes never left Larry's face. She put another forkful of food in her mouth, chewing slowly. Her face lit up as she listened.

Larry leaned forward. "I do have some concerns. Doesn't every mine in Bolivia have their Tío?" He paused for a moment, then continued without waiting for a response. "Many townspeople who work in the mine say there is no Tío here."

Mayda closed her eyes as if receiving an answer to her prayers. "That is true, *ingeniero*."

"But how can that be? Does the company forbid it?" I asked.

Tomás answered, "The company is not the problem, not really. The management just doesn't care one way or the other if there is a Tío. All the company wants is a smooth operation."

Mayda added, "We are mining about 180,000 tonnes per day. Think of it. It means the two-hundred tonne trucks must make seven hundred trips every twenty-four hours. The management wants only to keep the operations moving and to get the mill construction finished on schedule." Mayda picked at her desert, no longer interested in food.

With great emphasis Tomás said, "They do not want *anything* to interrupt the flow of the work, so they will not allow the workers to take company time to pay their respects to El Tío."

"I understand that," Larry said. "What bothers me as much as the company is the townspeople's attitude, especially the youth. They seem so uninterested."

Now Soledad spoke up. "*Ingeniero*, perhaps it has something to do with such long work hours. Our lives are so different, and," she paused and lowered her voice, "you also have to realize that with so much discrimination here, people are careful about expressing their beliefs."

Mayda added, "We're from Potosí where traditions are still important. In Potosí, we would not even enter a mine without paying respect to El Tío. But many of the professionals here are from Santa Cruz or La Paz or outside of Bolivia. They'd laugh at us if we followed our traditions."

"We do want a Tío for the mine," Tomás said. "There has already been one death, just four months ago. It did not have to happen."

When Mayda and Tomás finished, Larry agreed, "There'll be more accidents. There'll be strikes. The silver will disappear, at least according to the legends."

Tomás added, "Without our own Tío, the mine will fail." His shoulders slumped in resignation.

"I have an idea," Soledad said.

Chapter 30

Superman's Return

Larry

January 2007

A few hours before midnight, three darkened figures slipped out of the village and hiked slowly north along the floor of the Montes Claras Canyon under ragged black clouds and gibbous moon.

We carried no lights, but distant flashes of lightning kept photographing us in black and white. The guards seldom ventured out when the rains were about to fall, reasoning that no sane person would enter the property on cold, windy, and soon-to-be-wet nights.

I was the oldest, a balding Gringo geologist a few hairs shy of sixty-three. The bottles inside my backpack were wrapped in a raincoat to prevent rattling. Also in the pack was an incredibly rich sample of silver ore and a flat, tabular object wrapped in a soft cotton cloth that nobody knew I carried. This one was personal.

I had left my wallet and all identification in the hotel room in San Cristóbal, as had Karen, who followed me by a step or two. She was as determined as I. We both chewed coca leaf and tried not to swallow the mulch. Karen carried a backpack with a similar load.

Taking the lead was Soledad. She also chewed the coca, and seemed not to mind the cold as she picked a trail around the rocks and clumps of *paja brava* grass, avoiding their sharp stabs. Lashed by rawhide ropes to her back was a soft bundle about three feet long and half as wide, wrapped in a bright red *aguayo* and covered in black plastic.

"It is good we chose this night," Soledad said in a soft voice.

"Do you really think we can make it?" Karen asked.

"We can try."

A flash of light ripped the western sky, the wind abruptly changed to push us from the rear, a rustling in the *th'ola* scattered a few dead blades of grass across our feet.

My heart was pounding. "Listen," I whispered, "Did you hear . . . ?"

We looked and saw only shadow.

"The wind. Let us hurry," Soledad said.

We hiked for an hour and a half up the canyon nearly to the abandoned house of Esperanza and Canuto. Here the canyon split into several tributaries; we chose the one to the left which led uphill to the west toward the mining camp. Soledad pointed to the right, down beyond the main canyon. In the next lightning flash we could just make out the little cross above Esperanza's grave near her ruined garden terraces. Canuto would join her soon.

We pressed on to a chain-link fence topped by three strands of barbed wire. We had no idea how to scale it.

Out of the darkness a voice spoke, almost casually, "I know a place to cross." Behind us stood Senóbio.

"You came," Soledad said as she walked over and shook his hand. Karen gave him an awkward embrace, saying simply, "Thank you so much."

I was relieved to see him.

Senóbio led us along the fence to where some rocks rose high on our side. By standing atop the rocks we needed to clear only about three feet of barbed wire. He threw his *aguayo* to cover the wire, and one by one we climbed over and dropped heavily to the water-softened ground. As we hid among some boulders, Senóbio struggled to get the *aguayo* untangled from the barbs, ripping it in a few places.

"The guards come by here. We must not leave any sign that we crossed." Jabs from some *th'ola* sticks loosened the incriminating fibers snagged on the wires. They blew away onto the other side of the fence. "The wind is on our side," he said.

"How will we get back over?" Karen asked.

"I do not know."

We slogged in the mud along the washed-out roads of the Toldos Mine, about two kilometers from the site of the old town. A light rain with specks of sleet blew horizontally, its icy needles pricking our faces. A wet spot on my shirt was beginning to stick to my shoulder.

We traversed down the tributary canyon that leads north from Toldos and then bends westerly to join the main Río Toldos Canyon. As we approached a narrow road, Soledad motioned for us to hide in some abandoned prospect pits.

"This is the route of the guards. They drive ATV motorcycles, and each carries a radio. We will wait until the next one passes and then cross over," she said.

I pressed myself against the rock walls of the pit. It felt good to be out of the wind. I kept shivering and pulled my coat close around me.

A feeble, bouncing light approached on the narrow road above our hiding spot. We hugged the pit walls and listened to the motorcycle sputter and cough its way down the road, passing us on the left. Soledad eased her head up and motioned for us to climb out and cross the road and drop into the small arroyo below. We continued downhill for about three hundred yards, picking our way through fields of boulders.

The wide, light streak of the new haulage road shone wet below us near the bottom of the canyon. We had to cross it to reach the base of the Tres Gigantes. The cave was there.

Large boulders in the gulch provided cover as we studied the movement of the company vehicles. Senóbio took off his brown *aguayo* and put it around my shoulders.

"You keep it," I said to him.

"No, the cold and I are old friends."

I nodded to him and said, "I am glad you came."

"It had to be," he said to me, quietly so the others could not hear. "You know a man cannot leave his gods." He grinned.

I grinned back, "Yes, I know."

I turned to watch the movement on the road below us. The rain had stopped, temporarily, and the moon shown even brighter. A loaded truck splashed down the road with its headlights flashing on the fronts of the boulders. Coming up the other side was an empty truck, forcing us to move slowly around the sides of the boulders to keep pace with the shifting shadows. After both trucks had passed, we ran across the road and dropped into the deep canyon beyond.

Our hike here was easier, the sand wet but packed, and except for a large boulder occasionally in the way, the path quick.

"The cave is just off the road, there, to the right, just below where El Soldado used to be," Soledad said.

We struggled to climb the hill around the protruding vertical outcrops. Rain fell, stronger this time. The rain-saturated soils were beginning to flow on the slopes. Shadows somehow had become darker. Soledad had spent her entire life on these cliffs and ledges. She knew where to lead us. The cave was there, just as it always had been. It felt good to be dry and out of the wind.

The cave mouth faced the haul road. By bending to the right we could see the site of the leveled village, now covered by over a million tonnes of stockpiled sulfide ore waiting to be shipped by conveyor when the crusher began operations. To the left the edges of Tres Gigantes were visible. As each truck passed, headlights flashed a moment inside the cave then swept across the cliffs and away. For those few seconds, small barite crystals in the grainy sediments sparkled with their announcement that yes, barite was here, that faithful mistress of silver.

"It is perfect," Senóbio said.

Soledad insisted Karen and I should unwrap her bundle. Karen helped place it upright in the cave. The plastic bag was removed, exposing two red-painted horns about six inches long with yellow tassels at their tips, the horns protruding from a mass of bright yellow polyester hair cut from the head of a plastic doll. Karen had made two cones from the stiff front and rear covers of my recent copy of *Foreign Affairs*. A touch of red paint and a few staples to hold the yellow tassels, and they became the horns of a devil.

His face began as two white eyes staring through the slits of a black ski mask stretched over a soccer ball. Soledad's artwork added pupils of blue with thin red lines for veins. She had painted razor-sharp teeth in a mouth full of blood. Completing this face was a poorly trimmed mustache and beard of uncarded llama wool sewn to the ski mask.

Soledad unwrapped the protective *aguayo* and fastened it with nails to the wall of the cave behind the head, like a curtain draped behind a throne. Removing more black plastic, I exposed the body below the head, its chest covered by a yellow, long-sleeved child's cotton shirt emblazoned with "*El Regreso de Superman*," The Return of Superman, bought in a used clothing store in Uyuni.

"That is very appropriate," Senóbio said, with a chuckle. We had sewn llama wool gloves stuffed with paper to the ends of the arms. A child's pair of Levi pants made up the rest.

With those children's clothes and cartoon face, he didn't look much like those Tíos of the mines of Potosí and throughout the Andes, but ours was a Tío none the less, and we had brought him home.

Soledad tossed confetti into the air around the little cave, covering the walls and El Tío. The sparkling colored pieces stuck on him and dangled from a myriad of invisible spider webs attached to the walls. A seed necklace Karen had purchased from an Argentine hippie passing through Uyuni was draped around his neck.

"We must now *ch'allar*," Senóbio said. He popped the cap off the bottle of beer and sprayed brown foam over El Tío, the *aguayo*, and the cave walls. "All of the beer has left the bottle. It is a good omen. He had a good drink."

"Now you must do the same," he said to Karen, handing her the orange soda.

As Karen sprayed, the interior of the cave became dripping wet. More confetti was thrown, clinging to the wet surfaces. Flashing headlights of another truck turned the cave into a crystal-lined geode of sparkling pink, red, blue, purple, and white. Soledad hung colored paper streamers from nails she pounded into fractures in the cave walls.

We scattered handfuls of coca leaf as an offering. Many leaves stuck to the head and clothing of El Tío. By then our cheeks bulged with coca mulch. Senóbio offered a round of cigarettes, saying we all must *pij'char* and smoke, to show our benign intent. We lit up, offered one to El Tío, and chewed *la hojita.* As we sprinkled drops of wine and *cingani* to the cardinal directions, we asked that he grant our wishes: safety for the workers and much silver for the mine. More coca leaf was sprinkled about, until his eyes stared from behind a mask of green foliage.

"*Es buena hora,*" Senóbio said.

"*Es buena hora,*" we all said in turn. The remaining cigarettes were put into the small pocket of El Tío's pants and the coins, plastic bottles of *cingani* and wine were placed at his feet, along with the sample of high grade silver ore.

"We are done," Soledad said.

"Look, his cigarette is completely burned down to the filter," said Senóbio. "This is a very good sign."

"It burnt some of his mustache," Karen pointed out.

"Even better," Senóbio said.

Everyone turned to go, crouching as they dropped down to the low ditch beside the road, splashing into a few inches of gray water. I held back, shouting that I'd return in a minute.

I crawled back into the cave and sat beside El Tío, leaning against the sticky, colorful wall. I offered more coca leaf and sprinkled a few loose pieces of confetti on his head. He merely stared at me. I lit two cigarettes and put one into his mouth.

"Thank you, El Tío. For all you have done. The gift, the new lives, the gains, the losses, the chance to change."

His blue eyes stared straight ahead, his teeth as sharp and eager as before. He gave no sign he was listening.

"The people, they took your gift and ran with it into the new world. They are much better off, but it caused them to forget you, just as you said it would. But you gave it anyway, knowing it would be your suicide."

We sat and smoked together for a minute more. I had no blood to spread before him, the beers and *cingani* were gone, the confetti already stuck to his body. I pulled the flat object from my backpack and unwrapped it, presenting it as my offering to El Tío. "Karen and I brought you home to your cave so you may watch over your silver, but also to pay back a debt I owed to the people of San Cristóbal."

I placed the remainder of my cigarette in his mouth next to the other one, now becoming two red dots in the dark cave. I thanked him once again as I left.

At the cave entrance I saw a truck curve by with its load of black ore, its lights sweeping across the fissured rocks at the base of the Tres Gigantes, their shining minerals reflecting a million tiny starlights from within the dark shadows. I looked back and saw El Tío staring out from his throne at the powerful new world his gift had created. As the smoke from the cigarettes curled around his horns, I could see that El Tío was smiling.

Like all the Tíos of all the mines of the Andes, this one stands above his piles of coca leaf and small coins, his yellow hair and pointed horns covered by streamers and confetti glued together by stale beer and sticky soda. But this one, our Tío, has draped across his shoulders a bright green ribbon holding a brass medallion, the Thayer Lindsley award for the discovery of the San Cristóbal silver deposit, my small offering to satiate the hunger of this most generous god.

Epilogue

Karen

Twelve year ago Larry asked me, "What right do we have to say these people shouldn't take advantage of the only opportunity to come their way in centuries?" I can no longer answer whole-heartedly as I did back then, "Leave them alone."

We'd like to believe that our story ends happily-ever-after and perhaps if it were fiction, we could make it so. But with all the positive and negative results of the mining project, ours is an evolving story, one without end and one with outcomes that are difficult to judge.

After an absence of two years, Larry and I traveled back to San Cristobal in 2009. The town had continued to grow and now counted two thousand residents. Double story adobe homes lined the streets, dwarfing the pre-fab, company-built houses. Businesses had flourished: a beauty parlor, a bank, restaurants, and even a take-out chicken joint. A new car wash had plenty of customers now that people owned cars and trucks.

The clinic-hospital boasted a doctor, dentist, nurse and ambulance driver. Octavio, the *enfermero auxiliar*, informed us he was soon to change his career of twenty-five years to work in a warehouse at the mine.

Not all was rosy: Octavio reported anemia had replaced mal-nutrition to plague the town's children as they now filled their bellies with purchasable sweets, and though the children of the outlying *estancias*, still reliant on the traditional incomplete diet, escaped this new affliction, they remained malnourished.

Break-ins and thefts had become such a problem that people dared not leave their house unoccupied even for short periods. The influx of new people had eroded the three laws—do not steal, do not lie, and do not be lazy, the very foundation of Quechua society.

Fourteen-day shifts of twelve hours each, followed by one week off, still prevented most people from attending the traditional ceremonies.

As with all major change, the benefits have a cost. Many have suffered, especially the older folks who simply couldn't adapt and those young men who turned to drink. Others, however, had their dreams fulfilled: college educations, sufficient food and medical care, an escape from poverty.

"Come see." Soledad beckoned. Outside her family home, a humongous Volvo 18-wheeler stretched half-way down the block. This monster outdid the photos she had hung on her wall many years ago when she dreamed of being a truck driver.

"Yours?" Larry asked, incredulous.

"Bought with my severance pay and some help from my family. I am now my own boss. I will transport goods for the mine and for anyone else who needs my services."

Senóbio also appeared to be living out his dreams as he sat in front of a computer in the Foundation offices. Still stiff with newness, his blue jeans replaced the worn slacks of his teaching days, and his flannel shirt stretched tight around a middle-aged paunch on this once thin man. As we sat in his office, he repeatedly turned a bronze nameplate so that our eyes would not miss it, *S. Condori, Personnel Manager*. He had quit teaching as he realized this new job would enable him to provide for his ever-expanding family. A visit to his home revealed that one of his smudged-faced daughters had blossomed into a beauty and now cradled Senóbio's second grandchild in her arms. Yet another adobe building was being constructed in his backyard. As before, kids were everywhere.

Senóbio shared that he had visited El Tío in the cave at the mine just weeks before. Our Superman remained honored with more offerings of confetti, money, and cigarettes. The company even permitted the workers to do *ch'allas* on occasion.

"And what does the Gringo Tío look like?" Larry asked. After all, an inflated ball comprised his head.

"He's aged a bit, the ball deflated into a mass of wrinkles. He is more scary than ever," Senóbio conceded with one of his heart-warming laughs. Markawi was still a well-kept secret and Los Tres Gigantes had somehow survived the blasting of the town, at least for now.

Soledad's and Senóbio's dreams were not the only ones realized. Several years prior during one of our visits to San Cristobal, an adolescent boy, Cornelio Gonzales, had sought me out at the hotel. He'd requested tutoring in English and arrived promptly at our designated time for lessons each day. His motivation was impressive. He studied long hours into the night and his days were spent reading, writing, and practicing his English with anyone who would listen.

As the time for my return to Ashland had approached, Cornelio told me, "My one wish in life is to study English in the United States."

Without a second thought, I'd scribbled down my email address and said, "Write me when you are ready to come." I thought I would never hear from this young man again.

I received an email in 2007: *I am ready to come to study English in the United States. Saludos, Cornelio Gonzales.*

Cornelio has been living with us in Ashland, Oregon, for three and a half years, and is now a junior in the local university. His adaptation to our way of living is a book in itself, one which we hope he will write one day. His determination to succeed has helped him overcome many deficits in his early education.

His goal? "One day I would like to be Minister of Education and ensure that every Bolivian receives an education that will truly prepare him for life."

Cornelio has shared stories of growing up in the old San Cristobal, many of which we incorporated into our book. He became our fact-checker as we questioned whether we understood certain cultural rituals and events. He also reflected the nostalgia a child feels for a place that gave him his identity while at the same time, he expressed his appreciation for catching up with the more developed world, an opportunity afforded by the mine and the move of his village.

Would Cornelio go back to the old town and way of life? Would I wish him and the other residents of San Cristobal this possibility? I have no simple answer to this question. When I lived in a state of naiveté, I could claim with certainty that no culture should be disrupted for the sake of development. But that naïveté disappeared with my experiences in San Cristobal. I no longer rush to label development good or bad, but rather try to understand the complexities involved. Remaining open without judgment can feel uncomfortable, but relying on uninformed preconceptions is no alternative. Each project for development and each culture that will be impacted is unique. There is no universal formula. Nothing is all good or all bad.

As far as my relationship with Larry goes, this is the happily-ever-after part without an ending because our marriage continues to grow stronger. Our experiences in San Cristobal forced us both to look at the world differently. I watched my husband bond with the people, partake in the cultural rituals, and cry at the loss of their customs. His genuine desire to make the world better for these impoverished people, his willingness to experience a very strange and different culture first-hand, and his openness to examine strongly embedded beliefs only deepened my love and respect for him.

Larry

We started out at opposite poles, two points of view looking at the world from different angles, acute against obtuse. Karen saw injustice where I saw opportunity. She imagined a healthy, vibrant culture, and I, only dysfunction and despair. Our images of the world were focused by prisms cut concave and convex; hers, I thought, rose-colored; mine, she thought, opaque as coal.

It's funny how a shared experience can prove that neither of us was right.

The reality of poverty removed that rosy hue from Karen's vistas; the grace and honor of the people of San Cristobal began, ever so slowly, to infuse translucence into my darkened vision.

Karen has spoken above. I told you she was honest, that she would report the truth. And I, once so certain that God and faith and culture were only for the lonely, the lost, the desperate; I finally accepted what El Tío intended as his gift for me: the understanding that the hard reality of mathematics and science can be, indeed, must be, complemented by the vitally necessary world of spirituality and myth.

Return, November 2015

Six years have passed since we visited San Cristobal. As we enter the town, our eyes widen at the sign painted on the side of an adobe wall, "VOTE SENOBIO ALCALDE. CAMBIO SEGURO." (Vote Senobio mayor. Sure change) Our dear friend and dreamer, once the poorest man in the village, now sits in the mayor's seat, and it is he who decides how to spend San Cristobal's share of the royalties generated by the mine, this year bringing eleven million dollars to his village.

News travels fast, and soon Larry and I find ourselves in the back seat of a chauffeured car, Senobio up front next to his hired driver. A few wrinkles are testimony to the passing years, but Senobio is as animated as ever, bobbing up and down with excitement. He must show us his office, a three-hour drive across the salt flats from San Cristobal. Looking out at the remote sandy desert and spreading his arms in a wide arc, Senobio asks what we think of a possible golf course here or perhaps wind surfing to attract tourists.

The county seat where Senobio works resembles the old San Cristobal with its adobe houses with thatched roofs, a contrast to the modern San Cristobal where Senobio lives. Senobio unlocks the door to a modest building and enters his office where his small frame is lost behind a huge desk. A wooden sign sits upon the desk with Senobio Condori, ALCALDE inscribed in bold letters. Senobio waves his arms in a welcoming gesture for us to sit across from him. Portraits of Bolivia's heroes in stiff uniforms, Sucre and Bolivar, look down at us with stern expressions, contrasting with the relaxed, grinning Senobio who sports a running outfit with the Bolivian teams colors.

Senobio explains how the three Quechua principles, *Ama Sua; Ama Llulla;* and *Ama Qhella*–Don't lie; Don't Steal; and Don't be Lazy—inspire him to do right by his constituency spread out over forty five villages. "If we follow these laws," he explains, "all will be well."

Presiding over one of Senobio's shelves is a wooden statue of El Tio, surrounded by his bottle of beer and some coca leaf. His devil's horns are as pointy as ever and of course, he sports a huge erection. Our god of the underworld who promised the gift of silver proudly surveys what his prophecy has wrought. Perhaps his people have not yet forgotten him. We are told the el Tio we left in the cave near the mine still exists. His clothes decaying, the ball that comprised his head shrunken like a prune in the desert, he lives on, at least in the minds of our friends who helped place him there that dark rainy night.

I am not sure whose grins are bigger, Senobio's or ours.

Eleven million dollars in royalties each year is a lot of money, and Senobio is proud of what has been accomplished, mostly in San Cristobal. We have already witnessed the spectacular new gymnasium with a capacity for 1000 people offering a venue for sports events and exercise. A large, modern hospital awaits equipment due, they say, next year. Not only is health care provided, but also dental care, and several of the adolescents display braces when they smile. We see fewer gaping holes in people's mouths.

Youth attend a modern brick high school, and a second elementary school will open next year. No more crumbling adobe buildings and jagged glass in the broken windows that I recall from the old town, where I feared for the welfare of the children. In place of the rocks where children once scampered like mountain goats, a new swing set and jungle gym invite the younger ones to enjoy a playground.

An Institute offers high school graduates tuition-free, three-year programs in electronics, mechanics, and tourism with the goal of providing young adults with professional skills. Upon entering the classrooms, we receive smiles and waves from several of these older students who recall singing the Hokey Pokey with me.

San Cristobal, originally a town of 441 people, has grown to 3,000. There are jobs now, and people come from all over the country to take advantage of them. The town mushrooms outward into the surrounding desert, new houses under construction everywhere. Salaries range between $1000 to $4000/month where ten years ago the best paying jobs, if you could get one at all, paid $100/month. The townspeople can now afford the luxuries of a new truck, a modern two-story house with heat and electricity, and opportunities to travel to the Chilean coast. I am surprised and delighted to find a bottle of imported olive oil on the table of a family who has invited us for dinner!

However, with money come losses. The people have long work hours at the mine: twelve hour days, seven days a week, then seven days off. "Too long," Larry says. "They need more rest for safety reasons." The townspeople speak of five minutes to change shifts as closure of operations for even a few minutes would cost the mine millions of dollars.

Further, young workers can afford alcohol and vehicles—always a bad mix. The road between Uyuni, the city an hour away, and San Cristobal, is dotted with crosses where these young people have met their deaths.

"It's hard to have a sense of community with so many new faces and with everyone working long hours," our friends lament. We see what they mean about newcomers: it's difficult for us to strike up conversations with the women who have moved to San Cristobal from other places. They hide their faces when they see us walking down the street with our cameras. We are just tourists to them.

Yet our friends are adjusting to the changes with time. "It's getting easier," they report, "and our children have opportunities we never had. The high school band of 72 students, playing modern instruments, won a regional competition!" I've lost track of the number of kids now attending colleges.

Cornelio, the young man who lived with us in Oregon and graduated from Southern Oregon University, went on to receive his Masters Degree from the University of East Anglia in England and spent several years in Thailand. Now he's returned to San Cristobal and has been hired by Senobio to be the Educational Coordinator of the forty-five villages, including San Cristobal. His international studies of education have led him to recognize the necessity of replacing the curriculum of rote learning with critical thinking. Perhaps he's on his way of attaining his dream of becoming Education Minister of Bolivia.

Cornelio's father, Octavio, welcomes us with a meal. As we learned in our visit in 2009, Octavio still works in the mine, no longer serving as the town doctor. Occasionally, he delivers a baby when asked because "the townspeople trust me." A brand new Toyota Hillux truck is parked outside his door. No more pushing that cheap motorcycle!

And what about customs? Is the animistic culture lost, the belief the rocks have souls? Some say "yes" and some say "no." The *Achupalla*, the rock where so many ceremonies were performed, survived the move to the new town, though propped with metal braces. *Ch'allas*, asking the gods to grant wishes, are still performed there. Quechua and Aymara languages are taught in the schools, and children dance the *Tinku,* though to canned music, not to traditional instruments. Some older women dress in traditional garb, but the majority sport jeans and Nike sneakers. Quechua customs are still taught in the school curriculum thanks to Evo Morales, the Bolivian president, who wants to preserve his own indigenous roots and those of his people.

Llamas still wander the hills, but the townspeople working in mines can now afford to hire others to guard animals or tend their crops. Farming has become mechanized, quinoa now an important exportable crop. No longer tilling the earth by hand, the people hire tractors with drivers. Acres and acres sprout quinoa plants.

As for the mine, it is a massive hole in the ground where humongous trucks lumber back and forth carting their prize to the mill. This mine will have a long life span, promising work for several generations. I feel a little lost as I stand high on a ledge overlooking the open pit. The only familiar sight is three monolithic rocks rising out of the earth, Los Tres Gigantes, the guardians of the town, still tall and proud.

And of course, there's Soledad, happily driving one of these 220-ton trucks. It's her week off when we finally find each other on the school playground. She runs to greet me and as we hug, a little girl with big bright eyes and two black braids clings to Soledad's leg. "Meet my daughter," she says. "Her name is Karen." Soledad smiles as I gaze down through happy tears upon my namesake.

Acknowledgments

Larry and Karen

I had a lot more hair twelve years ago. My baldness and Karen's recent streaks of grey are the inevitable result of a twelve-year wait for the story of San Cristóbal to unfold before we could write the final chapters. In the beginning neither of us imagined the journey would be so long and certainly not so interesting, and how could we have known that Karen's idea to jump into the life of the Quechua would become the high point of our lives. For this gift we must thank first and foremost the warm-hearted generosity of the people of Bolivia, especially the patient, hard-working, curious, and at times perplexing citizens of San Cristóbal.

Our interaction with each villager, no matter how minor or profound, added to our love of the little village we came to call "home." Every contact added to our appreciation; sometimes just the poetry of a spoken phrase caught our imaginations, as when Santitos told us of his faith: "We are like castaways . . . alone in these vistas without end, leagues and leagues from anywhere, alone on a dangerous sea." Others, like Senóbio, who became our mentor, *compadre, copadre,* and friend, guided us by way of his flexible definitions into the often labyrinthine cosmology of the local Quechua, and yet it all made sense in the end. Young Soledad, now the loveliest truck driver in all Bolivia, shared with us a depth of knowledge of her culture that was well beyond her age.

The value of what they offered is more than we can ever repay, and although until this paragraph we have not used their actual names in this book, we must thank them personally here. So to the following incomplete list of people, we offer our love, thanks, and admiration: Segundino Quíspe, Cornelio

Gonzales, Máximo Gonzales, Nora Quíspe, Johnny Delgado, Francisco Obregón, Juan Mamani, Benito Calcina, Delfín Flores, Ana Calcina, Hilarion Quíspe, Carlos Murillo, Roberto Mantilla, and Anastasio Gonzales. And, of course, for our now-departed friend of twinkling eye and sore knees, don Juan de la Cruz Quíspe, may *El Rey* bring forth water as you so command.

Neither Karen nor I would have visited San Cristóbal, not even the first time, were it not for the generosity and vision of my boss and our friend, Thomas Kaplan. A wiser and more decent person does not exist; except, just maybe, for my old prospecting partner of nearly fifty years, Jon C. Gelvin.

All those who struggled through the numerous rough drafts—which I stopped counting at about 25—deserve praise: Fran Curtis, Steve Neuberger, Diane Schapira, Bert Anderson, Selene Aitken, Meg Kaufman, Alice Padwe, Shamus Fatzinger, Phyllis Douglas, Norm Bornstein, Joan Kalvelage, Dan Rowe, Deb Richards, Dami Roelse, Anne Chambers, and Jon Gelvin.

Our writing coach and superb editor, Molly Tinsley, worked with us for over seven years on this book . . . we apologize in advance for not learning all that she tried to teach us. Maybe someday, Molly. And to our new friends at FUZE Publishing, Karetta Hubbard, Elizabeth Whitmore, and Jennie Dunnington, Cezara Windrem, William Leung and Shannon McMahon we say again, it would not be possible without you.

Glossary

Abuelo (Spanish): grandfather.

Achachila (Aymará): the spirit of the rocks and mountains. In S. Bolivia, a gremlin-like spirit of the rocks who causes mischief for people, especially at night.

Achupalla (Aymará): pineapple. A mushroom-shaped rock formation on the edge of the San Cristóbal soccer field.

Aguayo (Spanish): a rectangular woven cloth, often of bright colors, about the size of a shawl.

Aguita (Spanish): diminutive of "water."

Alma (Spanish): soul.

Alumnos (Spanish): students.

Anastomosing (English): the pattern made by a braided stream.

Anciano (Spanish): old person.

Andesite (English): a fine-grained igneous rock containing less than 10% quartz whose feldspars are a mixture of calcic- and sodic-plagioclases.

Angelitos (Spanish): little angels. The dead children.

Barite (English): barium sulfate. A mineral that crystallizes in flat, shining plates, so commonly associated with silver mineralization that it has come to be known as the "mistress of silver."

Boliviano (Spanish): currency of Bolivia, at time of writing about seven Bolivianos to one US dollar.

Caballo Blanco (Spanish): white horse. A large, white rock of silicified andesite found at the foot of the Tres Gigantes that turns into a dangerous, rampaging steed at night.

Cancha (Spanish): field, soccer field.

Ch'alla (Aymará): sprinkling. A ceremony where offerings are given to the gods in return for granting of favors.

Chango (Spanish): monkey. Adolescents who work as assistants to adults.

Charango (Spanish): a South American stringed instrument similar to a lute traditionally made from the shell of an armadillo.

Chola (Spanish): originally a term of derision given by Spaniards to the Indigenous people, now an Andean woman who continues to wear traditional multi-layered skirts, aprons, and a bowler hat.

Cholita (Spanish): a young *chola.*

Coca (Spanish): see Hojita below.

Comedor (Spanish): dining room. The company-built dining hall provided for workers at the mine camp.

Compadre (Spanish): friend, companion.

Copadre (Spanish): name given to godfather of your child.

Corregidor (Spanish): one who corrects. Mayor of a small community.

Cosecha (Spanish): harvest.

Curandero (Spanish): people possessing supernatural powers to heal disease.

Dacite (English): a fine-grained igneous rock of the same general composition as andesite (see), often associated with silver mineralization.

Desert varnish (English): a thin, shiny coating composed of iron and manganese oxides forming on the exposed surfaces of rocks in desert regions after long exposure to the elements.

Dios (Spanish): God.

Dios mio, que difícil (Spanish): my God, how difficult.

Dique (Spanish): dike. A thin, long, planar-shaped igneous intrusion that cross-cuts surrounding strata.

Dome (English): a hypabyssal (near-surface) igneous rock with a deeper, narrow stem and a flared-out mushroom-shaped cap nearer the surface, commonly associated with mineralization, especially if dacitic.

El Altar (Spanish): the altar. A dark-colored cliff found on the northwest side of the village containing numerous cave-like openings.

El Dia de los Muertos (Spanish): Day of the Dead.

Enfermero Auxiliar (Spanish): auxiliary nurse. Government-paid nurses with twelve to eighteen months of training, sent to live in small villages to provide a modicum of health care to local residents.

Es buena hora (Spanish): it is a good time. A phrase spoken in all *ch'allas* signifying it is the proper time to speak to the gods, spirits or demons.

Fallas (Spanish): faults. A fracture in the rock which has experienced slippage of the opposing blocks of rock.

Hojita (Spanish): little leaf. The leaves of the coca plant, *Erythrozylum coca*, of the family *Erythroxylaceae*, native to northwestern South America. Best known for its alkaloid, cocaine.

Hydrothermal (English): a geological process whereby hot, subterranean waters charged with dissolved salts and metals precipitate mineral deposits.

Ingeniero (Spanish): engineer. Said in place of "Sir" or "Mister" as a sign of respect.

Jayula (Aymará): place where salt is found. Cerro Jayula, the highest peak in the San Cristóbal Range where the expanse of the Uyuni salt flat can be observed.

Lacustrine (English): formed in, related to, or deposited by lakes. The bedded sediments on Tesorera Ridge, just west of the village, which are extensively mineralized.

Lo siento (Spanish): I am sorry.

Me dejó solo (Spanish): he/she left me alone.

Mesa (Spanish): table. In S. Bolivia a table-like platform on which are placed offerings to the gods during *ch'alla* ceremonies.

Mita (Spanish): the number of days per year of compulsory labor required by the Spanish of every indigenous male, following up on a similar system that had been imposed by the Inca.

Pachamama (Aymará and Quechua): mother world. A benign goddess of all things above the earth.

Padrino (Spanish): godfather, sponsor, caretaker.

Paja brava (Spanish): angry grass. A perennial sharp-pointed grass of the Poaceas family that grows at high altitudes in the Andes.

Pampa (Spanish): plain.

Patrón (Spanish): a) a generally wealthy or powerful person who gives or donates aid or comfort to a less well-off person in exchange for loyalty or some service offered to the donor, or b) the patron saint, as in the *Patrón,* San Cristóbal.

Pij'char (Uncertain derivation): the practice of chewing coca leaf to ensure the sun returns in the morning.

Piñas (Spanish): pineapple. a) the small rocks given off as fruit by the Achupalla, or b) any rock taken to a different position from a place of respect to ensure the spirits of the rock formations also travel to the new site.

Pyrite (English): pyrite. A shiny yellow mineral, iron disulfide, aka "fool's gold."

Que buena suerte (Spanish): what good luck.

Quintal (Spanish): one hundred kilograms. Actual quantity varies according to local usage.

Q'orpa (Quechua): clod of dirt.

Quena (Quechua): Traditional flute of the Andes usually made of bamboo, with six finger holes and one thumb hole, open on both ends.

Ratito, un (Spanish): short space of time, "just a minute."

Riqueza (Spanish): richness, wealth.

Romanos (Spanish): Romans.

Salar (Spanish): salt flat.

Samiri (Uncertain derivation): a sacred place where the god Wiracocha hid the ancestors before the ancestors.

Soroche (Spanish): originally an illness caused by toxic emanations from ores in mountains, now altitude sickness, usually attended by severe headaches, nausea, and sleeplessness.

Sulfide (English): a sulfur-bearing mineral.

T'anta gua gua (Quechua): little girls' braids, referring to braided bread used in ceremonies

Tesorera (Spanish): treasurer. The ridge to the west of San Cristóbal which is developed on a major portion of the San Cristóbal silver orebody.

Th'ola (Quechua): a desert woody shrub, *Parastrephia lepido-phylla,* similar in outward appearance, but considerably shorter in height, to the North American sagebrush

(*Artemesia tridentata*), common from 3700 to 5000 m. above sea level.

Tía (Spanish): Aunt. Name given to any older women as sign of respect.

Tinku (Quechua): encounter. A dance incorporating a form of ritual combat in which teams of dancers from nearby communities or kin groups attempt to injure one another in order to give the Pachamama an offering of blood, believed to assure good harvests.

Toldos (Spanish): umbrellas. An abandoned silver mine located on the edge of the Río Toldos Canyon, two kilometers south of San Cristóbal.

Tonne (English): metric ton, 2204 pounds.

Vizcacha (Spanish): a large burrowing rodent (*Lagostomus trichodactylus*) of the family Chinchillidae, a food source for the people of the Altiplano.

Wira Wira (Quechua): grease, fat. *Senecio nivalis*, a low-growing plant reportedly useful for treating headaches, fevers, infections and warts.

Yacho (Quechua): shaman.

Zampoña (Spanish): pan flute. An ancient musical instrument based on the principle of the closed tube, consisting of usually five or more pipes of gradually increasing length bound together.

Questions for Discussion

1. With so many different belief systems discussed in the book (liberal vs. conservative, scientific vs. spiritual, animist vs. Catholic, etc.), what have you concluded about such conflicting views? Can they each be correct at the same time?

2. What would you like to see happen with the way poor countries are developed? Is it best for international corporations to get involved, and if so, to what extent should their involvement be? Do you, as citizens of a developed country, have the right to prevent development which may bring economic improvement to poor communities? Should the citizens affected by that development have the right to decide for themselves?

3. One major theme in *The Gift of El Tío* is the dual nature of change: it may offer positive benefit, but it always seems a price must be paid. Refusal to allow development has an obvious cost: a continuation of the status quo, thus continuation of the poverty. On the other hand, can we ever know in advance what the true cost of development may be?

4. Prior to reading the *Gift of El Tío*, with whose initial perspective did you identify more, Larry's or Karen's? After reading the book, do you still identify with one or the other?

5. As she witnesses the reality of poverty, what challenges does Karen's initial perspective face? What challenges do Larry's initial skepticism and his dismissal of spirituality face as he becomes absorbed into the cosmology of the Quechua community?

6. Is El Tío real? Prior to the prophesied year, thousands of experienced and hard-working geologists had combed the San Cristóbal hills and found nothing. But around that

year, Larry and his team spent a mere four hours and recognized a bonanza was present. How could that be? With
all the possible places in the world that Larry could have
been exploring, what do you think led him to this specific site on this particular date—was it coincidence
or was he led there to fulfill the prophecy of El Tío,
a prophecy that he would not learn of until several
years later?

7. What do you think will happen to the *new* San Cristóbal
once the orebody is depleted and the mine shuts down?
If the town goes back into relative poverty, do you think
the move with the temporary improvement in economic
conditions is worth the loss of culture and ceremony?

8. As a guest in a foreign country, what behavior do you feel
is appropriate when you encounter classism and/or rac-
ism? How would you have behaved when Soledad was not
allowed to eat with the authors in the *comedor*?